LOVE AND WORK ENOUGH

THE LIFE OF ANNA JAMESON

Anna Jameson

CLARA THOMAS

Love and Work Enough

The Life of Anna Jameson

"... one can but have one's heart and hands full, and mine are.
I have love and work enough to last me the rest of my life."

ANNA JAMESON TO ROBERT NOEL, 1841

UNIVERSITY OF TORONTO PRESS

TORONTO BUFFALO LONDON

© University of Toronto Press 1967

Reprinted in paperback 1978
Toronto   Buffalo   London
Printed in Canada
LSBN 0-8020-6346-2
LC 67-3186

To MKT and the DG of C
contributors to the making of this book

Preface to the Paperback Edition

IN ITS BASIC INTENTION *Love and Work Enough* is a profoundly feminist book, written out of my respect for Anna Jameson's ambitions and achievements. Its writing was the culmination of a great adventure in searching for and finding all the scattered records of Anna Jameson's life and work. Like Mrs. Erskine and Professor Needler, who wrote of her before me, I had first been fascinated by the cosmopolitan dimension of her life, her large circle of acquaintances and her warm friendships with Fanny Kemble, Ottilie von Goethe, the Brownings and Lady Byron. But I speedily became aware that thirty-five years of a writing career was the central factor in any understanding of the life of Anna Jameson and I became increasingly respectful of the quality of her professionalism. Her lifelong drive was towards the education of women, herself first and always and then all the other women she could reach. Through her particular combination of talent, ambition, energy and determination, she eventually succeeded in informing and influencing the taste of a large reading public in both England and America. She was no dilettante, practising writing as a gracious and acceptable feminine hobby, but a professional writer who supported herself and her family by her work. She was also a research scholar of unremitting energy, though the term had no currency in her time, certainly not as descriptive of a woman.

Since *Love and Work Enough* was published in 1967, Anna Jameson's various works have attracted a variety of attentions. In Canada, Eve Zaremba anthologized portions of *Winter Studies and Summer Rambles in Canada* in *The Privilege of Sex* (1973), linking her work to Marxist thought, a compliment that would certainly have astonished her. The actress, Pauline Carey, has written, produced and toured in a complete, one-woman show called, simply, *Anna Jameson,* and based on her months in Canada. Coles' Canadiana series has reprinted the three-volume, 1838 edition of *Winter Studies and Summer Rambles* and *Love and Work Enough*'s frontispiece portrait has been featured in a calendar of women notable in Canada's past and present. In Britain Margaret Maison has written an account of Anna Jameson's life for *The Biographical Dictionary of Modern British Radicals* and the scholarly lineage of her *Legends of the Madonna* is evident in Marina Warner's *Alone of All Her Sex* (1977). In the United States the art historian, Adèle Holcombe, has published research on the art criticism, and Lee Holcombe, social historian, has dealt with Anna Jameson's influence on the nineteenth-century feminist struggle. In *Victorian Ladies at Work* (1973), Ms. Holcombe has cited her influence on the early activists for higher education for women; in her extensive work on the Married Women's Property Act she has extended that citation into a more detailed account of Anna Jameson's influence on the Rights of Women movement. Most important, in *Literary Woman* (1976), Ellen Moers explores in detail the powerful influence of Mme de Staël and especially of her *Corinne* on nineteenth-century women writers. Nothing was more striking, in my own work on Anna Jameson, than the realization of the importance of Mme de Staël to her as both practical "role-model" and fantasy ideal. Ellen Moers rightly calls her an "important Corinne disciple" and her *Diary of an Ennuyée* "one of the most charming English imitations of *Corinne*: a hybrid work, part novel, part diary, part guidebook, in which the author suppressed the governess and presented herself as a highly improbable English *Corinne*."

All of these works, with their consequent expansion of interest in Anna Jameson, are a part of the creative and scholarly enthusiasm which has stemmed from the Women's Movement of the last decade. We have now come some distance from the blinkered vision with which generations of Canadian historians and literary scholars read and quoted *Winter Studies and Summer Rambles* as a minor phenomenon of trenchant observation, seldom relating it to the abundant totality of Anna Jameson's work. The photograph which is reproduced on the cover of this edition was taken by the pioneer photographer, Octavius Hill. It is a fine study of a strong woman, a pioneer herself in the fields of biography, travel literature, literary criticism and art history. She made a minor, but still unique contribution to the fabric of nineteenth-century society and she, herself, was an early, and unflagging, professional woman.

CT

York University, 1978

Preface

ANNA BROWNELL JAMESON (1794–1860) was a popular writer of the nineteenth century, widely read in England and America for her criticisms of literature and art and for her travel biographies. Her concern for the "Position of Women" ensures a place for her in the roster of feminist propagandists, as her eager friendships with Victorian celebrities guarantee a certain degree of curiosity about her own life and character. For Canadian readers her interest is enhanced by her *Winter Studies and Summer Rambles in Canada,* a vivid report of her travels and one of the best existing accounts of Upper Canada in the nineteenth century.

In his reminiscences of literary figures, Henry Crabb Robinson said of her: "She makes books for the great publishers, and having taste and a knowledge of the market is able to edit and be well paid for editing works of taste or commenting on pictures, etc."[1] The statement is true, but its baldness is misleading: years of apprenticeship in the building of her reputation preceded the eminence of Mrs. Jameson's later years and her choice of an area of concentration. Her writing career began in 1826 with *Diary of an Ennuyée* and was consolidated by the publication of *Characteristics of Women* in 1832. This work, a consideration of Shakespeare's heroines, added a considerable Continental reputation to her growing prestige in England and America; by the time she came to Canada in 1836 she was a practised and a confident professional woman of letters. For the last twenty years of her life it is not an exaggeration to say that she could have written about a very wide choice of subjects and had been read by a devoted public on two continents. A combination of family background, training and taste and, above all, the availability of a market for such work in the England of the forties and fifties determined her choice of art criticism as the major field of the last two decades of her writing. In *Consort of Taste*, a modern assessment of influential figures in nineteenth-century art criticism, John Steegman adds a solid testimonial to her importance: "She was rather a compiler than a thinker, perhaps; but she was a woman of wide experience and immense industry in her field, whose labours still bear fruit. . . . [A] most important link between old and modern criticism."[2]

There are three major sources for biographical material, all of them now out of print: *Memoirs of the Life of Anna Jameson*, written by her niece, Gerardine Macpherson, and published in 1878; *Anna Jameson: Letters and Friendships*, edited by Mrs. Steuart Erskine and published in 1915; and *Letters of Anna Jameson to Ottilie von Goethe*, edited by Professor G. H. Needler, published in 1939.

The first of these works was written by Mrs. Macpherson as a family memorial to her aunt, with the secondary motive of defending her memory from certain unflattering remarks made by Harriet Martineau in that astonishing Victorian phenomenon, her *Autobiography*: "Lady Morgan and Lady Davy and Mrs. Austin and Mrs. Jameson may make women blush and men smile and be insolent; and their gross and palpable vanities may help to lower the position and discredit the pursuits of other women. . . ."[3] Understandably, Mrs. Macpherson's account is coloured by family pride in Mrs. Jameson as a public figure. It is also marked by her own guilty feelings for having chosen marriage in preference to the role for which she had been trained, that of her aunt's research assistant and engraver for the art works always in progress between 1845 and 1860.

Mrs. Erskine's book adds a mass of material to Mrs. Macpherson's *Memoirs*. It maintains the respectful view taken by Mrs. Macpherson and its image of Anna Jameson, famous authoress, correspondent with the great and the near-great, adds interest and breadth to the earlier account. In no way, however, does it contribute a new dimension of depth to the picture of Anna Jameson, woman and writer.

Professor Needler's collection of letters from the Goethe Archives at Weimar is the latest published and a better source of revealing biographical data. Although his Introduction follows the Macpherson-Erskine pattern of unstinted admiration for Mrs. Jameson, the letters themselves leave an impression of her personality which disturbs one with its pathetic, possessive emotionalism and which underlines one's conviction that to estimate the achievement of a lifetime by biographical detail alone is less than justice and less than truth.

Besides these sources, which I have freely used to enlighten the process of her development, I have worked with a multitude of printed references and manuscript letters. A letter to Mr. Malcolm Elwin on the publication of his *Lord Byron's Wife* in 1963, led me to the Lovelace-Byron papers and two hundred letters to and from Lady Byron and Anna Jameson. A Canada Council grant enabled me to go to England where Mr. Elwin's hospitality was unforgettable and his advice of incalculable benefit; the letters, which Lord Lytton, their owner has permitted me to use, were of absorbing interest and great value to the further understanding of my subject.

In answer to a letter sent out to many American and British libraries and to the Goethe Archives in Weimar, I was informed of the existence and the whereabouts of some six hundred letters to and from Anna Jameson. Most of these, indeed all that have any important bearing on her life and writings, I have seen, thanks to the notable co-operation of many reference librarians in both public and university libraries. In particular I am indebted to Miss Edith Firth of the Baldwin Room, Toronto Public Library, for leading me to unpublished letters concerning Robert Jameson; to Professor Heinz Bluhm, Leavenworth Professor of German Language and Literature, Yale University, for his interest and advice and for his staff's provision of letters from Yale's Goethe collection; to Dr. Hahn, of the Goethe and Schiller Archives in Weimar; to Miss Hannah French and Mrs. Hazel Godfrey of the Wellesley College Library for making quickly available to me the Browning-Jameson letters and to Sir John Murray for his permission to quote from them; to Mr. George Johnson of the Osgoode Hall Library, Toronto, for his help in unearthing records of Robert Jameson's tenure as Upper Canada's Vice-Chancellor; to Miss Sybille Pantazzi of the Art Gallery of Toronto; and to Mr. Alfred Bennett, Secretary of the Law Society of Upper Canada. Important letters were made available to me by the staff of the Houghton Library, Harvard; the Armstrong-Browning Library of Baylor University; the Detroit Public Library; the libraries of Duke, Cornell and Columbia and of the universities of Texas, Illinois and Rochester. In addition the librarians of a host of other institutions answered my queries with far more interest and assistance than I could reasonably have expected.

The editorial assistance of Miss Francess Halpenny and Miss Diane Dilworth, of the University of Toronto Press, has been invaluable to me; Mrs. M. Moëns, Mrs. F. Knight, Miss V. Fairbairns, Miss S. Bracken, Ian Cameron and Stephen Thomas have assisted with both patience and industry. This work has been published with the help of a grant from the Humanities Research Council of Canada using funds provided by the Canada Council, and from the Publications Fund of the University of Toronto Press.

Through all the time that the work was in progress, the late Professors A. S. P. Woodhouse and G. H. Needler of the University of Toronto, were unfailingly encouraging. To them, and to Professor Northrop Frye, who first agreed with me that the life of Anna Jameson required twentieth-century investigation, I owe my greatest debt of gratitude.

In presenting Mrs. Jameson's life, I have made use of letters wherever possible, allowing them to speak with their own authenticity for the events and the people who were important to her. Critically, I have examined each of her works, from *The Diary of an Ennuyée* to the final two volumes of her *Sacred and Legendary Art* series, published posthumously in 1862. I have considered the influences having a bearing on its writing, the public for which it was designed, and, most important, its reception by the nineteenth-century literary world as demonstrated by contemporary periodical reviews. Anna Jameson's rise in prestige can be charted from the review of *The Diary* by the relatively minor *Monthly Review,* to the rough but valuable experience of "Christopher North's" criticism in *Blackwood's* beginning in 1829 and to her first notice in the *Edinburgh Review* in 1834. Finally she was accepted and given consideration by all three of the "Royal Reviews," the *Quarterly,* the *Edinburgh* and the *Westminster,* a distinction which began in the forties after the publication of *Winter Studies and Summer Rambles in Canada. Sacred and Legendary Art,* whose volumes were the major preoccupation of the last twelve years of her life, was received with enthusiasm on two continents and Anna Jameson, secure in her reputation, could and did speak with increased temerity and influence beyond the range of art criticism into the vexed "Rights of Women" field, always one of her subsidiary concerns.

The process of growth in literary reputation along with the cumulative interaction of the people, events and works which produced it has been an absorbing study. No final and completely authoritative unravelling of all the complexities of pattern is possible to any biographer; some degree of illumination of an interesting life and of a considerable achievement has, perhaps, been established.

CT
York University, 1966

Contents

Illustrations between pages 114 and 115

Abbreviations

ABBREVIATIONS in square brackets throughout the text are references to the following works:

Char	*Characteristics of Women* by Anna Jameson
CB	*A Commonplace Book of Thoughts, Memories and Fancies* by Anna Jameson
Diary	*The Diary of an Ennuyée* by Anna Jameson
E	*Anna Jameson: Letters and Friendships, 1812–1860* edited by Mrs. Steuart Erskine
FS	*Memoirs of Celebrated Female Sovereigns* by Anna Jameson
K	*Records of a Girlhood* by F. A. Kemble
LP	*Memoirs of the Loves of the Poets* by Anna Jameson
M	*Memoirs of Anna Jameson* by Gerardine Macpherson
ME	*Memoirs and Essays on Art, Literature and Social Morals* by Anna Jameson
N	*Letters of Anna Jameson to Ottilie von Goethe* edited by G. H. Needler
SLA	*Sacred and Legendary Art* by Anna Jameson
VS	*Visits and Sketches at Home and Abroad* by Anna Jameson
WSSR	*Winter Studies and Summer Rambles in Canada* by Anna Jameson

LOVE AND WORK ENOUGH

THE LIFE OF ANNA JAMESON

I

Emigrant's Daughter

ANNA BROWNELL MURPHY emigrated with her parents from Dublin to Whitehaven, Cumberland, in 1798, shortly before the outbreak of the rebellion in which many young revolutionaries died and the names of Robert Emmet and Lord Edward Fitzgerald were added to the roll of Ireland's patriot martyrs. She had been born on May 19, 1794, the eldest daughter of Denis Brownell Murphy, a young artist, and his English wife. Her mother had come to the fashionable Dublin boarding-school of Mme Dumoulin to be trained in the deportment and skills becoming a gentlewoman. While there, she and Mr. Murphy met and later married, settling in Dublin in a lively social circle with, at first, every hope of professional success.

Denis Murphy's removal to England was in the nature of a retreat with honour: responsible for his wife and three small daughters, it was only prudent for him to consider a move to the best market for the miniature painting which was his special talent; as a vociferous patriot Irishman, it was providential that his opportunity to emigrate came before the storm broke and the bloody purge began. Anna's two younger sisters were left behind with a family near Dublin, but she participated with her parents in the great adventure. A sense of urgency and drama attended her earliest memories as did a feeling of being the chosen one; time enhanced both—Anna Murphy felt herself special and she enjoyed every moment of being the centre of attention.

A fourth daughter was born in Whitehaven before the family moved to the more important town of Newcastle-on-Tyne in 1802. There, living over the shop of Mr. Miller, the bookseller and publisher, the precursor of the firm of John Murray in London, Denis Murphy's fortunes prospered sufficiently to send for his two children from Ireland

and the family was united—Anna, Eliza, Louisa, and Camilla. In 1803, the family moved to Hanwell, near London, and in 1806 to London itself, settling in a rather fashionable district near the Mall. Charlotte, a fifth daughter, was born here and from this time on, London was the centre from which Denis Murphy worked. He was successful in terms of the rank of his patrons and the number of his commitments, though doubtfully so in point of money payment or providence for the future.

For several years the Murphys were able to afford a governess for their daughters—Miss Yokeley, who had brought Eliza and Louisa from Dublin to Newcastle and who later married Mr. Murphy's brother. She was the daughter of a Frenchwoman, one of the Duke of Leinster's secretaries, and Anna's proficiency in French certainly began with her training. Miss Yokeley was not beloved, and though Anna looked back on her as "one of the cleverest women I have ever met with," she resented her authority and exulted in possessing a dream world of adventure which her power could not reach. [CB 118] Even more revealing of the resentment which the strong-willed child felt at being dominated is this passage from her Commonplace Book:

I recollect that when one of those set over me inflicted what then appeared a most horrible injury and injustice, the thoughts of vengeance haunted my fancy for months; but it was an inverted sort of vengeance. I imagined the house of my enemy on fire and rushed through the flames to rescue her. She was drowning and I leaped into the deep water to draw her forth. She was pining in prison and I forced bars and bolts to deliver her. If this were magnanimity, it was not the less vengeance, for observe, I always fancied evil, and shame, and humiliation to my adversary; to myself the role of superiority and gratified pride. [CB 111]

The most important source of information about Anna Murphy's education is "A Revelation of Childhood," probably written at the request of her friend, Harriet Martineau, whose story of her own childhood is a similar sort of confessional. Although Anna's account, published in her Commonplace Book in 1854, is written in far-off retrospect and with the hopeful purpose of improving the educational methods and the upbringing of children in mid-nineteenth-century England, she certifies as true its every word: "What I shall say here shall be simply the truth as far as it goes; not something between the false and the true, garnished for effect,—not something half-remembered, half-imagined,—but plain, absolute matter of fact." [CB 109]

Of her formal education Anna says little. "I had the usual desire to know and the usual dislike to learn, the usual love of fairy tales, and hatred of French exercises." [CB 109] She deplores the teaching of religion as she experienced it:

I was taught religion as children used to be taught it in my younger days, and are taught it still in some cases, I believe—through the medium of creeds and catechisms. I read the Bible too early, and too indiscriminately, and too irreverently. Even the New Testament was too early placed in my hands; too early made a lesson book as the custom then was. . . . The histories out of the Bible (the Parables especially) were, however, enchanting to me, though my interpretation of them was in some instances the very reverse of correct orthodoxy. To my infant conception our Lord was a being who had come down from heaven to make people good, and to tell them beautiful stories. And though no pains were spared to "indoctrinate" me, and all my pastors and masters took it for granted that my ideas were quite satisfactory, nothing could be more confused or heterodox. [CB 123]

Anna was precocious and made her abilities recognized, for she speaks of a clergyman who lived nearby—"a famous Persian scholar, [who] took it into his head to teach me Persian (I was then about seven years old), and I set to work with infinite delight and earnestness." [CB 127] She does add, in modesty of reminiscence, that all she learned was soon forgotten, but that the delight in Oriental literature was reawakened some years later by a volume of Sir William Jones's work. For some time, her "Eastern studies" were represented by a map of India in her bedroom on which she had her sisters trace routes of travel as she told them thrilling stories of adventure along these eastern roads. Indeed, her first recorded prose effort, written for the amusement of her sisters, was "Faizy," a long and conventional Oriental tale, later renamed "The False One" and printed in *Visits and Sketches*.

Her own reading is recalled in more vivid detail than any formal schoolroom training, even in the years of Miss Yokeley's domination:

A great, an exquisite source of enjoyment arose out of an early, instinctive boundless delight in external beauty. . . . It was the intense sense of beauty which gave the first zest to poetry: I loved it, not because it told me what I did not know, but because it helped me to words in which to clothe my own knowledge and perception, and reflected back the pictures unconsciously hoarded in my mind. This was what made Thomson's *Seasons* a favourite book when I first began to read for my own amusement and before I could understand one half of it; St. Pierre's "Indian Cottage" ("La Chaumière Indienne") was also charming, either because it reflected my dreams, or gave me new stuff for them in pictures of an external world quite different from that I inhabited,—palm-trees, elephants, tigers, dark-turbaned men with flowing draperies; and the "Arabian Nights" completed my Oriental intoxication which lasted for a long time. [CB 123]

Anna enjoyed forbidden books and even defends them in comparison to some thought fit for childish reading as "it was not the forbidden books that did the mischief, except in their being read furtively. I remember impressions of vice and cruelty from some parts

of the Old Testament and Goldsmith's "History of England" which
I shudder to recall." [*CB* 123] Shakespeare was on the forbidden shelf
but Anna, who was later to establish a firm literary reputation by her
criticism of his heroines, read all the plays surreptitiously.

I had read him all through between seven and ten years old. He never did
me any moral mischief. He never soiled my mind with any disordered
images. What was exceptional and coarse in language I passed by without
attaching any meaning whatever to it . . . though the witches in Macbeth
troubled me, though the Ghost in Hamlet terrified me (the picture that is,
—for the spirit in Shakespeare was solemn and pathetic, not hideous),—
though poor little Arthur cost me an ocean of tears,—yet much that was
obscure and all that was painful and revolting was merged on the whole
in the vivid presence of a new, beautiful, vigorous living world. . . . It may
be thought, perhaps that Falstaff is not a character to strike a child, or to
be understood by a child:—no, surely not. To me Falstaff was not witty
and wicked, only unmistakably fat and funny; and I remember lying on
the ground rolling with laughter over some of the scenes in Henry the
Fourth,—the mock play and the seven men in buckram. But the Tempest
and Cymbeline were the plays I knew best and liked best. [*CB* 124]

A scholarly young parish clerk lent her the *Odyssey* and the *Iliad*,
which left certain highly personal and vivid impressions on her mind.
Anna obviously collected available books from any willing source,
and she records her first experience of pious tracts by Hannah More,
lent to her by the same clerk:

It is most certain that more moral mischief was done to me by some of
those than by all Shakespeare's plays together. These so-called pious tracts
first introduced me to a knowledge of the vices of vulgar life, and the
excitements of a vulgar religion,—the fear of being hanged and the fear
of jail became coexistent in my mind; and the teaching resolved itself into
this,—that it was not by being naughty, but by being found out, that I
was to incur the risk of both. [*CB* 123]

Sometime between Anna's ninth and twelfth birthdays Miss Yokeley
left the family. The sisters' education progressed, henceforth with Anna
in charge, in an ambitious but understandably uneven fashion. The
Murphys' schoolroom probably contained the standard equipment of
the day—from globe to Mrs. Jane Marcet's "Conversations" series, the
currently popular question-answer textbooks. Few schoolrooms, however, have contained as dynamic and despotic a sister-governess as
Anna is reported to have been by her sister Camilla: "She it was who
settled how long a time was necessary for the learning of the lessons,
a process very easy to herself, which, with delightful childish inconsequence, she decided must be equally easy for her sisters." [M 16]
We are not surprised to learn that Anna's own education progressed

"chiefly at her own will and pleasure, with an extensive breadth and desultory character as conspicuous as its ambition. . . . She worked hard, but fitfully at French, Italian and even Spanish." [M 12]

As Anna fought, cajoled or bullied her sisters, leader among them both by nature and by circumstances, so Denis Murphy's personality dominated all the household. Witty, convivial and a gay talker, Mr. Murphy was patient with his daughters and proud of them, especially of his clever eldest who was reported among his friends as having "thoughts beyond her years" and asking all sorts of questions that no one could answer. [M 3] Often Mr. Murphy's commissions took him into the great homes of the wealthy. His tales of living with the aristocracy lost nothing in the "Irish" of their telling and his readiest listener was the eager Anna, desirous of his approval and her own improvement. In an early letter to her father, she says, "I am going on very quick with my Italian and am writing Exercises from french into Italian, what makes me apply myself to it is the hope of going down to you." [E 20]

Anna's Italian studies were continued to the point where she became a fluent reader at least. During her first Italian tour she says, "I never read anything but Italian, not having any French or English books, except Shakespeare." [E 66] Earlier she had reported to her family that her "only extravagance . . . is having an Italian Master regularly. . . . I denied myself a winter dress that I might have an Italian master." [E 48]

As a child, she was an industrious novice in poetry writing as well as in the prose tale, and even when he was away from home she evidently looked confidently to her father for criticism and encouragement in her efforts:

. . . I take the opportunity of Sending you a little Effusion which has been ready written since the last Parcel went off! I am not quite satisfied with it myself. I hope you will resolve me a few questions in the first verse and third line, whether I should say "thy form I spied" or thy "bloom I spied"; in the same verse I use the pronoun you and directly after thou and thy which though Pope and even Milton have been guilty of I am sensible is a great inelegancy; how shall I correct it? I also use the word flower a great deal too often. I beg leave to dedicate to you my last thing which you said you liked. [E 19]

This passage resounds with priggish self-importance in our ears, but in that day literary "effusions" were a standard part of the education of the young lady. It is unusual in any day for a child to look with such confidence to her father for advice on the proper word. Though training in precision is attributed to Miss Yokeley, Denis

Murphy must also have been an interested and a valuable mentor. Miniature painting is a particularly exacting and detailed art form and Mr. Murphy, who had considerable skill in "making the great small," encouraged his daughter to be exact and careful in observation and record, both in her writing and in her sketching. His training she carried into all of her later work.

An "effusion" on Lord Collingwood, famous after the battle of Trafalgar in 1805, and a small poem called "The Bat" are the only recorded pieces of Anna's early verse, obviously preserved more by a family cherishing mementos of their famous one than because they have any poetic merit. The Collingwood poem was written with commendable fervour if deplorable spelling, sometime shortly after Trafalgar when she was about eleven. Its hero never returned to "veiw" his native land but in 1810 "sunk in death" at sea, like Nelson:

> With Fame and Victory following in his train,
> *Collingwood* veiws his native land again!
> To songs of praise each joyous harp is strung,
> And happiness resounds from every tongue
> E'en I, unskilled in poesy's magic art,
> Will sing brave Collingwood's exalted part,
> For the first time to him will tune my lyre,
> While *Nelson* shall my humble verse inspire.
> Now raised alike in glory and in name—
> Britain shall boast another son of Fame,
> Who, born each honour from Napoleon's head
> To snatch, and deck the gallant Nelson dead,
> As yet another champion bold shall rise
> And, as a hero, claim the exalted skies.
> While Victory loud proclaims, though Nelson's slain
> Still Britain reigns o'er Neptune's boisterous main.
> Though first in honour and though first in place,
> Though first in favour and though first in grace,
> Though Fame shall weave fresh laurels for his head,
> Yet still he mourns victorious Nelson dead.
> But rise! nor yield to unavailing greif;
> Though yet we mourn the dear departed cheif;
> 'Tis you must snatch from a usurper's hand
> Those rights which Freedom gave to every land.
> Our second hero every danger braves,
> And conquering Britain dares the bellowing waves,
> Blesses the place where Collingwood drew breath,
> But mourns the hour when Nelson sunk in death. [M 18]

Like all we know of her early years, Anna's early writings show drive, confidence and eagerness to do and to learn. The desire to give and to receive affection was very strong in her nature, but at times it was submerged, at times distorted and at times defeated in the strength of her desire to dominate and to make a place and a name for herself. Several passages in "A Revelation of Childhood" are illuminating—she describes her childish aversion to discordant sounds, her highly emotional response to music and her impulse to be the "star turn" of any scene: "The music of "Paul and Virginia" was then in vogue, and there was one air—a very simple air—in that opera, which, after the first few bars, always made me stop my ears and rush out of the room. I became at last aware that this was sometimes done by particular desire to please my parents or to amuse and interest others by the display of such vehement emotion." [M 16] Her recollected early response to others is perhaps the most important key to her emotional nature in childhood and in maturity as well: "I did not, like the little Mozart, ask of everyone around me, "Do you love me?" The instinctive question was, rather, "Can I love you?" Yet certainly I was not more than six years old when I suffered from the fear of not being loved where I had attached myself, and from the idea that another was preferred before me, such anguish as had nearly killed me." [CB 110]

Twice in childhood she evolved and put into motion wild travel schemes involving her sisters and herself. Once, rebellious under Miss Yokeley's care, the group, led by Anna, set off from Newcastle on a planned runaway to join their parents in Scotland. Later, in London, when she was twelve, Anna proposed to take her sisters to Brussels where they would all learn lace-making to reinforce the family's finances. Only on the eve of departure, with the defection of Louisa and Camilla, did the plan crumble; Anna was affected by no such pangs of sentiment as undermined the younger girls and stood firm, ready to go, but unable to do so alone.

Anna assumed, or was saddled with, an early maturity regarding her family's welfare and began very early to consider it her right and duty to be chief protectress of parents and sisters. These lines occur in a letter written to her father when she was twelve: "On account of your late illness, we can hardly expect our Debts paid in the next parcel but shall be put off a little while longer." [E 20]

At sixteen, Anna was ready to begin a career as governess. She had been educated in the accepted pattern for the young lady of her day, but her achievement in certain directions was outstanding: by talent and training her sketching was beyond the level of polite accomplishment; her skill and interest in languages were unusually developed, and a measure of experience in teaching was hers through her experiences with her sisters. Most important, the confidence of an aggressive nature which never left her was Anna's most valuable asset.

She was always to rely strongly on her personal impressions and to dramatize herself as the centre of every situation; her writings took life from this tendency, although at times her personal relationships suffered. She began early and intensely to relate her reading to herself: "Altogether I should say that in my early years books were known to me, not as such, not for their general contents, but for some especial image or picture I had picked out of them and assimilated to my own mind and mixed up with my own life." [*CB* 125]

The miniature painted by her father at this time shows an auburn-haired, fair-skinned girl in white with touches of pastel pinks and blues, in tones suggestive of a Romney portrait. Anna's features and attitude are an emphatic denial of the impression of softness in the delicate colouring. She looks totally alert and almost pertly confident, with a humourless firmness in her set of chin, tilt of head and admonitory pointing finger. A sixteen-year-old does not often take herself lightly; by nature and by circumstances Anna was encouraged to take herself very seriously indeed. The "effusion" written by Lady Byron many years later with this miniature as its subject, though regrettable as a poem, may well have expressed Anna's own youthful feeling about herself and her aspirations:

> In those young eyes, so keenly, bravely bent
> To search the mysteries of the future hour,
> There shines the will to conquer, and the pow'r
> Which makes that conquest sure,—a gift Heav'n-sent
> The radiance of the Beautiful was blent
> Ev'n with thine earliest dreams; and towards that star
> Of thy first faith, oft dimm'd, and always far
> Still hast thou journey'd on, where'er thy tent
> O never yet in vain such pilgrimage
> Witness the poet-souls of every age:
> Long ere the Magi hail'd the prophet-beam,
> Or Worship own'd an altar and a shrine;
> The few who felt how real the dream
> Thus gaz'd, and thus imbib'd th' "etherial stream"
>
> [E Frontispiece]

2

A Governess' Career

ANNA MURPHY'S THIRD ATTEMPT to assist her family and gain independence for herself was undertaken at the age of sixteen, when she became governess to the four small sons of the Marquis of Winchester. The position was considered a prize: Anna suddenly became both onlooker and participant in the life of one of England's great noble families. For the next fifteen years she was intermittently a governess. Her experiences, both as recorded in contemporary letters and written in retrospect, add their weight and interest to the volumes written in fact and fiction about the nineteenth-century governess.

In 1810, too, Denis Murphy was appointed "Painter in Enamel" to the Princess Charlotte, daughter of George IV and Queen Caroline. He set about making miniature copies of Lely's portraits of the ladies of the court of Charles II, the so-called "Windsor Beauties," hoping to sell them to his patroness, but unfortunately without any definite arrangement or understanding. During the long period of the work an apartment at Windsor Castle was allotted to him and he was well known to an aristocratic circle. Anna's poem on Lord Collingwood is written on the back of a note from Georgina, Duchess of Devonshire, authorizing Mr. Murphy to copy some pictures for her.

Mr. Murphy, with five daughters to provide for, was doubtless glad to have his clever eldest placed advantageously. Understandably, he hoped that she would "get on" with her employers and gain preferment and possibly even the social recognition that he could not give her. The pleasure he felt in his daughter's successful employment is expressed in a letter written to Anna in 1812. The satisfaction that the rich merchant might take in having his child presented at court, the poor painter feels in having his daughter so highly placed and well regarded as a governess:

I went to Windsor two or three days ago and saw Miss Egerton who was eager to know how you and Lady W. [the Marchioness of Winchester] went on together. I told her all I knew of the matter which has pleased her much. She says Lady W. has a *treasure* in you and that she is sensible of it—this will make you proud of yourself, but carry or bear "your faculties meekly." You will do very well thank God—and your mother and I are quite satisfied at your conduct every way and delighted at the appearance of your future prosperity. [E 23]

She certainly took first rank among the sisters and probably came more and more to be Denis Murphy's confidante.

In 1812, while she was still with the Marquis of Winchester, he wrote to her of the "Court Beauties," the miniatures upon whose sale the Murphy family's hopes of prosperity depended. He had been encouraged by an audience with the Queen and the four princesses, all of whom had received him warmly and had admired his paintings. Princess Charlotte, in particular, "bad me *keep up my spirits* and [said] that when she was able (and that time may not be too far distant) *she would take them herself.*" [E 23] Princess Charlotte, however, died without finding the means to buy the miniatures. After her death, in 1818, Denis Murphy appealed to her husband, Prince Leopold of Saxe-Coburg, but was coldly received by Sir Robert Gardiner, the Prince's secretary: "His Royal Highness expressed no wish to become a purchaser, but enquired if I knew the amount you valued them at." [M 57] Prince Leopold refused the copies; it was more than ten years before they were purchased.

Anna stayed at her first post about four years. In a letter to her mother, near the end of this time, she says, "My mind is not well; I feel as if it were stretched beyond its strength, as if a little repose would save me, my head at least." [E 24] The similar recollected instance which Anna reports in *Of Mothers and Governesses*, a pamphlet written after she had become a recognized authoress, may well have been a memory of her own:

I recollect an instance of a young girl of twenty, with the best will and intentions, and some qualities admirably suited to her task who, within two years, became languid, nervous, hysterical, and at length utterly broken down. She was obliged to give up her situation. Here, though great and lasting injury was inflicted, no unkindness was intended—I should say, on the contrary, all *kindness* was intended; and the services of the young lady were well paid and highly valued. The mother was full of lamentations at her own loss, and her friends condoled with her. The whole scene, which I witnessed, reminded me of an anecdote told by Horace Walpole: how my Lord Castlecomer's tutor broke his leg, and how everyone exclaimed, What an exceeding inconvenience to Lady Castlecomer! [ME 273]

The five years which intervene between her leaving the Winchester household sometime in 1814 and the known engagement by the Rowles of Bradbourne Park, Kent, are without documentary record of any kind. These, the years between twenty and twenty-five, Anna Murphy probably spent in her own home, sketching, educating herself as she saw fit and moving about the city with freedom. Always a poor young lady, she was emancipated because of her poverty to a degree that the wealthy could not know. Later, when travelling with the Rowles, she described herself as having no "weak timidity" and as being accustomed to walk the streets of London.

There is very probably a connection between the disappointment of the "Court Beauties" and Anna's acceptance of a post as governess with the Rowles family. She writes in 1819: "I live upon home letters, remember. . . . I cannot be happy even with Mrs. Rowles without them. . . . I go on very pleasantly here, Mrs. Rowles is extremely kind and even affectionate; we are almost inseparable companions and begin to *know* each other better." [E 24] The desire for affection, the warm attachment to friends and the determination to ingratiate herself with them which were strong characteristics of Anna are here evident as they are in many references to Mrs. Rowles: "In the evening Laura and Henry ride out and Mrs. Rowles and I drive in the Barouche or wander about the garden and grounds which are wild and beautiful. It is clear that I am becoming rather a favourite and I will try and keep up my credit you may be assured." [E 25]

Anna Murphy's first trip to the Continent was taken in 1821, still in the employ of the Rowles family. Clearly, she was well treated, devoted to Mrs. Rowles and very conscious of the opportunity of travel, probably a cherished dream since the early unsuccessful runaway plans with her sisters. The pleasure of the trip far outweighed its disadvantages, though she considered herself a poor traveller and was quite exhausted every evening. In most of her letters enjoyment is uppermost; only occasionally do poverty, ill health and personal annoyances dim the picture.

The poverty, in great part, was because Anna undertook to settle her sister Louisa in Paris for a year's training in French and general teaching accomplishments and to support her out of her own funds. In the winter of 1821, Anna Murphy was twenty-seven. Louisa was, at most, four years younger, above the usual age for the beginning of such governess-training. This attempt at augmenting the family fortunes by producing another wage-earner was probably engineered by Anna's enthusiasm—with what degree of sisterly co-operation we do not know:

I hope you like the arrangement I have made for dear Louisa. She will have this advantage above all the rest, without which I should not have felt able to have left her in Paris, the MacGowans will be within a short distance and she has them to have recourse to in any difficulty. I wish very much that it had been in my power to spend a week gaily with her before I left Paris; I mean to have taken her to the theatres and some interesting sights, but this cannot be. . . .

In pursuit of her plan, for Louisa and, ultimately, for the benefit of the entire family, Anna practised a rigorous personal economy:

I find that the difficulty is to take care of one's small change. Here there are no bank notes and but very little gold, all the money is in small silver and one is tempted every moment by some cheap article of beauty or convenience which is thought a great deal of in England. . . . I have now resolved, and keep to my resolution, to spend *no* money whatever. I find that to pay my washer-woman is as much as I can do, for washing is the diable. [E 29]

Postage is also the "diable" and the temptations to colourful baubles continue, though Anna, both pathetic and priggish, disclaims personal desire: "I have managed my money matters with such rigid economy that I have six guineas to receive on the 26th. I had a wish to buy a coral necklace at Naples, which I manfully resisted; not that it required much self-denial, as I do not much care about those things, but I thought you girls would have liked it amongst you." [E 63]

She enjoyed languages and had considered an Italian master her one luxury during the trip, but she dismissed him to have "the £15 due to Madame Aubert on the 27th of January," [E 53] for Louisa's board. Finally, as her tour nears its end, she regrets that she must come home with no presents for the family, "rather a disappointment, but it cannot be helped." [E 65] But for all such deprivations, there were major compensations, not least among them the personal satisfaction of finding Carlo Dolce's *Poetry* painted with "*red* hair, literally as red as mine, and it did not strike me as ugly." [E 47]

Travelling with the Rowles meant "luxury living *à la Milor Anglais*" [E 80] with consideration shown for the governess as well as for the family: "I go in the close carriage with the children early in the morning while the air is chill; about eleven there is a general *turn out* and the servants turn in. I go either in the barouche with Mrs. R. or on the box with Mr. R. Louisa [a daughter] and I take this seat by turns." [E 35] Anna Murphy identified herself with the family; her discomforts were theirs as well. Even when they moved from a magnificent hotel on the Boulevards to cramped quarters in the Rue St. Honoré and, instead of a suite of three rooms, Anna had not even a schoolroom, "these are trifling inconveniences." [E 31]

The children in her care were a joy and no problem:

Today Mrs. Rowles dines out; she has left me the carriage and I shall take all the children to St. Cloud immediately after an early dinner. We shall spend the rest of the day there, sup in the gardens upon coffee, cream and fruit (a la francaise [sic]) and return at bedtime. I shall make the little elfs as happy as I can. How you would enjoy such a day! All of you! [E 31]

Laura, her eldest pupil, was her pride and there was none of the envy of her favoured position which might well mar a governess' thoughts: "Laura has got a nice little horse and a stylish hat and feathers, and she is the admiration of all Florence; she looks the picture of health and loveliness." [E 47]

For all pleasures beyond the very fact of "beholding these objects of which I have *dreamed* from my very childhood" [E 50] she was totally dependent on her employers. Theatres, opera, sight seeing—all these were beyond her means, though for all of them she had a lively longing: "Tonight we go to the Opera, or at least Mrs. Rowles goes and I have some hopes of going too." [E 41] In Naples she felt herself "a kind of prisoner" and from Rome she reports an irksome consciousness of "my dependent situation [that] cuts one quite out of society and I have felt it more abroad than anywhere." [E 50]

"Mrs. Rowles is very kind to me," she wrote, "Mr. Rowles very tiresome—a complete wet blanket." [E 38] She disliked the "parade and fuss" with which they travelled, although she termed Mr. Rowles "an excellent Chef de Voyage" and described vividly the imperious behaviour to which, presumably, the European peasants were accustomed: "The scenes which occur sometimes at the little inns where we *munch* are the most amusing you can imagine. We seize upon the people's eatables, take possession of their frying pans, lift up their *pot-lids*, open their cupboards" [E 36] but Mr. Rowles pays well for all the fuss he makes—"I must say that he does not spare money." [E 43]

Fortunately, she could depend on Mrs. Rowles to include her in many sight-seeing expeditions, and sometimes, as in Florence, she went alone, "on the sly," to feel herself "satisfied with beauty" as she gazed on a statue of Venus in the Gallery. She resolutely subdued her desire to be constantly sight-seeing, reminding herself of her governess' duties—"with this I must be satisfied." And finally, as their trip in Italy neared its close, Anna wrote, "I have received a hint from Mr. R. that Mrs. R. wishes to have a French governess for Laura when we are at Paris; that sounds very inconsistent with all the professions Mrs. R. has always made me, but, however, I may feel it, I shall take it all as a thing of course, and we shall part very good friends." [E 61] She was to attach herself warmly to woman friends throughout her life. This may have been her first disillusion as to the quality of their friendship; it was to be by no means her last.

This first experience of the Continent was one whose importance Anna fully appreciated and whose pleasure she was always wishing her family could share: "My dear Mamma how I wish you were here—how you would enjoy these glorious scenes, and this delicious climate. . . . I wish for dear Papa and other dear people whom I will not *individualize,* who would truly feel and enjoy it all, and help me to enjoy it more than I do." [E 59]

The dependence of her position must have been somewhat balanced by the independence of movement and the venturesome spirit permissible in a governess but not in the ladies of the family. Her reported adventure on Vesuvius is a foretaste of the intrepid Mrs. Jameson's Canadian travels of many years later:

I had an opportunity of witnessing a most magnificent spectacle, an eruption of Mount Vesuvius and ascended the mountain during the height of it, in company with Mr. Rowles and Mr. Copeland. I was exposed, at one moment, to imminent danger from an immense red-hot stone which came bounding down the mountain, and saved myself by an exertion of presence of mind, which (though I say it that should not say it) was hardly to be expected from a woman at such a moment. I was then within fifteen yards of a stream of lava, which, glowing red-hot or rather almost to a white heat, rolled along like a cascade of fire. [E 61]

In both Florence and Rome, Anna set out by herself to see the sights, impatient of the delay in waiting for the family. In Rome she made a solitary evening excursion, and from Florence she writes, "We have not been to the Gallery yet, but I have *on the sly;* my impatience would not wait." [E 45]

Her enthusiasm for Rome was unbounded, a part of the fashion of her day for things Italian, but much more a personal predilection, a foreshadowing of her lifelong love of Italy and her future preoccupation with its art:

I have visited St. Peter's three times, the Vatican twice, the Pantheon, the Capitol, the Coliseum, the Forum, the pillars of Antonine and Trajan, the Borghese, the Corsini, the Barberini Palaces, and last of all the Pope in his pontifical splendour in the chapel of the Quirinal Palace—*a good week's work* as Mr. Rowles calls it." [E 52]

I shall leave Rome with great regret. I have got acquainted with it as with a friend and it contains so much of interest that I shall leave many things unseen for want of an opportunity, for I cannot be so absurd as to suppose that I am abroad merely to walk about where and when I like, instead of performing those duties which belong to my situation; but all I could see and learn, I have seen and learnt. [E 66]

After her return home in the early summer of 1822, she evidently had hopes of establishing a school, for in August she writes, "I have purchased a good reputation in the world, am now rather well known; if I were to head an establishment with my sisters, aided by them, I should perhaps succeed." [E 69] This project, however, was not realized, perhaps from lack of sisterly co-operation, but more probably because of lack of capital. Instead, she accepted another position as governess, this time to the children of Mr. Littleton, afterwards Lord Hatherton. In September 1822 she is writing to her family from Teddesley, the Littleton residence in Staffordshire.

The Littletons were a family of wealth and position, tracing their lineage to an eminent fifteenth-century judge. Mrs. Littleton, niece of the Duke of Wellington, was celebrated for her beauty. Anna speedily became attached to her and particularly to the eldest daughter, Hyacinthe. During her tenure Anna wrote *Much Coin, Much Care*, a moralistic little drama for the children to perform; here also she probably wrote and published *Little Louisa*, a child's vocabulary of useful words. This dictionary could well be republished for children today: its definitions are both simple and interesting and its differentiations of meaning are eminently clear and reasonable.[1]

Anna stayed with the Littleton children until her marriage in 1825, a seasoned teacher whose earlier references to the "little elfs" in her charge had changed to more realistic and considerably more spirited comments. In a postscript to a letter marked 1824 she writes, "There are two d—— lookers-on peeping over my shoulder or I would say more."[2]

Her association with the Littleton family was one of lasting and mutual esteem. After her marriage they remained her friends and throughout her life she made periodic visits to Teddesley. In 1831 Robert Jameson writes to his wife from Dominica, "I hope this will reach you at Teddesley—and that you will be enjoying the delicious frost and snow of England." [E 85] Fanny Kemble, writing in 1837 to Anna Jameson who is absent in America, reports Lady Hatherton's interest and regard: "Lady Hatherton, whom I met the other evening at old Lady Cork's was speaking of you with much affection; and all your friends regret your absence from England."[3] In January, 1839, shortly after the publication of *Winter Studies and Summer Rambles in Canada*, Mrs. Jameson is again staying with the Hathertons:

We have had a large aristocratic party—the Wilmot Hortons, the Earl and Countess of Cavan, the Lady Lambarts and junior Bentincks, Vernons, Bagots, all very gay; but my chief delight has been the society and affection of my *ci-devant* pupil, Hyacinthe Littleton. My book has made me very *notorious*, and I have been praised and abused *à toute outrance*. [M 155]

Here is a culminating triumph indeed for the former governess and one senses Anna's enjoyment of both the society and the acclaim.

Although her fifteen years of intermittent teaching were by no means all discontent and oppression, she wrote of the profession later with considerable bitterness. The young woman who could enjoy the advantages which governessing brought and make light of its inconveniences became the mature authoress who, in "Of Mothers and Governesses" (1845) could not condone a single thing about it. "I have never in my life heard of a governess who was such by choice," [*ME* 281] she says, and gives as a reason for the deteriorating lot of the governess the increasing difficulties of marriage. "Forced celibacy with all its melancholy and demoralizing consequences" [*ME* 255] has made governesses a class so numerous that the supply exceeds the demand.

In Carlylean tones of doom she cries war on the class system, before she comes to the real core of her article—an insistence that some improvement in training for governesses is necessary. She was always, by our standards, a very moderate, even a timid feminist. She rejects at the outset the idea of a college for governesses in an argument whose validity is doubtful, but whose appeal to the editorial protectors of the hearth and home would be certain:

For myself, I should not much like to take into my family a woman educated expressly for a teacher. . . . A college expressly to teach women the art of teaching would be very useful; we want good and efficient female teachers for all classes, and there is no reason why we should not have female professors of distinct branches of knowledge, as grammar, arithmetic, the elements of mathematics, music, dancing, drawing;—but I do not trust to a woman professing them all in a lump: and, farther, I am of the opinion, that the same qualifications which might render a woman an admirable teacher of one distinct branch of knowledge would not render her a desirable governess; for to instruct is one thing, and to educate is another;—it requires a training of quite a different kind from any that could be given in a college for governesses. [*ME* 262]

She is forcefully outspoken about the contrast between the social position and prospects of the male tutor and the governess. The profession of tutor implies the "education of a scholar and a gentleman" and is one means by which a young man may make his way in the world without demeaning himself, jeopardizing his social position or shutting himself off from advancement. But for the governess, a woman whose "proper sphere is home," "the occupation of governess is sought merely through necessity, as the *only* means by which a woman not born in the servile classes *can* earn the means of subsistence." [*ME* 253]

Anna Murphy is caught in her time; though no one could have enjoyed the fruits of independence more than she, though no one was more industrious, she rejects the position of governess as something demeaning to one of her background and education. She resents women of her class having to work, almost as much as she deplores the lack of available training for such work. Therefore, either by choice, or expedience and obedience to public opinion, she is conveniently vague, the theoretical reformer of some halcyon time rather than the practical pusher of one specific scheme for improvement in conditions as they are: "It is very possible, that the necessity of having private governesses, except in particular cases, may . . . be done away with by a systematic and generally accessible education for women of all classes; and that some other means of earning a subsistence may be opened to the earnest woman, willing and able to work. . . . [*ME* 259]

To the mother looking for an employee and the governess seeking a post she gives sound advice, somewhat obscured in the governess' section by an overlay of complaint which would surely foster self-pity instead of the firm resolve she advocates: "After all, the best preparation is to look upon the occupation to which you are devoted (I was going to say *doomed*) as what it really is,—a state of endurance, dependence, daily thankless toil; to accept it as such courageously and meekly, because you must,—cheerfully, if you can;—and so make the best of it." [*ME* 285]

"Of Mothers and Governesses" has less logic than emotion and its effect would be less salutary on the governess class than shaming to the mothers and perhaps to the fathers and legislators of the day. The incidental suggestion of a future college for women may well be as clever a piece of propaganda as the final listing of cases on the records of the Governesses' Benevolent Institution is a clever gambit: no one who reads this evidence of responsibility beyond the means to bear it could dismiss Anna Jameson's foregoing words as a mere emotional tirade.

She was one of a host of nineteenth-century daughters who supported or helped to support their families, as is illustrated in the concluding statistics in "Of Mothers and Governesses": "Is obliged to maintain an invalid sister, who has no one else to look to."—Cases 6, 31, 34, 78, 81, 83. . . . "Supported both her aged parents, and three orphans of a widowed sister."—Case 65. . . . "Devoted all her earnings to the education of her five nieces, who all became governesses."—Case 93. [*ME* 297]

Anna Murphy pushed herself out of the governess class by her marriage and by the exertion of her considerable talent. Like her fictional contemporary, Becky Sharp, she did well from a humble beginning as governess; like Becky, her hair was of a sandy red and again like Becky, she was adept at seizing opportunities for self-improvement. There the comparison stops, for, unlike the notorious Becky, Anna was a woman of firm convictions, deep and responsible family attachments and many scruples. In 1845, in "Of Mothers and Governesses" she was writing for a cause from a position of assurance. Her own years of teaching had been by no means unproductive nor had the experience been as embittering as her pamphlet would lead one to believe.

3

Courtship and Marriage

ROBERT SYMPSON JAMESON of Ambleside, who became Upper Canada's first Vice-Chancellor and the first Speaker of the Legislature after the union of the Upper and Lower Canadas, was born in 1798, one of a family of three boys and a girl, children of Thomas Jameson of Somerly, Hants.[1] The little we know of his early life comes from his association with the Coleridge family in Ambleside where his mother and the children lived after his father's death. Robert's brother Joseph became a clergyman and for many years was Minor Canon and Precentor of Ripon Cathedral. He was a protégé of Wordsworth, the subject of a warm letter of recommendation to Archdeacon Francis Wrangham:

He has a Mother and a younger Brother dependant upon his exertions; and it is his wish to take pupils to encrease his income, which, as a Curate, you know cannot be but small.—He is an excellent young Man, a good Scholar, and likely to become much better, for he is extremely industrious. Among his talents, I must mention that for drawing; in which he is a proficient having at one time designed himself for that profession. . . . I [am] much interested in his welfare and that of his Family.[2]

Like his brother, Robert Jameson was talented in painting and sketching—his interest in art and literature was later to provide the basis of the mutual attraction between Anna Murphy and himself. He was the special boyhood friend of Hartley Coleridge, the son of Samuel Taylor Coleridge; a memoir of his brother by Derwent Coleridge attests the affectionate regard of all the Coleridges for Robert Jameson, but especially Hartley's friendship: "One friend he [Hartley] had, a resident in the town, though not a schoolfellow, Robert Jameson, to whom he afterward addressed a series of beautiful sonnets."[3] For some time in 1821–2, Jameson and Hartley Coleridge were evidently living together in London and on one occasion at least, Jameson was deputy-correspondent for Hartley to the Coleridge family: "My dear Father; You have probably, ere this, received Robert's letter, acqainting you that I am well in bodily health."[4]

Both Hartley Coleridge and Robert Jameson became the protégés of Basil Montagu, son of the fourth Earl of Sandwich and his beautiful mistress, the actress Martha Ray, whose shooting by a jealous young curate was a *cause célèbre* of the late eighteenth century. Montagu was a colourful, wealthy and influential man, a well-known lawyer and friend of the artistic *élite*. Hartley Coleridge lived with the Montagus for some time after the loss of his Oriel Fellowship and Henry Crabb Robinson reports a similar kindness to Robert Jameson: "Basil Montagu was fond of playing the patron. He did give the use of his chambers and instruction to Jameson, a poor lad from Westmoreland. . . ."[5]

These young men and others, encouraged by Montagu, formed an enthusiastic literary circle, hanging on the edges of the older group and at the same time drawing their famous elders into new ventures, notably *Fraser's London Magazine*. Charles Lamb writes: "Frazer, whom I have slightly seen, is Editor of a forthcome or coming Review of foreign books, and is intimately connected with Lockhart etc. so I take it that this is a concern of Murray's. . . . I have stood off a long time from these Annuals which are ostentatious trumpery, but could not withstand the request of Jameson a particular friend of mine and Coleridge."[6]

Through the years until 1828 there are various references in Lamb's letters to a continued association with Jameson:[7] in 1827 he writes of sending material to "Frazer's" through Jameson. A month later, Jameson is acting as Lamb's legal agent. In 1828, he is again doing some legal business for Charles Lamb who writes to Thomas Allsop:

I do not invite or make engagements for particular days; but I need not say how pleasant your dropping in any Sunday morning would be. Perhaps Jameson would accompany you. Pray beg him to keep an accurate record of the warning I sent by him to old Pam, for I dread lest he should at the 12 months' end deny the warning. The house is his daughter's but we took it through him and have paid the rent—to his receipts for his daughter's. Consult J. if he thinks the warning sufficient.[8]

Henry Crabb Robinson, a lawyer, friend and follower of the literary set, knew Jameson both socially and professionally. In 1821, Robinson "became acquainted with one [I] call a *strange* young man, a pupil of Basil Montagu's. He had taste, was, though merely an amateur painter, able to send landscapes to the Exhibition, [I] never became much acquainted with him."[9] Robinson's reminiscences of his professional career contain references to a "Jameson" with whom he was associated. On two occasions "Jameson prosecuted and he was not sufficiently master of himself to give any effect or spirit to his case. In a hurried manner he stated the law and the facts."[10] Later, Crabb Robinson was given a case through the agency of Jameson: "My attorney was a stranger. He had offered the brief to Jameson who declined it from a consciousness of inability to speak and recommended me."[11] Ominous as these sound for his future in law, they fit the picture we are later given of Robert Jameson by his wife and friends. He was never able to express himself orally with ease or warmth.

In the early twenties, however, his legal career was hopeful. He was called to the Bar in 1823 and taken under the patronage of the eminent Lord Chancellor Eldon in whose court he became a reporter. His respect for Lord Eldon and his decisions, termed excessive by later colleagues in Canada, was understandable in any young attorney, particularly so in a penniless young man with his way to make. The publication in 1824 of his *Cases in Bankruptcy*[12] set his feet up another rung in the legal ladder and perhaps his subject matter strengthened a predilection for money—his detractors always called him tight-fisted.

Early in his London career, in the winter of 1820–1, Robert Jameson was introduced to Anna Murphy by a North County friend of her father's, John Harden of Brathay Hall. Mr. Harden was a convivial hospitable Irishman whose doors were always open to a large group, including Samuel Coleridge and his sons, Wordsworth, John Wilson, the "Christopher North" of *Blackwood's*, whose own estate was not far distant, and, obviously, Denis Murphy.

The meeting flowered into courtship, but from its early days the relationship of Robert and Anna was an unstable one—their engagement in the spring of 1821 was broken off before Anna went to the Continent with the Rowles family. This trip may have been a kind of consolation prize; certainly its literary fruit, *The Diary of an Ennuyée*, leads us to believe that its writer was inconsolable from an unfortunate love affair. On the other hand, it would be by no means inconsistent with Anna's character to grasp at the chance for travel, resolutely breaking her engagement for it if necessary. Her letters home are by no means consistently, or at any time convincingly, broken-hearted—nor is Robert Jameson forgotten. After a month away she enquires about him: "Louisa mentions that Mr. Jameson has some intention of going to Switzerland. I wish you would find out when and how he goes, and what part of Switzerland he is going to visit. . . . If a small parcel has been left for me pray take *extreme* care of it as I value it particularly, and send it by Mr. Jameson if he comes or by the first opportunity." [E 32] In the fall, she is agitated by not hearing from him: "I promised Mr. Jameson I would write to him on a certain condition. I have written twice from Paris and Geneva; tell him so." [E 44]

Obviously still interested in keeping a hand on her rejected lover, she was suffering from some degree of both ill health and mental anguish. There are enough references to it in her letters to give a basis of truth to the subsequent *Diary*—the fictionalized story of her trip:

November 1, 1821 . . . I must now give some account of myself—and first assure you my dearest Mamma that I am much better than I have been for some time past and am beginning to grow fat and "well-favoured." I shall live to return to England in spite of prognostics and astonish you all with the wonders I have seen. [E 41]

November 29 . . . I continue better in health and have reason to be grateful for it; I have suffered so very much, I cannot well bear fatigue, but I take care never to utter the least complaint and to be as cheerful as possible. . . . though *real* pain of heart has a good deal damped my natural disposition to excitement and enthusiasm, I like to keep my mind tranquil and my imagination free and alive to all impressions of pleasure. [E 48]

She was taking a certain amount of pleasure from the self-dramatization to which she gave full treatment in the *Diary*. Such lines as these involve her family in the drama and presumably keep up the sympathies already engaged in the romantic *Sturm und Drang* of their eldest:

I found a letter here [Rome] from Mr. Jameson, which, by reviving that struggle in my heart which I thought I had subdued, has rendered me rather unhappy; but we must suffer in this world and whether we suffer from one thing or another makes no difference. I wrote to him—I do not know whether he will like my letter or answer it. [E 54]

As the trip nears its finish, she rejoices in the prospect of home—and it is surely significant that Mr. Jameson's Madonna is to be purchased at the forfeit of gifts for others:

How glad I shall be to see you all again! . . . In your letter mention all friends—Mr. Jameson and everybody. . . . I shall bring home no presents to anybody; that I feel rather a disappointment, but it cannot be helped. I wish to purchase the Madonna for Mr. Jameson which he commissioned me to buy—but the finest, which I long to get for him, the Dresden Madonna—is beyond my reach in point of price. [E 66]

It is difficult to remember from the tone of her letters home and particularly from the published *Diary*—misleading in respect to age—that Anna Murphy is not a young girl, but is rather a woman of twenty-eight with twelve years of a governess' career behind her and twice that many years of dominating her sisters and being the centre of family attention. Her soul-sufferings sound exaggerated and the entire trip takes on the appearance of a calculated risk as one begins to suspect that she had no intention of losing Jameson or his attentions to her.

However, it is evident from letters written after her return in the summer of 1822 that, though the courtship is re-established and Jameson is as eager as the absent Anna could have wished, she feels a basic incompatibility in their characters which warned her away from him once and is to continue to do so for another three years. Immediately on her return, in July of 1822, she writes to her mother that "Mr. J. is very unhappy and persevering and vehement, and makes me uncomfortable without meaning or wishing to do so. I do not change without cause and I cannot change again; it is not my nature or character." [E 68] The family, as usual, was involved in her romance and Eliza writes soon after: "Her spirits, I am sorry to say, are not what they used to be, but she is resigned and thoughtful. . . . She has made up her mind never to see Jameson again, which I believe is a sacrifice, and is chiefly the cause of her present lowness. I am in hopes that, in a few days, she will be better able to give me an account of her travels, which as yet she has very slightly mentioned." [E 68]

Anna had been both disappointed and disgruntled when the Rowles dismissed her in Paris to engage a French governess, cutting short her Continental stay. It is both easy and tempting to accuse her now of adopting a role and playing it to the hilt, with all the fitting dramatic trappings. The dramatization of herself as heroine did occur here, as it occurred again and again throughout her life; the impulse which led her to it was no superficial one but was deeply ingrained—the key to her behaviour on many occasions and a prime cause of both her triumphs and *débâcles*. She was certainly confused about her feelings and motives regarding Robert Jameson, but all the pressures around and within her—society, family and the desire for a married woman's status—pushed her toward surrender.

Denis Murphy obviously favoured this match, though he ruefully questions the wisdom of marriage in general:

What you say of Anna and Jameson, I had anticipated and wrote to Camilla about it. I should have spoken to Jameson long ago, but Anna herself prevented me. I am quite sure he is all honour and affection . . . but why should we urge these young people to marry and get into want and perplexities and ill humour? We must at all events wait until Jameson speaks for himself. [E 69]

In August of 1822 we have the longest and perhaps clearest analysis of the "strangeness" of Robert Jameson and his attraction for Anna Murphy that we are ever to get from her:

Papa has *settled* everything between Mr. Jameson and myself rather too hastily—in the first place I do not like to hear him called *poor Jameson*—in the next place, we are on just the same terms. I have the firm conviction that there exists a disparity between our minds and characters which will render it impossible for me to be *quite* happy with him, and yet I think that he will have me simply because I shall not, in the long run, be able to stand out against my own heart and his devoted affection, which is continually excited by the obstacles and the *coldness* which I throw in his way. There exists not a more amiable, excellent being. . . . [E 69]

By August 17, she was living at Teddesley Park, governess to the Littleton children. Jameson was again an accepted, if not encouraged suitor:

I have sent Mr. Jameson my phiz; by the by, were you sorry to part with it? and my little MS. book of Rhymes to which I added those written abroad. He has sent me a beautiful etching of his own performance. I hope you have seen it; I thought it was beautiful before I knew it was his. He writes delightful letters and shows his character and feelings in *them*, more than in his conversation. [E 70]

No doubt the artistic and literary affinity between Robert Jameson and Anna Murphy played a vastly important part in their courtship. He had friends among the respected authors of England and one can imagine the impression to be made on a clever young governess with literary aspirations by talk of evenings at Charles Lamb's or conversations with Coleridge. In his turn, Robert Jameson was sincerely impressed by Anna Murphy's talents and eager to help her develop and display them. His own interests were largely expended on patronage, encouragement and on playing the agent, rather than on original work of his own. But the references to Jameson's ease in writing and stiffness in conversation are ominous, recurring again and again throughout their association. While the indefatigable letter-writing habits of our nineteenth-century forebears are to be admired, their letter-courtships were surely a most unrealistic match-making exercise, particularly liable to disillusion when the participants were subjected to the realities of marriage.

For some three years, however, the relation was maintained in courtship, while Anna Murphy taught and Robert Jameson's legal career progressed favourably. He encouraged her to write for publication. A passage from a letter to her mother, dated 1822, shows her working at his request:[13]

. . . and the consecration of many of my short evenings to a little literary attempt made at Jameson's request and which he wishes to publish in the London Magazine. I have finished it, and it is by this time in the hands of Barry Cornwall; it was almost all written at Rome and Florence in the form of notes and now re-written, connected and corrected. I do not know what success it will have, nor do I hope for much. [E 71]

The June and September, 1822, issues of the *London Magazine* contain unsigned articles entitled "Sketches on the Road," dealing with travel in Italy; these may be the work to which Anna refers. On the editorial page of the November 1822 issue is a poem, signed A.J., which afterwards appears in *The Diary of an Ennuyée* as "A Farewell to Italy." These, as far as we have record, are her first appearances in print.

Finally, in 1825, after five years of hesitation and delay, Anna Murphy and Robert Jameson were married. She was thirty-one, well above the usual marrying age for her day; he, four years younger, though seemingly gentle and tractable, could be stubbornly independent, at least about petty issues. A rift occurred in the very first week: according to a family legend, on the Sunday after their marriage, Robert insisted on visiting the friends with whom he usually had dinner. Anna protested, as she did not know them, but finally, dressed in her wedding white, she set out with her husband. When it began to rain, she refused to continue and he left her to walk back to their rooms in the rain. He went on, had dinner and spent the evening with the friends, as usual. This tale is usually told as a black mark against Jameson, but might rather serve to indicate an early clashing of two strong wills.

For some time Mr. and Mrs. Jameson lived smoothly enough, setting up housekeeping in modest lodgings in the respectable but unfashionable neighbourhood of Chenies Street, Tottenham Court Road. As a protégé of Lord Eldon, Mr. Jameson's prospects were hopeful, but without family means, he was dependent for the present on a small income. He and Anna lived frugally, their social pleasures residing in Robert's *entrée* to literary circles.

It may be that he was spending his spare time on the revision of the Johnson and Walker *Dictionary of the English Language*. Though no mention of such a project occurs in the Jamesons' personal records, the British Museum catalogues the second edition, printed in 1828, "with an introduction by R. S. Jameson, Esq. of Lincoln's Inn," explaining and justifying the changes in Walker's pronunciation and announcing the addition of several thousand words.[14]

He continued his encouragement of Anna's work, securing the publication of her *Diary of an Ennuyée* through his friendship with Thomas, the eccentric cobbler-bookseller who knew all the literary *élite* of London. Thomas offered to print it at his expense and Anna, with no confidence in her work, jokingly asked only the promise of a Spanish guitar should it be successful. The work, first published as *A Lady's Diary*, was successful; it was speedily bought by Mr. Colburn the publisher for the sum of fifty pounds, ten of which Thomas spent on a guitar for Mrs. Jameson as promised. Colburn republished it in 1826 as *Diary of an Ennuyée* and its author, whose identity speedily became known, tasted the first fruits of success.

Anna's various protestations about the chance publication of her first work and her modest trepidations regarding it leave the reader with a tongue-in-cheek reaction, particularly in view of the earlier *London Magazine* efforts stemming from the same trip. Then too, in letters to her family during the trip, she had spoken of her practice of keeping two journals, one of them a diary record of places and events, the other, always kept "under lock and key," a faithful account of her own impressions, of interesting anecdotes and descriptions of scenery: "I have been very careful to be exact and accurate and *true* in every respect." [E 43] Several months later she had reported from Rome on work in progress:

As I have never failed noting down exactly and sincerely in my journal the impressions of every day, I think I shall be able to amuse you all, dear girls and Mamma and Papa, with some of my *scribbles.* . . . I have filled one note book and half another and have quite filled two thick journals, securely locked up, and have just bought a third, so I am not idle. I have collected material which, if I live and Heaven grants me health and that peace to which I have long been a stranger, I will turn to good account. . . . [E 65]

This, besides the self-dramatization to which she was addicted, sounds like a writer determined to make the most of her labours, rather than a bashful, modest diarist so uncaring and unsure of success that she jokingly bartered her book for a guitar. With knowledge of the indefatigable writer within Anna Jameson, it seems far more likely that she was anxious to have her work published at any price and that the initial reward was unimportant compared to the sight of her book in print. There is no reason, however, to disbelieve the story of the cobbler, the *Diary* and the guitar; in fact Mrs. Jameson was celebrated among her friends for musical ability and brought a guitar to Canada with her. It was probably the same instrument, an enduring, if small first literary profit.

4

The Diary of an Ennuyée

ANNA JAMESON'S FIRST PUBLISHED BOOK, a product of her tour with the Rowles family, was a fictionalized travel-biography, dressed up with Graveyard School sentimentality and catering to no fewer than three current vogues: notebooks on Italian travels, fiction and fact joined in Italian travel, and the Childe Harold's parade across Europe of a mysteriously broken heart. Its frontispiece introduction, however, takes care to claim that all that follows is fact, not fiction:

The following Diary is published exactly as it was found after the death of the Author; varied only by the omission of certain names. As a real picture of natural and feminine feeling, the Editor hopes that it may interest others as much as it has interested him. The asterisks mark the places where even more leaves had been torn away by the writer; and where there may sometimes appear a want of continuity. The little Poems interspersed were found in another volume, the companion of her travels; and have been inserted with regard to their dates, when dated, or to some evident connection with the feelings expressed in the Diary. [*Diary* Preface]

Charles Peter Brand in his study, *Italy and the English Romantics*, charts the course of popularity of things Italian among the English. He finds that beginning with a growing interest in Italian history after the publication of Gibbon's *Decline and Fall* and a growing interest in Italian artists which had been fostered by Sir Joshua Reynolds, the fashion for Italian travel rose and then declined as interest in the Romantic poets waned. Brand charts the numbers of travel books on Italy, finding a peak year in 1820 when thirteen new books appeared, and a continuing output throughout the twenties. Gradually the subject became so hackneyed that writers were driven farther and farther from the usual tourist routes until Maria Graham "ventured to spend *Three Months in the Mountains East of Rome* and Keppel Craven to explore the *Southern Provinces of Naples.*"[1]

Anna Jameson was also using quite freely the method and plan of Mme de Staël in *Corinne*, published in 1807, a travel account in fictional guise of the beauties of Italy. Mme de Staël, while she is said to have identified herself with her lovely, brilliant, broken-hearted heroine, is avowedly writing a novel. Anna goes further than the celebrated Baroness—nowhere does she admit that her work is fiction. She becomes her own heroine, the governess apotheosized into a romantic high-born young lady and, partly in truth, but mostly in fiction, she makes capital of her own "broken heart."

There is ample evidence in both her work and her letters that she was well aware of Anne Louise Germaine Necker, Baroness de Staël; that lady was the perfect idol for a governess with a romantic imagination, intellectual leanings and a degree of writing talent. In a letter home, she describes a visit to Coppet, Mme de Staël's Swiss home for a part of her long exile from France: "The Chateau is in itself beautiful and you may imagine with what reverence I visited every room. . . . a picture of Mme de Staël, when young, exhibited a figure and countenance the most striking and expressive I ever beheld." [E 37]

In both letters home and the *Diary* itself, she mentions *Corinne* as a valued travel-guidebook and Mme de Staël's methods of description as superbly effective. In the *Diary*, her violent reaction to *Corinne* becomes a useful part of her self-characterization as romantic heroine:

Nov. 28 . . . "Corinne" I find is a fashionable vade mecum for sentimental travellers in Italy; and that I too might be *à la mode*, I brought it from Molini's today, with the intention of reading on the spot, those admirable and affecting passages which relate to Florence; but when I began to cut the leaves, a kind of terror seized me, and I threw it down, resolved not to open it again. I know myself weak—I feel myself unhappy; and to find my own feelings reflected from the pages of a book, in language too deeply and eloquently true, is not good for me. I want no helps to admiration, nor need I kindle my enthusiasm at the torch of another's mind. I can suffer enough, feel enough, think enough, without this. [*Diary* 116]

The Childe Harold motif is recognizable in the mystery which surrounds her heroine's broken heart:

Ah! let me remember the lesson of resignation I have lately learned; and by elevating my thoughts to a better world, turn to look upon the miserable affections which have agitated me *here* as——.
The sentence which follows is so blotted as to be illegible.—Ed. [*Diary* 45]

There is tantalizing suggestion of a passion which must surely be guilty to cause so much pain:

Why was I proud of my victory over passion? Alas! what avails it that I have shaken the viper from my hand, if I have no miraculous antidote against the venom which has mingled with my life blood, and clogged the pulses of my heart! [*Diary* 45]

Finally, as the tour ends, there is ever increasing tragic suffering and death:

Lyons, 19. . . . If the cloud would but clear away, that I might feel and see to do what is right! but all is dark, and heavy, and vacant: my mind is dull, and my eyes are dim, and I am scarce conscious of anything around me. . . .

Yet if they would but lay me down on the roadside, and leave me to die in quietness! To rest is all I ask.
24. . . . St. Albin. We arrived here yesterday.
The few sentences which follow, are not legible.
Four days after the date of the last paragraph, the writer died at Autun in her twenty-sixth year, and was buried in the garden of the Capuchin Monastery, near that city.—Editor. [*Diary* 380]

Byronic suffering apotheosized into lady-like Christian resignation is celebrated in poetry:

> It is o'er! with its pains and its pleasures,
> The dream of affection is o'er!
> The feelings I lavish'd so fondly
> Will never return to me more. . . .
>
> But a spirit is burning within me,
> Unquench'd, and unquenchable yet;
> It shall teach me to bear uncomplaining,
> The grief I can never forget. [*Diary* 4]

Alongside these sentimental effusions, Anna Jameson displays a very healthy instinct for bookmaking. Her *Diary*, introduced as the "Diary of a Blue Devil," with a graceful tribute to Matthew's *Diary of an Invalid* and to "old Evelyn's," begins with and continues a chronological travel account across Europe from June 25 to July 27, according to the route described by Brand as the most popular one at that time. It is interrupted until August 25 by the insertion of a romantic and tragic tale, avowed true, and so given a touch of authenticity by Edmonds, a visitor to the heroine.

To her mixture she adds, on September 3, some Wordsworthian nature musings, judiciously placed after a brief account of a visit to the Pont des Arts:

Are there not times when we turn with indifference from the finest picture or statue—the most improving book—the most amusing poem; and when the very commonest, and everyday beauties of nature, a soft evening, a lovely landscape, the moon riding in her glory through a clouded sky, without forcing or asking attention, sink into our hearts? They do not console,—they sometimes add poignancy to pain; but still they have a power, and do not speak in vain: they become a part of us; and never are we so inclined to claim kindred with nature, as when sorrow has lent us her mournful experience. At the time I felt this (and how many have felt it as deeply, and expressed it better!) I did not *think* it, still less could I have *said* it; but I have pleasure in recording the past impression. [*Diary* 29]

Sometimes she describes natural scenery in ecstatic hyperbole, beginning by denying any ability to do justice to it and carrying on with lengthy enthusiasm: "I am so tired tonight, I can say nothing of the Jura, nor of the superb ascent of the mountain, to me so novel, so astonishing a scene; nor of the cheerful brilliance of the morning sun . . . nor of the far distant plains of France . . . nor of Morey, and its delicious strawberries and honeycomb; . . ." [*Diary* 33]

Interspersed with descriptions are anecdotes, often of contemporary or recent history. Anna produces for these an air of authenticity by such devices as quoting stories told by her boatman whom she describes in detail as "a fine handsome athletic figure. . . . He had been in the service of Lord Byron, and was with him in that storm between La Meillerie and St. Gingough, which is described in the third canto of Childe Harold. . . . Our boatman had also rowed Marie Louise across the lake, on her way to Paris." [*Diary* 35] Anecdotes from the lips of one who was there bear the seeming stamp of truth, as do those of "M. le Baron M--n, whom we knew at Paris, and who told me several delightful anecdotes of Josephine: he was attached to her household, and high in her confidence." [*Diary* 36]

Judiciously, the name of Lord Byron is kept before the reader. In his copy of Isaac D'Israeli's *Essays on the Literary Character*, lent to her in Venice, the Ennuyée finds marginal notes: "What was rumoured of me in that language, if *true*, I was unfit for England; and if *false*, England was unfit for me. But 'there is a world elsewhere.' I have never for an instant regretted that country,—but often that I ever returned to it." [*Diary* 78]

A brush with banditti was a titivating episode for a book on Italian travel and according to Brand, almost a prescribed part of the formula for writing such a book. Accordingly, Anna relates with horrific relish her trepidations at a mountain inn where some years before a series of traveller-murders had been committed: "Last night we slept in a bloodstained hovel. . . . " Even in her letters home, she mentions the imminent possibility of the whole party being kidnapped for ransom, thus adding the zest of danger to her travels, though without the Gothic flourishes of the *Diary*'s description: "O for the pencil of Salvator, or the pen of a Radcliffe. . . . At length, after passing the crater of a volcano, visible through the gloom by its dull red light, we arrived at the Inn of Covigliajo, an uncouth dreary edifice. . . ." [*Diary* 88]

The guide-book quality of the work and her special preoccupation with art are joined in reports on the various galleries, fearlessly confident in judgment and intensely personal in reaction:

The Dutch and Flemish painters (in spite of their exquisite pots and pans, and cabbages and carrots, their birch brooms, in which you can count every twig, and their carpets, in which you can reckon every thread) do not interest me; their landscapes too, however natural, are mere Dutch nature (with some brilliant exceptions), fat cattle, clipped trees, boors and windmills. Of course I am not speaking of Vandyke, nor of Rubens. . . . [*Diary* 111]

At this early stage, **her art criticism** is more a drawing of attention to works of the masters with rhapsodic praise or with blunt and personal dislike than it is an attempt at a reasoned appreciation:

There is a picture by Michel Angelo, considered a chef d'œuvre, which hangs in the Tribune to the right of the Venus: now if all the connoisseurs in the world, with Vasari at their head, were to harangue for an hour together on the merits of this picture, I might submit in silence, for I am no connoisseur; but that it is a disagreeable, a hateful picture, is an opinion which fire could not melt out of me. . . . a Virgin, whose brickdust coloured face, harsh unfeminine features, and muscular, masculine arms, give me the idea of a washerwoman (con rispetto parlando!) an infant Saviour with the proportions of a giant: and what shall we say of the nudity of the figures in the background; profaning the subject and shocking at once good taste and good sense? [*Diary* 108]

In later editions of the *Diary*, this passage is footnoted with an apologetic "This was indeed ignorance! (1834)."

A strong personal preference for the ideally beautiful and not the realistic was to be a continuing criterion, as was her preoccupation with the idealized representation of the human figure as the peak of an artist's achievement. She also engages in the misleading and, to our minds, fruitless pastime of judging the quality of the painter's character by the attractive qualities which she finds in his paintings. She conveniently finds, of course, that her favourite painters have had the most endearing personal qualities. "Take Raffaelle, for example, whose delightful character is dwelt upon by all his biographers; his genuine nobleness of soul, which raised him far above interest, rivalship, or jealousy . . . where, but in his own harmonious character, need Raffaelle have looked for the prototypes of his half-celestial creations?" [*Diary* 338]

She finds objectionable many paintings which deal with horror and suffering, especially one of Judith and Holofernes in the Pitti Palace at Florence which, to her dismay, was painted by a woman. Though she finds painting analogous at times to tragedy and certain painted martyrdoms "so many tragic scenes wherein whatever is revolting in circumstances and character is judiciously kept from view, where human suffering is dignified by the moral lesson it is made to convey," she can at times wish wearily that "there were fewer of them." [*Diary* 336]

There is, however, in the most mawkish of her effusions and in her most shallow judgments, a saving involvement of the author, an eagerness and enthusiasm to observe and report which is always readable, and sometimes, in her best passages, keenly enjoyable. In Paris, emphasis on *la mode* astonished her.

The rage for cashmeres and little dogs has lately given way to a rage for Le Solitaire, a romance written, I believe, by a certain Vicomte d'Arlincourt. Le Solitaire rules the imagination, the taste, the dress of half Paris: if you go to the theatre, it is to see the "Solitaire," either as tragedy, opera or melodrame; the men dress their hair and throw their cloaks about them *à la Solitaire*; bonnets and caps, flounces and ribbons are all *à la Solitaire*; the print shops are full of scenes from Le Solitaire; it is on every toilette, on every work table;—ladies carry it about in their reticules to shew each other that they are *à la mode*. . . .

To retrieve my lost reputation I sat down to read Le Solitaire and as I read, my amusement grew, and I did in "gaping wonderment abound," to think that fashion, like the insane root of old, had power to drive a whole city mad with nonsense; for such a tissue of abominable absurdities, bombast and blasphemy, bad taste and bad language was never surely indited by any madman, in or out of Bedlam: not Maturin himself, that king of fustian,

"———— ever wrote or borrowed
"Any horror half so horrid!"

and this is the book which has turned the brains of half of Paris, which has gone through fifteen editions in a few weeks, which not to admire is "pitoyable," and not to have read "*quelque chose d'inouie.*" [*Diary* 28]

Finally, she faithfully reflects the usual point of view of the nineteenth-century English traveller, who looks on Italy as something between an awe-inspiring museum, a health resort and an entertaining sideshow, with an unconcealed impatience with the social and political facts of its uneasy, Austrian-dominated existence:

How I detest politics and discord! How I hate the discussion of politics in Italy! and above all, the discussion of Italian politics, which offer no point upon which the mind can dwell with pleasure. . . . Let the modern Italians be what they may, what I hear them styled six times a day at least,—a dirty, demoralized, degraded, unprincipled race,—centuries behind our thrice blessed, prosperous, and comfort-loving nation in civilization and morals; if I were come among them as a resident this picture might alarm me: situated as I am, a nameless sort of person, a mere bird of passage, it concerns me not. . . . I love these rich delicious skies; I love this genial sunshine, which even in December, sends the spirits dancing through the veins; this pure elastic atmosphere, which not only brings the distant land-scape, but almost Heaven itself nearer to the eye; and all the treasures of art and nature which are poured forth around me; and over which my own mind, teeming with images, recollections, and associations can fling a beauty even beyond their own. [*Diary* 310]

Like many other English of her time, Anna Jameson found it possible later in life to live in Italy without the "alarm" she mentions and to appreciate the cheapness of living there.

The *Diary*, as published by Colburn, was reviewed in the *Monthly Review* for April, 1826, a periodical which was kindly, in general, in its treatment of female writers. The active promotion of Mr. Colburn for his authors' works may well have been operating in Anna's favour. At any rate her work, its authorship unknown, was given an encouraging, but admonitory article:[2]

We confess that we have felt some embarrassment how to treat this little volume. If it be what it professes, the genuine diary of a young and broken-hearted woman . . . it is scarcely matter for cold and fastidious criticism. But if it be really all this, we would then say to the friends of the poor girl, that they ought never to have suffered its publication. There are, however, a few contributions in the volume and even some suspicious traces of bookmaking. . . .

The reviewer speaks of the triteness of the subject matter but he approves of the author's style: ". . . [It] is lively and sufficiently correct . . . where her melancholy is for a moment forgotten, her narrative exhibits flashes of animation and gaiety; and there are several indications in the volume of talent both for humorous sketches of character and graphic delineation of scene." He encourages the effusiveness which our day finds tiresome and insincere, but which the 1820s expected of lady authors and applauded in them: "There is often a pleasing turn of poetical fancy about her." However, the same characteristic is deplored in her poetic pieces, none of which "rise at all above mediocrity."

Solemnly, with avuncular kindness, the reviewer warns the female sex against an offensive freedom of expression:

... here we are bound to remark, that there is at times in the Diary rather more freedom of expression than is usually found in the untravelled English-woman of five-and-twenty. With a love of the fine arts, our fair country-women learn to acquire on the Continent a license of observation and criticism which we would not willingly see substituted for the retiring sensitiveness of their insular manners. When the characteristics of Titian's genius are examined in the Diary, we are told of "his love of pleasure and his love of woman"; that "through all his glowing pictures we trace the voluptuary," and that "his virgins are rather des jeunes epouses de la veille." ... Most true; but we could have forgiven less accurate description from the pen of a young English woman.

Finally, in spite of his disapproval, the reviewer is caught by the romantic story of the heroine, for he ends with a quotation of the book's last lines and the comment that, "[t]here is something affecting and mournful in these closing pages, written, as it were, between time and eternity, and yet noting the habitual current of thought, and filled to the last with the daily occurrences of a journey which conducted the young and heartstricken traveller only to a tomb."

The *Diary* was a considerable success, perhaps not what the book trade of the 1820s would consider a best-seller, but certainly part of "la mode" of the day. As the fame of the Ennuyée grew, she was not unwilling to make her identity known. Indeed, at the Montagu house in Bedford Square, regarded by the literary *élite* as "something between a hotel and a Parnassus,"[3] Mrs. Jameson became the literary "lioness" of the hour, a stimulating experience for a formerly obscure but ambitious governess.

There were some, however, who did not forgive her for what they considered the perpetration of a hoax. Henry Crabb Robinson never recovered from the impression of dishonesty given him by Anna Jameson and her book, and on meeting her, he formed an instant dislike which he never completely overcame:

I saw . . . Mrs. Jameson, the very clever authoress. My first impression I copy from the journal. . . . She has desired me to call on her, but I do not like the expression of her countenance, and therefore doubt whether I shall—she looks like old Mrs. Crabb." I might have said: "She has the voice, as well as the fair complexion, of Mrs. Godwin, whom Lamb always called the Liar." And I never could effectually banish that association. . . .[4]

He does not record the reading of the *Diary* until 1832; then he says of it:

Read walking, what I have since finished, the *Diary of an Ennuyée,* amusing gossip; the affected sentimentality of a pretended invalid very disgusting. A young woman in good health and at her ease pretends to be suffering and even dying of grief—disappointed affections—and we have an account of the author's death. She is the wife of my old acquaintance, Jameson.[5]

Anna herself evidently felt a continued embarrassment at having begun her rise by the use of the broken-hearted heroine mask in her *Diary.* Before its republication in the collection called *Visits and Sketches at Home and Abroad,* she prefixed a note which is unlikely to be totally sincere but is certainly a polite apology:

With regard to a certain little Diary, of which it has been thought proper to give here a new edition, . . . — what shall I say? If I have cheated some gentle readers out of much superfluous sympathy—as it has been averred— it was certainly without design. I can but repeat here the excuse already inserted in another place, "that the work in question was *not* written for publication, nor would ever have been printed but for accidental circumstances; . . . " I regret that even this deception was practised, but would plead in excuse that the basis of that little book *was* truth; that it was, in reality, what it assumed to be, "a true picture of natural and feminine feeling." [VS "The Author to the Reader"]

5

Anna Jameson and Fanny Kemble

THE EXPERIENCE OF BEING MILDLY CELEBRATED and socially sought-after was not one to which Anna Jameson was at any time averse. The new stature and the many friends and acquaintances it brought her rewarded her eager ambition and stimulated her to further effort. The most important result of this early recognition, at least from the standpoint of her future work, was Anna's friendship with Fanny Kemble.

Fanny, born in 1809, was the niece of Sarah Siddons, for two generations England's most celebrated Shakespearean actress; she was the daughter of Charles Kemble, actor, owner and manager of Covent Garden Theatre, younger brother of Mrs. Siddons; she was shortly to become, almost overnight, the most famous "Juliet" of her day. She reported her first meeting with Anna Jameson with rueful humour at her own gullibility about the *Diary*:

At an evening party at Mrs. Montagu's, in Bedford Square, in 1828, I first saw Mrs. Jameson. The Ennuyée, one is given to understand, dies; and it was a little vexatious to behold her sitting on a sofa, in a very becoming state of blooming *plumpitude*; but it was some compensation to be introduced to her. And so began a close and friendly intimacy, which lasted for many years, between myself and this very accomplished woman. [K 124][1]

Her impression of Anna's appearance at the time is the most flattering description we have of her:

When first I met Mrs. Jameson she was an attractive-looking young woman, with a skin of that dazzling whiteness which generally accompanies reddish hair, such as hers was; her face, which was habitually refined and *spirituelle* in its expression, was capable of a marvellous power of concentrated feeling, such as is seldom seen on any woman's face, and is particularly rare on the countenance of a fair, small, delicately featured woman, all whose personal characteristics were essentially feminine. Her figure was extremely pretty; her hands and arms might have been those of Madame de Warens. [K 129]

Mrs. Jameson was fifteen years older than Fanny Kemble; at the time of their meeting the one was thirty-four, the other nineteen. Anna was no doubt genuinely impressed by the young girl's exuberant, witty and warm personality, as well as by her latent dramatic and literary talent. She was also impressed by the entire Kemble clan, who were respected and courted in a great variety of England's social and literary circles. Furthermore, one of the family, a Fanny Kemble of the preceding generation, had been a friend of the Murphys in Anna's childhood.[2] The young Fanny Kemble was of the third generation of these gifted artists and solid citizens; she was capable of an appreciation of her family's social prestige and a shrewd appraisal of the reasons for it:

In England alone is the pervading atmosphere of respectability that which artists breathe in common with all other men—respectability . . . a power, which, tyrannical as it is, and ludicrously tragical as are the sacrifices sometimes exacted by it, saves especially the artist class of England from those worst forms of irregularity which characterize the Bohemianism of foreign literary, artistic and dramatic life. [K 5]

Fanny had studied at the fashionable Parisian school of Miss Rowden who had formerly kept a school at Hans Place, London, and who had instructed Mary Mitford and Lady Caroline Lamb. The young Fanny was perhaps typical of her age in being impressionable and romantic, and perhaps true to her family's dramatic heritage in being excessively so. In her *Records of a Girlhood* she recounts her early intense emotional response to Byron, which she later resolutely subdued by denying herself the stolen pleasure of reading his poems. Her reaction to the *Diary of an Ennuyée* was likewise violent and again accompanied by disturbing qualms, not so much about its contents or its writer, as about her own state of mind:

About this time I met with a book which produced a great and not altogether favorable effect upon my mind (the blame resting entirely with me, I think, and not with what I read). I . . . was possessed with a wild desire for an existence of lonely independence, which seemed to my exaggerated notions the only one fitted to the intellectual development in which alone I conceived happiness to consist. Mrs. Jameson's "Diary of an Ennuyée," which I now read for the first time, added to this desire for isolation and independence such a passionate longing to go to Italy, that my brain was literally filled with chimerical projects of settling in the south of Europe, and there leading a solitary life of literary labor, which, together with the fame I hoped to achieve by it, seemed to me the only worthy purpose of existence. [K 124]

As Fanny Kemble was in the mood to be impressed by the writer of the *Diary*, so Anna Jameson needed only the encouragement of their pleasurable meeting to begin courting the goodwill of Fanny and all her family. From 1828 until Fanny's marriage in 1834, the end of *Records of a Girlhood*, there are many letters pointing to a "friendly intimacy" on the Kemble side and enthusiastic regard on Anna's.

In the autumn of 1829, the Kembles were suffering one of the worst of their many financial crises with Covent Garden Theatre. In a desperate effort to improve the family finances, it was decided that Fanny should be presented on the stage as Juliet. Her triumph is a matter of theatrical history: the wildest of applause was hers, as was the most faithful of coteries. Overnight she became the toast of London and was thereby committed intermittently throughout her life to a career in the theatre which she always insisted she disliked and distrusted.

By this time, Anna Jameson was close enough to the family to give her advice on the dressing of the new Juliet:

Poor Mrs. Jameson made infinite protests against this decision of my mother's, her fine artistic taste and sense of fitness being intolerably shocked by the violation of every propriety in a Juliet attired in a modern white satin ball dress amid scenery representing the streets and palaces of Verona in the 14th century, and all the other characters dressed with some reference to the supposed place and period of the tragedy. Visions too, no doubt, of sundry portraits of Raphael, Titian, Giorgione, Bronzino,—beautiful alike in colour and fashion,—vexed her with suggestions, with which she plied my mother. . . .

In later years, after I became the directress of my own stage costumes, I adopted one for Juliet, made after a beautiful design of my friend, Mrs. Jameson, which combined my mother's *sine qua non* of simplicity with a form and fashion in keeping with the supposed period of the play. [K 189]

Fanny Kemble's reminiscences about the early days of her fame provide a lively record of life in her affectionate but authoritarian family. By night, she was a sudden star of London, sought after, pampered and praised by all of society and courted by the infatuated young FitzClarence, son of William IV and the actress Mrs. Jordan. By day, she was a dutiful daughter, very much in the sphere of her parents' influence. Even Anna Jameson, quite obviously admired by the young actress and respected by the parents, was rebuffed with noticeable decision when her invitations were so frequent and importunate as to threaten the rules of decorum. Intermittent signs of a strain which was always to mark the Jameson-Kemble family relationship are evident in a letter, dated March, 1831.

GREAT RUSSELL STREET, MARCH, 1831

DEAR MRS. JAMESON,

My mother is confined to her bed with a bad cold, or she would have answered your note herself; but, being disabled, she has commissioned me to do so, and desires me to say that both my father and herself object to my going anywhere without some member of my family as chaperon; and as this is a general rule, the infringement of it in a particular instance, however much I might wish it, would be better avoided, for fear of giving offence where I should be glad to plead the prohibition. She bids me add that she fears she cannot go out tomorrow, but that some day soon, at an early hour, she hopes to be able to accompany us both to the British Gallery. Will you come to us on Sunday evening? [K 370]

The Kemble family's wariness of Mrs. Jameson and perhaps of her influence (she was, Fanny tells us, lending her notices and criticisms of *The Cenci*), persisted throughout the spring of 1831. Several other letters from Fanny demonstrate their polite refusal of Anna's voluntary involvement in their lives: "She [Mrs. Kemble] bids me thank you very much for the kindness of your proposed visit, and express her regret at not being able to avail herself of it." [K 385] In a letter of 1830 about a suitable governess for her young sister Adelaide, Fanny writes: "I am sorry to say that the lady Mrs. Jameson recommended for her governess has not been thought sufficiently accomplished to undertake the charge." [K 284]

In 1830, Fanny's brother John, fired with youthful idealism, involved himself with a revolutionary Spanish movement. His family was desperately anxious about him and rightly so, for the movement was discovered, many of its supporters were imprisoned and some were executed. He escaped and his sister's subsequent letter to Anna carries an odd note of obligation as well as family gratitude for her sincere concern: "My brother John is alive, safe and well in Gibraltar. You deserve to know this, but it is all I can say to you." [K 334]

At certain times, Mrs. Jameson's determined companionship caused Fanny Kemble some embarrassment though this, judging from the tone of its recounting, was borne with good humour:

I was at this time sitting for my picture to Mr. Pickersgill. . . . Unluckily, Mrs. Jameson proposed accompanying me, in order to lighten by her very agreeable conversation the tedium of the process. Her intimate acquaintance with my face, with which Mr. Pickersgill was not familiar, and her own considerable artistic knowledge and taste made her, however, less discreet in her comments and suggestions with regard to his operations than was altogether pleasant to him; and after exhibiting various symptoms of impatience, on one occasion he came so very near desiring her to mind her own business, that we broke off the sitting abruptly. . . . [K 366][3]

The pattern of this friendship establishes a design that was to be repeated at intervals throughout Anna Jameson's lifetime. She is the seeker and the instigator; the subject of her enthusiasm, at first genuinely attracted and impressed, becomes alarmed and impatient at her insistence and cannot return in full measure her enthusiastic regard.

Hayter, a fashionable artist, drew a series of sketches of Fanny Kemble as Juliet and for these Anna wrote the letterpress. Fanny records "Mrs. Jameson's beautifully written but too flattering notice of my performance." [K 235][4] In 1834, she writes from Boston a direct rebuke of Anna's fulsome praise:

But without wishing to enter into any discussion about my merits or your partiality, I can only repeat that you are free to write of me what you will, and as you will; but, for your own sake, I wish you to remember that praise is, to the majority of readers, a much more vapid thing than censure, and that if you could admire me less and criticise me more, I am sure, as the housemaids say, you would give more satisfaction. [K 587]

In August of 1830 when the Kembles, father and daughter, are on tour in Liverpool, Fanny writes to her great friend, Harriet St. Leger, "You must not call Mrs. J. —— my friend, for I do not. I like her much, and I see a great deal to esteem and admire in her, but I do not *yet* call her my friend." [K 286]

It is disturbing to read the record of a friendship which seems on Anna Jameson's side over-anxious and on Fanny Kemble's side admiring, but slightly unwilling. Yet it is certain that the major benefit of this Kemble relationship must have gone Anna's way. Though her contacts through the Montagus and the Procters were many, and though her circle was increasingly enthusiastic about her talent, the various worlds and friendships opened to her through the Kembles must have been both useful and socially enjoyable. Furthermore, at the time, and perhaps for long afterward, Anna Jameson was stage-struck. Shakespeare's works were a favourite topic of conversation between herself and her young friend and it is certain that Fanny and the Kemble-Siddons' stage interpretations of his heroines played an important part in Anna's subsequent *Characteristics of Women*. Fanny speaks of Mrs. Jameson "threatening" to write a play, an ambition which was not realized:[5]

Friday 29th [April, 1831] . . . Mrs. Jameson paid me a long visit; she threatens to write a play; perhaps she might; she is very clever, has a vast fund of information, a good deal of experience, and knowledge and observation of the world and of society. She wanted me to have spent the evening with her on the 23rd, Shakespeare's birth and death day, an anniversary all English people ought to celebrate. [K 394]

There were other important social contacts in the years after the publication of the *Diary*. Mrs. Montagu, the wife of Basil Montagu, and her daughter, Mrs. Procter, wife of Bryan Waller Procter ("Barry Cornwall," the poet), were among the most admiring of her correspondents. Mrs. Procter's letter of June, 1827 is written in terms which sound over-enthusiastic to our ears until we realize that they are simply a part of the currently accepted vocabulary for sincere admiration:

When do you go into Devonshire? . . . pray write to me or I shall think that, like many ladies, my letter has lost me *my lover*. . . . You have all the faults of one . . . you spoil me, encourage my vanity, for I say really if Mrs. Jameson, who first of all is very sensible, then has a great deal of taste, has known so many agreeable people, etc., etc., etc., likes me, I must be charming. . . .
My dear Mrs. Jameson, I do not think this, I only think that I have more enjoyment in your society than in any one else's and I am very grateful to you for sparing me so much of your time. . . . [E 77]

Mrs. Montagu writes in a more restrained though equally cordial vein, at the same time paying tribute to one of Anna Jameson's most ingratiating talents, her ability to sketch and her readiness to present her friends with pleasant and flattering examples of her work:

In all this time, I have not said one word of what is nearest my heart. . . . I do not say "dear Mrs. Jameson" or "Sweet woman" or "talented creature" or any of those glib sentences which slide so easily off the tongue that one shrewdly suspects they are only to be found where deep waters take their course silently, while the inch-deep brook babbles to every passer-by and talks loudest when it has a hard and rocky bosom. You gave me a charming portrait of your Mary Ashworth, for so I think your fair relation is called, and today you have sent us a lovely Landscape which forms a delightful background to your figures; there should have been only one, for so lovely a Claude, but you put a swing between the elms and made a Watteau of it at once. . . . [E 79]

On more than one occasion Fanny Kemble mentions sketches which Mrs. Jameson has done for her and of her, always in tones of great appreciation: "Talking of stupid parties, your beautiful little pictures of me and my various costumes helped away two hours of such intolerably dull people here the other night. I assure you we all voted you devout thanks on the occasion." [K 479] She refers to these as "Mrs. Jameson's beautiful toy likenesses of me." Later she is delighted to find in the home of a friend, Lord Ellesmere, "a miniature of me copied from a drawing of Mrs. Jameson's by that charming clever woman, Miss Emily Eden." [K 578]

These were years of social success for Anna Jameson. In all the recorded impressions of her, only Carlyle joins Henry Crabb Robinson in being openly antagonistic. Since Carlyle was never noted for the sunniness of his nature, the violence of his reaction may be somewhat discounted as a dyspeptic tirade:

I got to Bayswater, and found the celebrated Mrs. Jameson on the point of arriving. Would she had never arrived! Did I lose my heart to her? Ach Gott! A little, hard, brown, redhaired, freckled, fierce-eyed, square-mouthed woman; shrewd, harsh, cockney-irrational: it was from the first moment apparent that without mutual loss, we might "adieu and wave our lily hands."[6]

In 1829, Robert Jameson left England for an appointment as puisne judge in the island of Dominica. Crabb Robinson gives to Basil Montagu the credit for Jameson's later appointment to Upper Canada.[7] Chief Justice Read, in his *Lives of the Judges*, emphasizes Jameson's patronage by Lord Eldon, the Tory Chancellor, remarking, with some sarcasm, that, though Mr. Jameson had been represented in his early days at the Bar as having learning beyond that of the average barrister, "it has not been represented whether this average was general average or special average." In a passage whose tone is totally unsympathetic, he concludes that the presence of outlying Colonies of the Empire was a saving boon to Mr. Jameson.[8]

By the time of Robert's departure, Anna Jameson was making no secret of her unhappiness in marriage. From this time forward, she was given to expressions of self-pity and she invited sympathy from her friends. Fanny Kemble writes to her with motherly concern:

I am sure you will believe me when I say that, without the remotest thought of intruding on the sacredness of private annoyances and distresses, I most sincerely sympathize in your uneasiness, whatever may be its cause, and earnestly pray that the cloud, which the two or three last times we met in London hung so heavily on your spirits, may pass away. It is not for me to say to you "Patience," my dear Mrs. Jameson; you have suffered too much to have neglected that only remedy of our afflictions. . . . [K 266]

Fanny again expressed her concern and her sense of Anna's depth of unhappiness in her diary in June, 1831:

Mrs. Jameson came and sat with me some time. We talked of marriage, and a woman's chance of happiness in giving her life into another's keeping. I said I thought if one did not expect too much one might secure a reasonably fair amount of happiness, though of course the risk one ran was immense. I never shall forget the expression of her face; it was momentary, and passed away almost immediately, but it has haunted me ever since. [K 423]

The separation further strained an already unsuccessful marriage; it may also have been an escape for both the Jamesons from a totally impossible union. An anonymous writer in *The Argosy*, probably Mrs.

Henry Wood, its editor, attributes the eventual complete separation to Robert Jameson's increasing envy of his wife's accomplishments and fame.[9] However true this theory may be, in the early years Jameson was certainly both admirer and patron of his wife's work.

He does seem to have had a personality well meriting Crabb Robinson's epithet "strange." Once in Dominica, his letters are affectionate and charming, with no sign of a rift and every indication of regret at separation, although he does discourage any idea of his wife joining him:

I am startled at the thought of your coming here as at something suicidal, though your society would make even this place happy to me, though the only object of my coming out here was that I might hereafter live in comfort with you. I dare not think of such a thing. I must return to England, or get a better appointment. Had I even a thousand pounds in my possession, I should be tempted to quit this country; anything rather than this wearisome banishment. . . .

. . . I have borne much very goodtemperedly hitherto, but it cannot be wondered at that I am not satisfied to go on thus, year after year, separated from you and all who are dear to me, a sot, contented to live and die among those whose most refined pleasures are eating Turtle and drinking punch and Madeira.

. . . I would ask a thousand questions about others, but it is sickening to think of the months that must elapse before they could be answered. I shall therefore rely upon your telling me what you know will be a matter of interest. Would to Heaven that before such answer could arrive, I might be on my way to England! The most tempestuous passage across the Atlantic would in itself be delightful, if it led to such a conclusion; in short, I am sick *for* home as *of* the West Indies. [E 86]

Robert Jameson voiced the homesick cry of hundreds of nineteenth-century colonial administrators who considered themselves exiled and lost among second-class citizens and who, all too often, turned to punch and Madeira as a cheap and handy anaesthetic for their homesickness. Whether or not Jameson's drinking was an early problem to him and whether this was a major factor in the failure of the marriage, we do not know. It was to become a debilitating factor during his later years in Canada.[10]

In the summer of 1829, after Robert Jameson's departure, Mrs. Jameson and her father accompanied a wealthy friend and patron, Sir Gerard Noel, on a Continental tour. Noel's reason for this particular journey is not known or not mentioned; perhaps he was on a picture-buying expedition with an artist-adviser along; perhaps Anna Jameson went as governess-companion to his young daughter, Harriet Jane, whom Anna describes as "a good little creature, with some of her father's caprices, much of his talent and more of his real benevolence."

Since Mrs. Jameson describes the trip as taken for mere amusement, it may have been one of the wealthy Sir Gerard's caprices to take Mr. Murphy and his daughter to Europe. In a letter home she gives a pleasant report of her father's enjoyment:

As to Papa, he is in excellent spirits and desires me to tell you that he behaves very well. He goes wandering about and admiring everything he sees and he has bought a pair of spectacles for ten pence which are the best in the world and a pair for Mama and a lantern for Edward to send up at his kite's tail, with other invaluable things, too many to commemorate, and I think I never saw him so happy or look better. [E 81]

If Anna and her father went hoping that the trip might have a profitable side effect, they were not disappointed: Sir Gerard bought the "Windsor Beauties" which, ever since the death of Princess Charlotte, Denis Murphy had been trying to sell.

In *Visits and Sketches* (1834), a work which is, in part, an account of this tour, Anna describes the party's mode of travel in terms which are a classically witty evocation of the nineteenth-century English gentleman's party abroad:[11]

We travelled à la milor Anglais—a partie carrée—a barouche hung on the most approved principles—double-cushioned—luxurious—rising and sinking on its springs like a swan on the wave—the pockets stuffed with new publications—maps and guides *ad infinitum*; English servants for comfort, foreign servants for use; a chess-board, backgammon tables—in short, surrounded with all that could render us entirely independent of the amusements we had come to seek and of the people among whom we had come to visit. [VS I, 21]

Sir Gerard is the subject of one of Anna's best sketches. With a warmth and sincerity coloured by gratitude, she delineates this eccentric Englishman in terms that bring to life a type of elderly aristocrat; hard-living, broadly cultured, gay, and gallant—one of a class carefully cultivated and cherished for some centuries, aggressively individual, and above all, English:

Our CHEF *de voyage*, for so we chose to entitle him who was the planner and director of our excursion, was one of the most accomplished and most eccentric of human beings; even courtesy might have termed him old, at seventy; but old age and he were many miles asunder, and it seemed as though he had made some compact with Time, like that of Faust with the devil, and was not to surrender to his inevitable adversary till the very last moment. Years could not quench his vivacity, nor "stale his infinite variety." He had been one of the prince's wild companions in the days of Sheridan and Fox, and could play alternately blackguard and gentleman, and both in perfection; but the high-born gentleman ever prevailed. He had been heir to an enormous income, most of which had slipped through his fingers *unknownst* as the Irish say, and had stood in the way of a coronet, which, somehow or other, had passed over his head to light on that of his eldest son. He had lived a life which would have ruined twenty iron constitutions, and had suffered what might well have broken twenty hearts of common stuff; but his self-complacency was invulnerable, his animal spirits inexhaustible, his activity indefatigable. The eccentricities of this singular man have been a matter of celebrity; but against each of these stories it would be easy to place some act of benevolence, some trait of lofty, gentlemanly feeling, which would at least neutralize their effect. He often told me that he had early in life selected three models, after which to form his own conduct and character; namely, De Grammont, Hotspur, and Lord Herbert of Cherbury; and he certainly did unite, in a greater degree than he knew himself, the characteristics of all three. [VS I, 22]

With a sensibility that would have done credit to Sterne himself, Sir Gerard indulged his emotions while his busy observer savoured and recorded his enjoyment:

[At the opera] I remember that on looking round after Donna Anna's song, I was surprised to see our chef de voyage bathed in tears; but no whit disconcerted, he merely wiped them away, saying, with a smile, "It is the very prettiest, softest thing to cry to one's self!" Afterward, when we were in the carriage, he expressed his surprise that any man should be ashamed of tears. "For my own part," he added, "When I wish to enjoy the very high sublime of luxury, I dine alone, order a mutton cutlet, 'cuite à point', with a bottle of Burgundy on one side and Ovid's epistle of Penelope to Ulysses on the other; and so I read, and eat, and cry to myself." And then he repeated with enthusiasm—
    "Hanc tua Penelope lento tibi mittit Ulysse:
    Nil mihi rescribas altamen ipse veni;" [sic]
his eyes glistening as he read the lines; he made me feel their beauty without understanding a word of their sense. [VS I, 31]

With such a host and hopeful prospects for sale of the "Beauties," Anna and her father followed an itinerary which is not completely known, since the published account of it is mixed with that of her next trip to Germany. Italy, the former tourist Mecca, was discarded in favour of a trip through the Low Countries, Germany and down the Rhine; perhaps there was some special reason for the itinerary, but it is more probable that they were following the current fashion which was switching at this time from Italy to Germany. At any rate the trip stimulated in Anna an interest in Germany's literature, art and society, an important influence on her for the rest of her life. It also provided the therapy of change and relief from tension. The opportunity of any trip was always a challenge, and this one was an especially welcome refreshment after the vicissitudes of her married state.

6

Memoirs of Poets, Sovereigns and Court Beauties

CARLYLE REFERRED TO ANNA JAMESON as one of "the swarm that came out with the annuals,"[1] those publications which came into being to supply the demand for entertaining and pleasantly improving reading for a great new interested public. *Blackwood's*, with its familiar tone of tongue-in-cheek, patronizing banter, traces the history of the great revolution which put light, polite reading into the hands of the well-to-do women of England:

. . . we simply assert, that in the times we allude to (don't mention dates) there was little or no reading in England. There was neither the Reading Fly nor the Reading Public. What could this be owing to, but the non-existence of periodicals? What elderly-young lady could be expected to turn from house affairs for example, to Spenser's Fairy Queen? It is a long, long poem, that Fairy Queen of Spenser's; nobody, of course, ever dreamt of getting through it. . . . As to Shakespeare, we cannot find many traces of him in the domestic occupations of the English gentry during the times alluded to; nor do we believe that the character of Hamlet was at all relished in their halls, though perhaps an occasional squire chuckled at the humours of Sir John Falstaff. We have Mr. Wordsworth's authority for believing that Paradise Lost was a dead letter and John Milton virtually anonymous. We need say no more. Books like these, huge heavy vols. lay with other lumber in garrets and libraries. As yet, periodical literature was not; and the art of painting seems to have preceded the art of reading. It did not occur to those generations that books were intended to be read by people in general, but only by the select few. Whereas now, reading is not only one of the luxuries, but absolutely one of the necessaries of life, and we no more think of going without our book than without our break-fast. . . . No mouth looks up now and is not fed; on the contrary, we are in danger of being crammed; an empty head is as rare as an empty stomach; the whole day is one meal, one physical, moral and intellectual feast; the

Public goes to bed with a Periodical in her hand and falls asleep with it beneath her pillow.[2]

Anna Jameson was one of the many who wrote to answer the steady demand, perhaps filled primarily by the periodical press, but also by other reading material, all of it advocating moral uplift and pleasant, not too taxing intellectual improvement. *Blackwood's* "elderly young lady" who could not be expected to find her way in and out of *The Faerie Queene*, could and did respond to *Loves of the Poets* and to *Lives of Celebrated Female Sovereigns*. Though not written for the annuals, they are cut to the same specifications; they are informative, moral, sentimental, and sometimes misleadingly prettied-up history, biography and criticism—a kind of pocket anthology for the gracious lady reader. They provide an ideal target for *Blackwood's* concluding parody on the annuals' style of writing: ". . . the sunshine strikes the intermingled glow and threatens to set the house on fire. But softly— they are cool to the touch, though to the sight burning. Innocuous is the lambent flame that plays around the leaves; even as, in a dewy night of fading summer, the grass brightening circle of the still glow-worm's light."[3]

The *Memoirs of the Loves of the Poets* are exactly what they announce themselves to be: a series of biographical sketches of women celebrated in ancient and modern poetry, with emphasis on their subjects' romantic attachments, determinedly pure and safely con-jugal in their stress. To these are added anecdotes of historical interest and a measure of innocuous and vapid criticism, largely in the form of quotations from the poems and rapturous comments upon them. The sketches are informative—in fact gratifyingly full of factual his-torical data. Mrs. Jameson had the instincts of a scholar: she had the grace to use footnotes and she refers to many authorities, but these are almost always historical or biographical and not critical.

Her method as a biographer-critic is the same as her method of art criticism. She relates the poetry to the life of the poet and she reacts personally and violently. She insists, for instance, that Milton was a tender lover, that any unhappiness in his relations with women was the fault of the women involved, particularly of the luckless Mary Powell and her relatives: ". . . to be obliged to regard the mighty father of English verse,—him 'who rode sublime upon the seraph wings of ecstasy' . . . to think of such a being as a petty domestic tyrant, a coarse-minded fanatic, stern and unfeeling in all the relations of life, were enough to confound all our ideas of moral fitness." [*LP* 251] Her denunciation of Johnson for his treatment of Milton and his domestic relations reaches ridiculous but very quotable heights: Milton like his own Adam, "radiant like another Moses" and Johnson, "the Hippopotamus of literature."

Her declared purpose is to illustrate "the influence which the beauty and virtue of women have exercised over the character and writings of men of genius." Various footnote references attest the continuing influence of Mme de Staël on her, as does the epigraph, "Il vaut mieux réunir tous ses efforts pour descendre avec quelque noblesse, avec quelque réputation, la route qui conduit de la jeunesse à la mort." [*LP* Preface]

The contemporary interest in Italian literature is well illustrated by the weighting of the material. In the first twenty-two chapters, eight deal with Italian poets and their loves, three with French, one with classic poets, the rest with English. The next ten chapters, which examine conjugal poetry, are divided into one classical, one German, four Italian, and four English. The final chapters, thirty-three to forty, deal with six English poets and two French ones. Obviously, German literature had not yet the interest for Anna Jameson and for the public that it was to have in the 1830s.[4]

Anna Jameson had ample intelligence to be aware of critical pitfalls, but no sense of responsibility about treating any poet or his poetry in a way that did not suit her declared purpose: "This, in general terms, was the progress of the lyric muse, from the poets of Queen Elizabeth's days down to the wits of Queen Anne's. Of course, there are modifications and exceptions, which will suggest themselves to the poetical reader; but it does not enter into the plan of the sketch to treat matters thus critically and profoundly." [*LP* 264] In *Loves of the Poets*, Anna is usually writing far below her own potential as a critic, as Professor Nethercot has implied by the rather grudging credit given her for being, along with Alexander Chalmers, one of the few "really perspicacious" nineteenth-century critics who made a distinction between John Donne's satires and much of his other verse.[5] Part of her purpose, and her protection from serious critical attack, is given her by the feminine audience she addresses: "It is for women I write; the fair, pure-hearted, delicate-minded, and unclassical reader will recollect that I do not presume to speak of these poets critically, being neither critic or scholar; but merely with a reference to my subject, and with a reference to my sex." [*LP* 22]

In so picking her subject, and in so treating it, she was once again writing for the public taste. She was never a radical, though a woman writer in her day was open to that suspicion. She would now be considered too conservative, too easily led by friends, publisher, public

taste, and ambition for easy fame into a distortion of her genuine
instinct for research and considerable facility in writing. Such passages
as the following comparison of Elizabeth of England and Mary Queen
of Scots are still readable and persuasive by their energy of imagination and grace of expression:[6]

These two queens, so strangely misplaced, seem as if, by some sport of
destiny, each had dropt into the sphere designed for the other. Mary should
have reigned over the Sydneys, the Essexes, the Mountjoys;—and with her
smiles, and sweet words, and generous gifts have inspired and rewarded the
poets around her. Elizabeth should have been transferred to Scotland, where
she might have bandied frowns and hard names with John Knox, cut off
the heads of rebellious barons, and boxed the ears of illbred courtiers.
This is no place to settle disputed points of history, nor, if it were,
should I presume to throw an opinion into one scale or the other; but
take the two queens as women merely, and with a reference to apparent
circumstances, I would rather have been Mary than Elizabeth; I would
rather have been Mary, with all her faults, frailties, and misfortunes. . . .
[LP 209]

The list of references which she used and acknowledged is impressive, not for its exhaustive scholarship or scrupulous honesty, for it
displays neither of these, but for its being there at all. It was quite
accepted, particularly for lady writers of her day, to romp happily
through any and every source plagiarizing as they would. Harriet
Martineau saw no need to acknowledge her sources for *Tales of
Political Economy*; the popular authoress Letitia Landon (L.E.L.),
whose personal life bears some parallels to Anna's own, came finally
to the very sad pass of quoting herself, reworking again and again
her own old material.[7]

Anna Jameson's incipient, if incomplete, scholarship is a positive
value in her work, one which impressed itself, no doubt, on her
reviewers and was a part of the reason for their encouragement. Their
approval did not, however, extend to encouragement towards objectivity or toward becoming a declared scholar-critic. Nor did her own
sights ever rise that high. One tires of her recurrent "nor . . . should I
presume to throw an opinion into one scale or the other" and the
even more frequent "none but the fair sex shall be my readers"; one
must recognize, finally, that this humility was only partly insincere, if
at all. Her critics at this stage in her career treated her always as a
lady-writer first and as a writer second; this she expected and, indeed,
of it she made capital. Her attitudes were those which society in her
day expected of her; they assured her of admirers and readers and of a
market for all she could produce. Most important, they aligned the
weapons of criticism for, and not against her.

Within these bounds, self-imposed and society-imposed, Anna Jameson could and did gradually gain influence, the confidence of the public and the franchise to speak as she would and be heard. If she was aware of any choice, she does not show it. She was untrained for depth of scholarship and, most assuredly, for objective criticism, as indeed were most of her contemporaries and readers. She got a great deal of what she wanted—recognition, admiration, encouragement, and, not least, money—for writing as she did. Her letters show not the slightest chafing under the rules. Had she written with less tact and more critical scholarship, her work might have been more satisfying to the twentieth century; it would not, perhaps, have been published in the nineteenth.

In September, 1829, *Blackwood's* reviewed *Loves of the Poets.* John Wilson, "Christopher North"—the reviewer identifies himself as "Old Kit"[8]—takes exactly the same complex tone as for his "Monologue on the Annuals." It is unctuous, often flattering; it matches effusion with an inflated effusiveness of its own; while praising it often manages to damn, for, though one may tend to read more sophistication into "Old Kit" than was actually there, one is convinced that he found the rapturous outpourings on the poets' loves a trial hardly to be borne. But although he shows every tongue-in-cheek indication of patronage to the ladies' literature, he does devote some fifteen pages to its consideration, pages filled with lengthy quotations. On the premise that any publicity is good, for a beginner at least, this wordage from *Blackwood's* must have been an encouragement, if also in part a considerable annoyance to Anna.

The review is a curious one; why would this periodical, already notorious for personal attack, gratuitously insult a woman and at the same time hold her book before the public, supposedly with esteem? "Christopher North," disclaiming malicious intent in any direction and adopting a pose of injured innocence in the face of past charges of slander, says:

To give the devil his due, Old Kit was still the Friend, Lover, Slave and Lord of the ladies.
And here it behooves us to set ourselves right with our readers in one particular. Is there, or is there not, such a thing in nature as an ugly woman—not comparatively, but positively? We do not scruple to answer—yes. We saw her—this very day. Red hair—a mouth that—But, to the surprise of Dr. Knox, let us run away from the subject. . . .
That the authoress of "The Loves of the Poets" is a beautiful woman, using that epithet in any one of its million meanings you choose, we lay no claim to a particular fine tact in having discovered from the nature of her volumes.[9]

Of course, John Wilson may not have known that the woman whose work he was reviewing was red-haired. Unless, however, he was attacking Lady Morgan, another red-haired Irish author whose work he also reviewed, he would seem to be deliberately attacking Anna's vanity. Indeed, his remark leads one to wonder whether he and Carlyle had compared notes on her appearance. In his memoirs he does not record meeting Mrs. Jameson until 1832 and then he reports to his wife frankly, but not cruelly, that the celebrated author of *King Charles's Beauties* is "very clever, middle-aged, red-haired and agreeable, though I suspect you would call her a conceited minx."[10]

"North's" review of *Loves of the Poets* begins by demolishing, but always in the guise of well-intentioned praise, the premises on which Anna Jameson bases her writing:

Nothing is a surer proof of genius than the choice of a subject, at once new and natural, and the *Loves of the Poets* is of that character. . . .

The *Loves of the Poets* is also a very ladylike theme;—for all truly great or good poets, from Homer to Hogg, have, in the only true sense of the word, been gentlemen. Indeed, it would not be too much to say that there never was, nor can be a finished gentleman not a poet. . . .

The manners of all Poets are delightful—in the long run. You may indeed come upon them in a paroxysm and are wellnigh frightened out of your wits. What savages! We have seen the author of the Lyrical Ballads look so like a cannibal, that it would have needed some nerve to accompany him on an Excursion. But, in the long run, the man is like an angel. . . .

The morals of all poets are good—in the long run. None of your trash about Burns and Byron. All the great Greek tragedians were excellent private characters. There never was a more harmless creature than Homer. Pindar was a paragon of decency and propriety—as a son, husband, and father. Horace was a good fellow, and Virgil would not have hurt a fly. . . .

But we must come to the book in hand. About the loves of some of the True Poets, the fair writer knows more than we do—about some, less—and about others pretty much the same; but we shall be happy to be led by so sweet a conductress through scenes of such enchantment. She shall wave us on with her own white arms—she shall, in her own silver voice, "tell the story of their loves."[11]

"Christopher North" wickedly parodies Anna's style with his own, continuing with a lengthy recital of the Petrarch-Laura and Dante-Beatrice sections in a tone and manner affecting entire approval, with passages of his effusive prose set beside the passages of hers, until at last he abandons comparison to "lay aside these very delightful volumes —perhaps to return to them, in a month or two—or some time during the winter. . . ."[12]

Although *Blackwood's* was not among the reviews which were notorious for bending the knee to a publisher's pressure, Leslie Marchand, in his book on the *Athenaeum*, gives evidence to show that it was not above the "log-rolling" practices then current.[13] "Christopher North's" final paragraph sounds like an admission of a publisher-motivated review: ". . . but if that part of the reading public which does not confine its midnight studies to Maga do not call for new editions, then we shall set their teeth on edge by a taste of some more fair and fresh fruit from the same tree."[14]

Whatever the motive and however reprehensible the methods, there was a considerable distinction in being reviewed by *Blackwood's*. Only the *Edinburgh* and the *Quarterly* surpassed it in point of prestige and Anna Jameson was to wait for some years for recognition by either of these "Royal Reviews." No doubt many copies of *Loves of the Poets* were bought because of Wilson's review. Anna had to pay for this, as all writers do, in terms of personal pride.

Memoirs of Celebrated Female Sovereigns (1831) is indistinguishable in kind from *Loves of the Poets*. Written also for female readers, it denies a primarily scholarly intention, "for the didactic form of history or biography has not always been adhered to; incidents and characters are not here treated in a political and historical, but in a moral and picturesque point of view." [FS Preface] In a criticism of the current education for young girls, the author deplores the stress on "facts, dates and names" as she condemns subjecting the feminine mind to historical tales of profligacy and cruelty:

. . . under the idea of inspiring a just horror for these things, it is as if we should teach our children humanity by introducing them into the shambles. . . .

It would be presumption to say that in this little work I have been able to avoid entirely the objections to which I have alluded; but at least, those great moral truths which are based on our religion as Christians, and lead to our best views of duty and happiness, are not lost sight of. . . . [FS Preface]

The text of this work is a series of biographical studies of twelve queens of widely differing times in history, from Semiramis to Catherine II of Russia, all written with a respect for factual historical material and with the sporadic acknowledgment of sources which was a remarkable feature of *Loves of the Poets*. The accounts are much less cloyed by moral didacticism than the Preface leads us to expect. Cleopatra, for instance, is not accorded the sternly moralizing treatment which the introduction suggests, because the authoress finds her outside the usual rules of conduct and refuses to demean her by pointing a commonplace moral: "[We] must needs leave her as we find her, a dazzling piece of witch craft, with which sober reasoning has nothing to do." [FS 27] Anna devotes a lengthy chapter, full of fact and anecdote, to Christina of Sweden and, although she finally sums her up as "unsustained by moral dignity, unenlightened by true religion," she is undoubtedly fascinated by her power: ". . . her mind resembled a chaos, in which the elements of greatness and goodness were mixed up confusedly with every perverse ingredient that ever entered into the composition of man or woman." [FS 260] The young lady who read the text of *Celebrated Female Sovereigns* would find it much livelier than the introduction would lead her, or her mother, to expect.

One effect of the work, as announced by the author in the Preface, is, by her assembling of historical evidence, to discredit militant feminism:

On the whole, it seems indisputable that the experiments hitherto made in the way of female government have been signally unfortunate; and that women called to empire have been, in most cases, conspicuously unhappy or criminal. So that, were we to judge by the past, it might be decided at once, that the power which belongs to us as a sex, is not properly, or naturally, that of the sceptre or the sword. [FS Preface]

Anna Jameson was a better writer and a more confirmed feminist perhaps than she knew, certainly than she would admit to her public at this stage in her career. Her readers would be apt to finish the book more impressed by these sketches of female power than sobered by the moral lessons drawn from them.

The long history of the "Windsor Beauties" in the lives and fortunes of the Murphy family did not end with their purchase by Sir Gerard Noel, though that seems to have given Mr. Murphy the opportunity of attempting to realize further profit from them. In 1831 they were engraved and published in a handsome volume called *Memoirs of the Beauties of the Court of Charles II*. This work is very much of the handsome "gift-book" variety, and its success was reportedly "literary and artistic . . . but [it] brought no pecuniary gain." [E 80]

In one of *Blackwood's* "Noctes Ambrosianae" dialogues, "Old Kit" and his friends put their seal of approval on Mrs. Jameson's account of the lives of the "Beauties":

SHEPHERD,
What lang, thin folios are thae you're lookin' at, Mr. Tickler? Do they conteen pictures?

TICKLER,
The Beauties of the Court of King Charles the Second . . . by Mrs. Jameson.

NORTH,

One of the most eloquent of our female writers—full of feeling and fancy—a true enthusiast with a glowing soul.

SHEPHERD,

Mrs. Jameson's prase aye reminds me o' Miss Landon's poetry—and though baith hae their fawtes, I wou'd charactereese baith alike by the same epithet—rich. I hate a simple style, for that's only anither word for puir. . . . There's nothing simpler nor water, and, at times, a body drinks greedily frae the rim o' his hat made intil a scoop; but for a' that, in the long rin I prefer porter. . . .

NORTH,

Let us close the fair folio for the present, my boys. I do not deny that many worthy people may have serious objections to the whole work. But not I. 'Tis a splendid publication, and will, ere long, be gracing the tables of a thousand drawing-rooms. The most eminent engravers have been employed, and they have done their best; nor do I know another lady who could have executed her task, it must be allowed a ticklish one, with greater delicacy than Mrs. Jameson. "She has nought extenuated, nor set down aught in malice," when speaking of the frail or vicious; and her own clear spirit kindles over the record of their lives. . . .

SHEPHERD,

That's richt. Mony a moral may be drawn by leddies in high life yet from sic a wark. "Dinna let puir Nelly starve!!!"[15]

The Beauties was reprinted in 1838, and this edition was the first of Anna Jameson's works to be reviewed in *The Times*, possibly thanks to a friend, Henry Reeve, who was at this time on its staff. The reviewer deplores the addition of notes and corrections by an editor, "a gentleman who has read Pepys and Evelyn, and is of a very proper and moral way of thinking." He found Anna's "little histories" far less solemn and more amusing than the note of her editor, a "stupendous political pyramid on her head," although, as was to be expected with such heroines as Nell Gwynne and the Duchess of Portsmouth, "the authoress, though she has told the truth, has not told the *whole* truth."[16]

7

Characteristics of Women

FROM 1830 ONWARD, Anna Jameson was engaged on her most ambitious project to date—a discussion of Shakespeare's heroines. Though her admiration for the plays and her familiarity with them went back to the avid reading of her childhood, much of the actual impetus towards this topic and its treatment coincided with her *entrée* into the Kemble family and the stagestruck admiration she felt for the talented young Fanny. She sought and received both encouragement and advice from her young friend. Scattered throughout Fanny Kemble's letters from 1830 to 1833 are references to the work in progress, not always showing the help that her correspondent wished, but always in a tone of admiration at her clever friend's writing ability:

DUBLIN, SUMMER, 1830

DEAR MRS. JAMESON:

I received your third kind letter yesterday morning, and have no more time today than will serve to inclose my answer to your second, which reached me and was replied to at Glasgow. . . . You surely said nothing in that letter of yours that the kindest good feeling could take exception to, and therefore need hardly, I think, have been so anxious about its possible miscarriage. However, "Misery makes one acquainted with strange bed-fellows," and I am afraid distrust is one of them. . . . You ask me for advice about your Shakespeare work, but advice is what I have no diploma for bestowing; and such suggestions as I might venture, were I sitting by your side with Shakespeare in my hand, and which might furnish pleasant matter of converse and discussion, are hardly solid enough for transmission by post. [K 269]

There follows a paragraph of enthusiastic effusion on *The Tempest* and then Fanny gives her opinion about a title: "I agree with you that there is much in the name of a work. . . . For myself, I prefer "Characters of

Shakespeare's Women"; it is shorter, and I think it will look better than the other in print." [K 275]

By March of 1831, the work was complete, or nearly so. Fanny Kemble reported to her friend, Harriet St. Leger, that Anna had read aloud to her a good deal of it. Fanny termed the characters "very pleasing sketches—outlines," but judged Anna's criticism and analysis "rather graceful than profound or powerful." [K 359] Two months later, the book was still very much a topic of discussion; while Fanny and a friend were trying on dresses they "talked all the while about the characteristics of Shakespeare's women with Mrs. Jameson, who had come to see me. I pity her from the bottom of my heart; she has a heavy burden to carry, poor woman." [K 513]

In July, 1831, the book was ready, but Fanny commiserated on the delay in its publication and about the state of Anna's health, particularly of her eyes, which had been badly strained by the laborious etching process that she had taught herself in order to use her own sketches for illustration. Fanny was philosophic about the book's postponement, in view of the general unrest prior to the introduction of the Reform Bill: "I have no doubt the booksellers are right in point of fact, for we are embarked on board too troublous times to carry mere *passe temps* literature with us. 'We must have bloody noses and cracked crowns,' I am afraid, and shall find small public taste or leisure for 'polite letters.' " [K 428]

By July, 1832, the book had been published. It was dedicated to Fanny Kemble, who was about to depart for an acting tour of America with her aunt and her father. This trip, an attempt by the Kembles to amass some money for the family white-elephant, the Covent Garden Theatre, was considered exile by Fanny. Because of it Anna had changed her first dedicatory etching to "A female figure in an attitude of despondency, sitting by the sea, and watching a ship sailing toward the setting sun." [K 531] Fanny's letter of thanks and acknowledgement was written a few days before sailing, and selects for special praise her own favourites, Juliet and Portia:

LIVERPOOL, JULY 22

MY DEAR MRS. JAMESON:

I fear you are either anxious or vexed, or perhaps both, about the arrival of your books, and my non-acknowledgement of them. They reached me in all safety, and, but for the many occupations which swallow up my time, would have been duly receipted ere this. Thank you very much for them, for they are very elegant outside, and the dedication page, with which I should have been most ungracious to find any fault. The little sketch on that leaf differs from the design you had described to me sometime ago and I felt the full meaning of the difference. I read through your preface all in a breath; there are many parts of it which have often been matters of discussion between us, and I believe you know how cordially I coincide with most of the views expressed in it. The only point in your preliminary chapter on which I do not agree with you is the passage in which you say that humour is, of necessity and in its very essence, vulgar. I differ entirely with you here. I think humour is very often closely allied to poetry; not only a large element in highly poetic minds, which surely refutes your position, but kindred to the highest and deepest order of imagination. . . . but I think, had I time, I could convince you of it. I acted Juliet on Wednesday, and read your analysis of it before doing so. Oh, could you have seen and heard my Romeo! . . . I am sure it is just as well that an actress on the English stage at the present day should not have too distinct a vision of the beings Shakespeare intended to realize, or she might be induced, like the unfortunate heroine of the song, to "hang herself in her garters." [K 531]

In September, with the season successfully begun in New York, Fanny writes of missing her discussions with Anna, although "I may not often confess to being convinced by your arguments in our differences," and of continuing to read her "pretty book. There are one or two points which shall 'serve for sweet discourses' in our time to come." [K 545]

The "preliminary chapter" which Fanny mentions represents a new departure in Anna Jameson's writing method, and a device which she was to use again and again in the future. The introductory dialogue between two characters served a variety of purposes. This method of imparting information by question and answer was, of course, a favourite, if not always a popular pedagogical method of the nineteenth century; Fanny Kemble's young sister Adelaide was, she says, "rabid against" "Nat. Phil." as she called Mrs. Marcet's *Conversations on Natural Philosophy*, one of the best known of this kind of lesson book.

As a teacher Anna had certainly used this kind of text book and she now adapted its method to her specifications. Through a dialogue between "Alda" and "Medon" (Anna herself and a gentleman friend), she was able to state her position on a number of matters and, particularly, to announce her intentions in this present book. After a humble disclaimer of all ambition in her undertaking, and an insistence that her work was done without a thought of fame or money—a point that contains more grace of expression than truth of intent—Alda refutes Medon's suggestion that she has written the book to maintain the superiority of the female sex over the male. Though in reality a criticism of Shakespeare's heroines, Mrs. Jameson insists that the book reveals, in fact, "Characteristics of Women." She finds in Shakespeare, she says, the answers to all the personality riddles presented by historical accounts of women and by observation of living women: "All I sought, I found there; his characters combine history and real life; they are complete individuals, whose hearts and souls are laid open before us—all may behold and all judge for themselves." [*Char* I, xxi] Shakespeare, whom she had earlier called "The Poet of Womankind," is the absolute authority, a kind of God among poets, one "who understood all truth"; "I wished to illustrate the manner in which the affections would naturally display themselves in women—whether combined with high intellect, regulated by reflection, and elevated by imagination, or existing with perverted dispositions or purified by the moral sentiments. I found all these in Shakespeare. . . ." [*Char* I, lii]

This Introduction may well have been written after the completion of the text, possibly at the publisher's instigation, possibly as a cautionary measure on Anna's part. Fanny Kemble, who had read much of the text, speaks of the Introduction as if she had not seen it before. It is, in its way, a masterful piece of fence-sitting. Any serious criticisms which might be levelled at its author are silenced by her statement that she was writing about women, not criticizing Shakespeare. Similarly, the many who might carp at a feminist crusade are silenced by the scholarly prestige of the magic word "Shakespeare." Finally, for the prudish minority who might doubt his invincible respectability, the author has this modest word:

It is objected to her [Portia], to Beatrice, and others of Shakespeare's women, that the display of intellect is tinged with a coarseness of manner belonging to the age in which he wrote. . . . Much has been said, and more might be said, on this subject—but I would rather not discuss it. It is a mere difference of manner which is to be regretted, but has nothing to do with the essence of the character. [*Char* I, xxxvi]

Certainly this policy of wide-scale appeasement explains Mrs. Jameson's choice of name for her work and her rejection of Fanny Kemble's choice, though the latter ("Characters of Shakespeare's Women") would seem to be a more honest description of the work in hand. [K 275] There is something for everyone in the introductory dialogue. When Alda and Medon are not joining hands to rhapsodize about Shakespeare's genius, Medon is giving Alda an opportunity of speaking in the voice of a strong-minded woman about a variety of subjects—the education of women, politics, the prevalence of satire in life and literature as she sees it, and the fundamental natural differences between man and woman.

There is a considerable amount of feministic propaganda here, and though the pills have been well-sugared with inoffensiveness, they may have been none the less effective. Her already familiar theme of educational improvement is restated:[1]

MEDON: . . . there are young women in these days, but there is no such thing as youth—the bloom of existence is sacrificed to a fashionable education, and where we should find the rose-buds of the spring, we see only the full-blown flaunting, precocious roses of the hot-bed. [*Char* I, xlvii]

ALDA: . . . Blame then that "forcing" system of education, the most per-nicious, the most mistaken, the most far-reaching in its miserable and mischievous effects that ever prevailed in this world. . . . Hence, the strange anomalies of artificial society—girls of sixteen who are models of manner, miracles of prudence, marvels of learning, who sneer at sentiment, and laugh at the Juliets and the Imogens; and matrons of forty, who, when the passions should be tame and wait upon the judgment, amaze the world and put us to confusion with their doings. [*Char* I, xliv]

Part tactful expedience and part personal conviction is her "How I hate political women!" The troubled and ultra-political times leading to the passage of the Reform Bill had delayed the printing of her book by a year. Moreover, a lady-writer desiring the widest approval, particularly one whose husband held one colonial post and very possibly lived in hopes of a better one, did well to clear herself of political pretensions. More than this, Anna Jameson seems to have been sincerely, and on principle, non-political. The same disclaimer of both interest and involvement occurs in the Preface to *Winter Studies and Summer Rambles in Canada* and indeed that work, considering that it was written in the months immediately preceding the Rebellion of 1837, seems remarkably free from political bias. Her remedy for the political ineptitude of her sex, as for virtually all their weaknesses, is an improvement in their education with a view to "their future destination as the mothers and nurses of legislators and statesmen."

She declares herself far from the position of asserting the superiority, or even the equality of the female sex to the male: "in Shakespeare the male and female characters bear precisely the same relation to each other that they do in nature and society—they [women] are not equal in prominence or in power—they are subordinate throughout. [*Char* I, xxiv] Ideally, the woman of the nineteenth-century was allotted a separate status and a preferred treatment from the male. In fact, there were injustices to women in education and in law which Mrs. Jameson never tired of pointing out. However, she was interested in preserving all the benefits of their separate status; hence she could say that women's position was false and injurious to both sexes and, with no sense of self-contradiction, make this distinction: "A man's courage is often a mere animal quality, and in its most elevated form, a point of honour. But a woman's courage is always a virtue, because it is not required of us. . . ." [*Char* I, liv]

The Introduction ends with the assurance that the book has, indeed, a moral, "a very deep one, which those who seek will find." Such a statement at the end of this long passage of general uplift would leave an author less consistently serious than Anna Jameson suspect of a certain tongue-in-cheek attitude toward her public's expectations. The sparkle of wit occurs infrequently in her letters or her writings, however, and when it does it is almost always a reported anecdote attributed to someone else. Indeed, the same Introduction states, in the strongest terms, her position on satire:

ALDA: I abhor the spirit of ridicule—I dread it and I despise it. I abhor it because it is in direct contradiction to the mild and serious spirit of Christianity; I fear it, because we find that in every state of society in which it has prevailed as a fashion, and has given the tone to the manners and literature, it marked the moral degradation and approaching destruction of that society. . . . [*Char* I, xiv]

Anna's high seriousness and sense of mission were advantages to the success of her career in her day, though they affect somewhat adversely the readability of her work in ours; she was not threatened by the spirit of fun, as was her young friend, Fanny Kemble, whose most solemn pronouncements often glitter with gay self-mockery.

The text of *Characteristics of Women* groups Shakespeare's women into four categories: characters of intellect, characters of passion and imagination, characters of the affections, and characters of history. The analysis of Lady Macbeth, a "character of history," is one of the best and one of the most interesting in the collection. In answer to Medon's "I hope you have given her a place among the women in whom the tender affections and moral sentiments predominate," Alda replies, "You laugh; but, jesting apart, perhaps it would have been a more accurate classification than placing her among the historical characters." [*Char* I, lvii]

Anna begins with a short sketch of the history involved in *Macbeth* and a denial of its importance: "The sternly magnificent creation of the poet stands before us independent of all these aids to fancy—she is Lady Macbeth: as such she lives, she reigns, and is immortal in the world of imagination." [*Char* II, 300] Here, however, the effect of the nineteenth-century star-tradition of Shakespeare presentation on Anna's interpretation must also be considered. Usually, and certainly demonstrably in the Kemble acting hierarchy, any play was considered a vehicle for its star. Fanny Kemble relates the steps leading to her debut in 1829 and one sees that she was to be "brought out" in the play considered most likely to guarantee success for her. She was dressed and coached for the part with very little reference to the rest of the cast and the play was not, in effect, Shakespeare's *Romeo and Juliet*, but Fanny Kemble's "Juliet." [K 187ff]

Anna's interpretation of the part, according to her stated plan, delineates Lady Macbeth as a woman, rather than a character having a certain contribution to the totality of the play, *Macbeth*:

Lady Macbeth's amazing power of intellect, her inexorable determination of purpose, her superhuman strength of nerve, render her as fearful in herself as her deeds are hateful; yet she is not a mere monster of depravity, with whom we have nothing in common—nor a meteor whose destroying path we watch in ignorant affright and amaze. She is a terrible impersonation of evil passions and mighty powers, not so far removed from our own nature, as to be cast beyond the pale of our sympathies; for the woman herself remains a woman to the last,—still linked with sex and with humanity. [*Char* II, 305]

Anna Jameson recognizes and remarks on the validity of Hazlitt's words on Lady Macbeth, but deplores that ". . . this masterly criticism stops short of the whole truth—it is a little superficial, and a little too harsh." [*Char* II, 310] Anna reveals a mentally superior, unselfish, wifely woman, ambitious for her husband and able to nerve herself to any effort to further his cause. Once the cause is achieved, however, she would never stoop to panic or cruelty as does her husband. Even in the act of murder she is recalled to her womanhood by Duncan's resemblance to her father, and it is by such touches that her feminity, perverted into crime and thus doomed, is kept before us. Macbeth leans upon her and she sustains him when necessary, but only when necessary, stiffening his flagging courage by strong words. Finally her feminine constitution revolts under this ruinous mistreatment, and Lady Macbeth suffers moral retribution in the terrors of her nightmare and later in madness. Anna comments, "conscience must wake sometime or other, and bring with it remorse closed by despair, and despair by death." [*Char* II, 315]

Such an intensity of focus produces a reading of Lady Macbeth which is as overdrawn in its way as the earlier criticisms Anna was seeking to amend were insufficiently perceptive. Balance in consideration of Shakespeare's plays was, however, no part of her purpose. She was looking for, and she found in the plays, portraits of women. Lady

Macbeth is the "star bright apostate" and her inevitable end is death. But her commentator insists on her pervasive femininity and in certain passages of comparison her words are persuasive:

But Lady Macbeth, though so supremely wicked, and so consistently feminine, is still kept aloof from all base alloy. When Shakespeare created a female character purely detestable, he made her an accessory, never a principal. Thus Regan and Goneril are two powerful sketches of selfishness, cruelty and ingratitude; we abhor them whenever we see or think of them, but we think very little about them . . . their depravity is forgotten in its effects. [*Char* II, 320]

In one instance, in a frenzy of partisanship for her womanly villainess, Anna's criticism reaches rarely scaled peaks of the ludicrous. She indignantly refutes a comparison of Lady Macbeth and Clytemnestra: ". . . but, considered as a woman and an individual, would anyone compare this shameless adulteress, cruel murderess, and unnatural mother, with Lady Macbeth? Lady Macbeth herself would certainly shrink from the approximation." [*Char* II, 321]

Fanny Kemble's aunt, Sarah Siddons, had been the great Lady Macbeth of the preceding two generations; indeed as she introduces her subject Anna announces her intention of, in part, dispelling the anaesthetizing effects of Mrs. Siddons' stage-hypnosis:

Those who have been accustomed to see it arrayed in the form and lineaments of that magnificent woman and developed with her wonder-working powers, seem satisfied to leave it there, as if nothing more could be said or added. . . . But the generation which beheld Mrs. Siddons in her glory is passing away, and we are again left to our own unassisted feelings. . . . [*Char* II, 302]

The interesting thing about Mrs. Siddons' characterization of Lady Macbeth is that it was imposed on her by the statuesque, compelling, dark, and majestic stage-presence for which she was famous, and was not her own conviction as to the true or best representation. She imagined Lady Macbeth to be very different, physically, from herself:

You will probably not agree with me as to the character of that beauty [of Lady Macbeth]; yet perhaps this difference of opinion will be entirely attributable to the difficulty of your imagination disengaging itself from the idea of the person of her representative [Mrs. Siddons herself] which you have been so long accustomed to contemplate. According to my notion, it is of that character which I believe is generally allowed to be the most captivating to the other sex,—fair, feminine, nay, perhaps, even fragile. . . .[2]

Thomas Campbell in his *Life of Mrs. Siddons*, goes to some length to attribute Mrs. Jameson's interpretation of the character of Lady Macbeth to Mrs. Siddons:

Whether Mrs. Jameson heard of Mrs. Siddons' ideas on the subject, which she might by possibility, as the great actress made no secret of them, I have never been in the least anxious to ascertain, because it is plain, from her writings, that Mrs. Jameson has a mind too original to borrow from anyone. But, in deprecating all suspicion of obligation on the one side, I have an equal right to exclude the possibility of its being suspected on the other. Mrs. Siddons showed me these "Remarks on the Character of Lady M" some nineteen years ago, so that there can be little doubt of their having been earlier written than those of the authoress of the "Characteristics."[3]

Campbell's seemingly gratuitous attempts to lay a charge of unacknowledged borrowing at Mrs. Jameson's door carried an undercurrent of personal animosity. In June of 1831, Sara Siddons had died and shortly thereafter Campbell had applied for her letters with a view to writing her biography. Anna Jameson was also an applicant, but was rejected in his favour. [K 452] As happened later, when she hoped to write the life of Mrs. Harry Siddons of Edinburgh (a daughter-in-law of the great Sarah, and Fanny's cousin), the Kemble clan was divided in its opinion of her or of her qualifications.

Shortly after her aunt's death, Fanny Kemble was volubly anti-Campbell, of whose application she said, "He has behaved badly about the whole business, and I hope Mrs. Fitzhugh [Mrs. Siddons' bosom friend] will not let him have them [her aunt's letters]." [K 452] Many years later she recalls the incident in tones of lasting dissatisfaction with Campbell:

Mrs. Jameson at one time contemplated writing a life of my Aunt Siddons, not thinking Boaden's biography of her satisfactory; in this purpose, however, she was effectually opposed by Campbell, who had undertaken the work, and, though he exhibited neither interest nor zeal in the fulfillment of his task, doggedly (in the manger) refused to relinquish it to her. Certainly, had Mrs. Jameson carried out her intention, Mrs. Siddons would have had a monument dedicated to her memory better calculated to preserve it than those which the above named gentleman bestowed on her. It would have been written in a spirit of far higher artistic discrimination, and with infinitely more sympathy both with the woman and with the actress. [K 128]

Thomas Campbell's words were motivated to a degree by resentment at having been less than the unanimous choice of the Kemble family. Understandably, he also wished to shield himself from the suspicion of "borrowing" from Mrs. Jameson. It seems reasonable to suppose, however, that the gist of his words was true and that Anna Jameson was well aware of Sarah Siddons' opinions concerning Lady Macbeth.

Fanny Kemble's journal for Saturday, March 10, 1832, a time when she was concerned about Mrs. Jameson's work-in-progress, refers to her aunt's character sketches:

Emily called. . . . She brought me my Aunt Siddons's sketches of Constance and Lady Macbeth. They are simply written, and though not analytically deep or powerful, are true, clear, and good, as far as their extent reaches. She thinks Constance more motherly than queenly, and I do not altogether agree with her. . . . Mrs. Siddons's conception of Lady Macbeth is very beautiful, and I was particularly struck by her imagination of the outward woman: The deep blue eyes, the fair hair and fair skin of the northern woman. . . . [K 517]

It is an interesting conjunction of names (in the case of Constance) and of dates (March, 1832), perhaps also an indication of current rumour and a certain area of sensitivity on the subject, that the Preface of the *Characteristics*, published in July, 1832, explains: "It has become necessary to state thus publicly what is known to most of my friends, viz. that the whole of this little work, with the exception of the historical life of Constance of Bretagne and the character of Desdemona, was written previous to October 1831, and sent to the press in March last [1832]. . . . [*Char* Frontispiece] The second edition of *Characteristics* (1833), and following editions, contain an explicit denial of plagiarism along with an admission of personal contact: "Mrs. Siddons left among her papers an analysis of the character of Lady Macbeth, which I have never seen; but I have heard her say, that after playing the part for thirty years, she never read it over without discovering in it something new."[4]

Much later in life, Fanny Kemble, in her *Notes upon Some of Shakespeare's Plays* (1882), repudiates both her aunt and her friend, discounting the femininity of Lady Macbeth and describing her as "that unusual and unamiable (but not altogether unnatural) creature, a masculine woman, in the only real significance of that much misapplied epithet. . . . Lady Macbeth's character has more of the essentially manly nature in it than that of Macbeth."[5]

One should not underestimate the importance of the acting traditions and methods of the Kemble family for the *Characteristics of Women*. Certainly Portia, the first of Mrs. Jameson's women of intellect, and the sketch for which she garnered most praise, was Fanny Kemble's favourite character. Portia the wise, the wealthy and most important, the womanly in every sense, is a compound of "all the noblest and most loveable qualities that ever met together in woman" [*Char* I, 5]; for Fanny, she is ". . . noble, simple, humble, pure; true, dutiful, religious and full of fun; delightful above all others, the woman of women."

[K 187] In her youthful enthusiasm for Portia, and her own or her family tradition of "method acting," Fanny Kemble speaks of any character she plays, but especially of Portia, as a living being: "Juliet, with the exception of the balcony scene, I act; but I feel as if I were Portia—and how I wish I were!" [K 249]

As critic, Anna Jameson distinguishes between the character in the play and the woman:

Of these four exquisite characters [Portia, Isabella, Beatrice, Rosalind], considered as dramatic and poetical conceptions, it is difficult to pronounce which is most perfect in its way, most admirably drawn, most highly finished. But if considered in another point of view, as women and individuals, as breathing realities, clothed in flesh and blood, I believe we must assign the first rank to Portia. . . . [Char I, 5]

But her dramatic young friend does not cloud her conception with such shades of differentiation. Her comments, sprinkled throughout her memoirs, are all testimonials to Portia's reality to her: "She is a very *superior woman* . . . her teasing her husband half to death afterward restores the balance of her humanity, which was sinking heavily toward perfection." [K 352] As she reads *Characteristics of Women*, Fanny records her pleasure and concurrence in Mrs. Jameson's view of Portia: "I have been reading over Portia today; she's still my dream of ladies, my pearl of womanhood." [K 532]

Mrs. Jameson finishes her consideration of Portia by a detailed comparison with Camiola in Massinger's *Maid of Honour*. This, too, had probably originated in conversations with Fanny who had been attracted to the part of Camiola: "The arrangement of Massinger for the family library by my friend the Reverend Alexander Dyce, the learned Shakespearean editor and commentator, was my first introduction to that mine of dramatic wealth which enriched the literature of England in the reigns of Elizabeth and James the First, and culminated in the genius of Shakespeare. . . . The part of Camiola is the only one that I ever selected for myself." [K 255]

Both Fanny Kemble and Anna Jameson find Camiola's character less noble and satisfying than Portia's and on substantially the same grounds. In the latter's estimation,

What in Portia is the gentle wisdom of a noble nature, appears in Camiola too much a spirit of calculation: it savours a little of the counting-house. As Portia is the heiress of Belmont and Camiola a merchant's daughter, the distinction may be proper and characteristic, but it is not in favour of Camiola. [Char I, 37]

Fanny, speaking of the two roles, states,

One can imagine the merchant's daughter [Camiola] *growing up* to the possession of her great wealth, through the narrowing and hardening circumstances and habits of careful calculation and rigid economy, thrifty, prudent, just, and eminently conscientious; of Portia one can only think as of a creature born in the very lap of luxury and nursed in the midst of sunny magnificence . . . like a perfect rose, blooming in a precious vase of gold and gems and exquisite workmanship. [K 368]

Finally, both quote the same passages from the plays to illustrate their contrast between the two heroines. [K369] [*Char* I, 37]

The considerable degree of influence of Fanny Kemble's, or her family's, characterizations on Anna Jameson's finished *Characteristics of Women* had no overt significance for the nineteenth-century reader of the work. For the reader of the twentieth century, however, a whole new depth of interest is given by its far from negligible debt to the Shakespearean interpretations of the Kemble dynasty.

Anna's preparation for her analyses went far beyond personal influence from any source—she had read widely and carefully both from the texts and from critics. Among the latter, she most often refers to Schlegel and then Hazlitt with approval, and reserves for early critics—Richardson, Cibber, Mackenzie, and particularly Dr. Johnson —a strong measure of disapproval and disagreement. Mme de Staël is most often quoted for epigrammatic *bon mots* about the female character; for matters of opinion on a variety of subjects Anna cites a variety of sources: Coleridge, Rousseau, Constant, Forster, Moore. She is knowledgeable about Shakespeare's source materials, in many cases outlining for her readers his modifications of the old tales. Analyses of historical characters are introduced by a complete historical sketch, against which she sets her reading of Shakespeare's heroine.

Her analyses commonly end with, or include, a judiciously chosen comparison: Portia—Camiola; Juliet-Schiller's Thekla; Lady Macbeth —Euripides's Medea; Cordelia—Sophocles's Antigone, and Cleopatra— Fletcher's Cleopatra. Some of her comparisons are suggested by Schlegel; in fact, one would judge that his *Lectures on Dramatic Art and Literature*, translated into English in 1815 by John Black, was an important working model.

At home and abroad, Mrs. Jameson reaped a considerable critical reward for *Characteristics*. Both *Blackwood's* and the *Edinburgh Review* published lengthy and very favourable commentaries. From the latter, though delayed until 1834, she received full appreciation and vindication for her tactful support of the woman's point of view:

Whether Mrs. Jameson could have written a good romance, or a popular poem, we can hardly say; but we are quite sure that she has acted more wisely in choosing a different department,—one of the few in which there really existed an opening for female talent in English literature.

But in the path of the eloquent and philosophic female criticism, there has certainly existed a great gap in literature since the death of Mme de Staël. . . .

With truth, therefore, we think it may be said that the female characters of Shakespeare have never yet had justice done to them; not that their mere outward and visible attributes have not been forcibly and correctly set forth; for in our own country, as well as in Germany, much has been written eloquently, and truly—as far as it goes—upon the subject.

. . . But many cases occur where the matter lies not so obviously on the surface. And it is in these, the debateable land, as it were of character, that the criticism of a woman of genius may so often throw light on the singularities or moral enigmas of the part. . . . this is the service which in many particulars Mrs. Jameson has rendered to the female characters of Shakespeare;—in some cases placing the whole character in a new light, in almost all, elucidating and bringing out unsuspected beauties in individual situations or speeches. . . . it is hardly too much to say that in these Characteristics the full beauties of Shakespeare's female characters have been for the first time understood or portrayed.[6]

The reviewer gives a lengthy appraisal, particularly of Mrs. Jameson's treatment of Portia, deploring, as she had in her text, "the superficial manner in which the character of Portia had been treated by Hazlitt and Schlegel." He reiterates his opinion that the author is not the equal of Mme de Staël, but is a worthy practitioner of the same kind of art. This would be heady praise to Anna who, in *Characteristics*, had likened Mme de Staël to Portia, as a woman "distinguished for intellect of the highest order . . . remarkable for this trustingness of spirit." [*Char* I, 21]

Blackwood's, with an air of proprietary pride, displayed Mrs. Jameson as a clever protégé. A "Noctes Ambrosianae" dialogue announced a forthcoming review, and in it "Christopher North's" tone was a far cry from the mocking condescension of his first reviews of her work. After a lengthy quotation and paraphrase record of the "characters of the affections" he places Mrs. Jameson beside Charles Lamb as the most sensitive interpreter of Cordelia and then goes on to deliver an encomium on Anna's total performance:

Never, till now, have Shakespeare's female characters, except when like stars they "were not in twos and threes," been done justice to on the luminous page of philosophical criticism. Mrs. Montague was a woman of much merit in her day; but compared to Mrs. Jameson, was an owl to a nightingale. . . . Mrs. Jameson, we should guess from her writings is a domestic character and fond of "Parlour twilight." She manifestly belongs to no coterie, but there is no society, however distinguished, that her fine genius, talents and accomplishments would not grace. In these, her exquisite commentaries on the impersonations of the virtues of her sex, she has "done the state some service" and they well know it.[7]

In Part III of the four-part review, North takes issue with Mrs. Jameson over the character of Ophelia, quoting at length from an 1818 essay of his own, professing himself persuaded by her reading, but lapsing into his own "heresy," and into the ironic manner which he had used in his review of *Loves of the Poets*:

Shakespeare and Mrs. Jameson were right. Ophelia herself knew that Hamlet loved her;—and Hamlet knew that Ophelia knew that he loved her, and *therefore he used her thus*; for no behaviour of his, he was well assured could ever make his "soul's idol" doubt he loved. That doubt would have broken Ophelia's heart. But Hamlet wished not to break Ophelia's heart, whatever else he may have wished; but what he wished is "hard to be scanned."[8]

In September of 1834, *Blackwood's* again refers at length and in terms of praise to Anna's work, while reviewing Campbell's *Life of Mrs. Siddons*. In this review the ironic knife is absent—"Old Kit" is a warm partisan. The *Characteristics*, he says, has "placed Mrs. Jameson in the first rank of our philosophical critics on Shakespeare."[9] He went to her defence against Campbell's imputation of her borrowing from the great Mrs. Siddons, as well as stoutly defending both the Siddons and the Jameson interpretations of Lady Macbeth:

Mr. Campbell, in other places, expressed the highest admiration of Mrs. Jameson's taste, feeling and graces, now universally recognized, though we have not seen her placed beneath the dais in either of the Royal reviews. That accomplished scholar Mr. Hayward, prose translator of Faust, in speaking of her extraordinary merits, says that hitherto justice has not been done her in our periodical literature. . . . She has said countless fine things on one and all of Shakespeare's Women, no doubt often felt before by millions, but never before expressed; and she tells us in a note to a passage in the second edition of the *Characteristics*, that she had never seen Mrs. Siddons's analysis of the character of Lady Macbeth. . . . The woman's heart, in both cases alike, revealed to them truths which seem to have escaped the perception of us male critics . . . and though from zeal, at once natural and noble, in defence of their sex, they may have relieved too much the terrible character of Lady Macbeth . . . they have both more truly than any others expounded the wonderful meaning of Shakespeare.[10]

However subjective, however indebted to her friend Fanny Kemble and to Schlegel, Anna Jameson had undoubtedly achieved a "first" in literary criticism. Not until 1839 was there another treatment of

Shakespeare's female characters—Heine's *Shakespeares Mädchen und Frauen.* Heine praised Mrs. Jameson, whom he mistakenly calls Scottish:

Obige Worte entlehne ich einem Werke der Frau Jameson, welches "Moralische, poetische und historische Frauen-Charactere" betitelt. Es ist in diesem Buche nur von Shakespearesche Weibern die Rede, und die ausgeführte Stelle zeugt von dem Geiste der Verfasserinn, die wahrscheinlich von Geburt eine Schottin ist. Was sie über Portia in Gegensatz zu Shylock sagt, ist nicht bloss schön, sondern auch wahr.[11]

In 1922, in a *Modern Language Review* article, Kenneth Hayens investigated the extent of Heine's debt to Mrs. Jameson and Hazlitt, "the two English writers on Shakespeare in whom he [Heine] professes to see some good."[12] Making use of a dissertation by Ernst August Schalles, "Heines Verhältnis zu Shakespeare" (Berlin, 1904), Mr. Hayens finds indication of a considerable debt to both Hazlitt and Mrs. Jameson, a debt which he sums up as "absolute dependence . . . on occasion." He finds six identical quotations in Heine and Mrs. Jameson which point, he believes, to the German writer's free use of the earlier work, and from various correspondences in the treatment of certain characters he deduces varying degrees of dependence.

Ludwig Tieck, whom Anna met in Germany in 1833, praised her work, with certain reservations recorded in his annotated presentation copy of *Characteristics of Women,* now in the British Museum. Its fly-leaf carries this notation:

Dieses Buch ist mir von der Verfasserinn im Winter des Jahres 1833 gesandt worden. Wegen einer Anmerkung die mich betrifft (tom. ii, p. 312), war sie in Verlegenheit und sie hatte ein Blatt über diese Stelle geleimt. Meine Neugier war so ungeschickt, dass sie im Ablösen die Anmerkung selbst fast ganz zerstörte. Um so sonderbarer, weil gerade meine Ansicht über Lady Macbeth ganz mit, der verständigen Verfasserinn (gegen Göethe und die meisten Critiken) übereintrifft.—L. Tieck. [M 69]

Like Christopher North, Tieck disagrees with her reading of Hamlet, and at the foot of the page containing her analysis of Hamlet's treatment of Ophelia, he has written, "Hier alles oberst lächerlich." [M 69–72]

Anna's work was disseminated in its own form, through translation into German in 1834, and to some extent through Heine's work, into the stream of European Shakespearean criticism. Her combination of introductory modesty and facile writing, freshness in point of view and ultra-respectability of theme added enormously to the growth of her literary reputation.

Without exception, contemporary reviews of *Characteristics* praised her work, even if they found it necessary to disagree about certain characters. Allan Cunningham, writing in the *Athenaeum*, spoke of Mrs. Jameson, who aided "the general causes of genius" and "with the most delicate tact and discrimination . . . made us acquainted with the female nature as it appeared to Shakespeare."[13] No reviewer took issue with Anna's stated purpose or felt that a discussion of the characteristics of women through a study of Shakespeare's dramatic creations was in any way anomalous.

The popularity of the work continued through an impressive number of editions. Jaggard's *Shakespeare Bibliography* lists seven before Anna Jameson's death in 1860 and sixteen before 1905 (his list omits the 1834 German edition). The British Museum and Library of Congress catalogues have a slightly higher total: ten before 1860—including two German editions and a total of twenty. The first New York edition (1837) is a product of her Toronto winter; revisions and certain new etchings were done for it shortly after her arrival in Canada. Indeed her interest in Shakespeare and her study of the plays persisted throughout her life. Her annotated copy of *Collier's Emendations* has marginalia which range from signs of full approval such as "! !" to strong-minded ejaculations of disagreement—"Rubbish."[14]

The *Characteristics of Women* is an early endeavour in the psychological criticism of Shakespeare's characters. Partly because of an effusiveness of style which often masks its true sensitivity—which in any case is tiresome to a modern reader—and partly because A. C. Bradley's work effectively swamped all smaller craft exploring the heights and depths of personality in Shakespeare, it is almost unread today. The high estimate which Christopher North accorded Anna Jameson in 1832 was, however, echoed at least as late as 1863. Gerard Manley Hopkins, who is unlikely to be accused of lack of perception or sensitivity in judgment, accords her a place among the most distinguished of Shakespearean critics:

You speak with horror of Shakespearian criticism, but it appears to me that among Shakespeare's critics have been seen instances of genius, of deep insight, of great delicacy, of power, of poetry, of ingenuity, of everything a critic should have. I will instance Schlegel, Coleridge, Charles Lamb, Mrs. Jameson.[15]

8

Parting and Beginning

IN JANUARY OF 1832, Robert Jameson wrote from Dominica of an anticipated change in position and of a forthcoming leave in England. This letter, as usual, seems to be the expression of an articulate individual, a husband eager to rejoin his wife, a man eager too to leave behind the stultifying boredom of his West Indian post:

Your letters are painfully interesting, but even in the pleasantest parts, not calculated to *tranquillize*, but, on the contrary, to stir up a tumult of hopes and wishes which I can hardly write of at this moment with proper coherence. I expect daily to hear matter of importance from England by the hands of our Governor, who has been, like the packets, kept back by contrary winds. The Government have promised, in the strongest terms, in consequence of things that have taken place here, that we shall immediately undergo a thorough change and I have reason to expect that I shall not be overlooked. At any rate, I will not be long separated from you, but I think it will be in England that we shall first meet again. I do not look with much complacency to any appointment in the West Indies. It is a dismal, vulgar, sensual, utterly unintellectual place to spend the best years of one's life in. There are no retiring pensions attached to these high sounding offices, as there are in the splendid East; and by the time a man can save enough to buy him an annuity of £25, for the remaining seven years of his miserable life, he is a poor old yellow unserviceable thing that has left its liver behind. . . . [E 94]

In 1833, Jameson returned to England. He and his wife spent several months together at the home of Anna's sister, Louisa, who had married an artist, Henry Bate. Then Robert left to become Attorney General of Upper Canada. It is tempting to attribute his appointment to his wife's rising prestige and influential friends, but there is no corroboration for this view, implied by Mrs. Jameson's former biographers. A letter to her father, dated 1835, does mention James Stephen, the powerful Under Secretary for the Colonies who would certainly have been instrumental in her husband's appointment, but there is nothing in the reference to suggest either intimacy or gratitude—indeed Anna misspells Stephen's name. It is likely that Robert Jameson was still known as a promising young lawyer and as a protégé of Basil Montagu and Lord Eldon; he may also have been considered an inoffensive choice for a touchy posting.

This was a time of reorganization of the Colonial Office and change in its attitude toward the Canadas. Robert Jameson was the last non-Canadian Attorney General and in the State Papers for Upper Canada his appointment is recorded thus:

Notice of appointment of Mr. [Robert Sympson] Jameson as Attorney General for Upper Canada. It is desirable that the new Solicitor General should possess local experience in public affairs, and the Lieutenant Governor is requested to make a nomination.[1]

The confidential enclosure to the Colonial Office's notice of his appointment gives an indication of the precarious situation existing in the Canadas in this restless decade preceding the 1837 Rebellion and of the Government's awareness of it.[2] It gives at some length suggestions amounting to instructions for appointing a Canadian Solicitor General. Jameson's appointment surely indicates some degree of confidence in his ability; it must also have presented a triumph and a challenge to him after the deadening boredom of Dominica. Financially, the reward was a respectable one, as Anna reports to her father: "The salary of the Attorney General will be 1200 a year including fees and contingencies." [E 144]

Part of the difficulty with the Jameson marriage was certainly financial. Henry Crabb Robinson, who had little sympathy with Mrs. Jameson, but even less with her husband, calls him "a mean and selfish man"; "His passion is said to be avarice."[3] As far back as 1830, Denis Murphy had voiced a similar sentiment in a letter to his daughter: "I am sorry to hear you have no accounts from Jameson lately. I am not surprised at this, as I never had much dependence on your pecuniary aid from the West Indies. Your comforts will most likely in future depend on yourself." [M 53]

Robert Jameson called upon the Kembles in New York on his way to his new post. Fanny and her father missed the call and although Charles Kemble tried to get in touch with him, Jameson had gone on his way to a new life that was to prove a complete abandonment of the old one. [K 578]

Anna reported her husband's arrival in Canada to her family in terms which speak well enough for his position there, but which indicate a general acceptance of marital trouble:

I found at Manheim a letter from Canada; as usual, very well-written, very cold and very vague. I do not think he is disappointed in his office; he has seen the Almas [John Alma and his wife Emily, of Niagara Falls] who are flourishing, he has stood godfather to Emily's youngest son. His books and papers have been shipwreck'd, which is a real misfortune and no small expense; he has not seen the falls of Niagara; there is a party against him, but the popular opinion is for him, being considered a *Whig* official. No Solicitor General is yet appointed, so that a double weight of duty falls upon him and he was just going the circuit (of more than 1,000 miles). . . . [E 104]

Meanwhile, Anna, with her youngest sister Charlotte, had set out for Germany. She was armed with a number of important letters of introduction from a new friend, Robert Noel. A cousin of Lady Byron's, an enthusiast for German art and literature, Noel had been introduced to Anna and Robert Jameson by Behnes Burlowe, a sculptor, whom Anna counted among her very close friends. She and Robert Noel entered into a devoted friendship, a sincere attachment of a high-minded and literary sort, which was important for many years to both its principals. As the friendship developed, its benefits were mutual, but in these early days, Anna's debt was the greater, for her *entrée* into German society through Noel's introductions was accomplished with ease and speed. She writes from Weimar on June 27, 1833:

My Dear Sir,—
    It is a pleasure I cannot deny myself—no less than a debt of gratitude to you—to write these few lines from Weimar. I must thank you in the first place for the kind and cordial reception I have met with. Your charming friend Mme de Goethe received me almost with open arms, and from Dr. Froriep and his amiable wife and daughters I have met with the utmost politeness and attention. . . . [M 79]

Though the convention of the day demanded letters of introduction, and though these were undoubtedly important to Anna's welcome, she was not without fame in her own right. Her *Characteristics* had penetrated into Germany, since Goethe's youth a fertile field for Shakespearean enthusiasm. Soon after their arrival, Charlotte writes the family a letter which is an attractive panegyric of youthful enthusiasm for her trip and for her sister's fame. In it, she mentions the German publication of Anna's book at Leipzig, though "unfortunately from the first edition." [E 98] Anna gives the same news with a correction of her sister's information, indicating a possible sensitivity about the Sarah Siddons—Lady Macbeth problem: ". . . my name is well known, for the English editions of some of my books are sold at Leipzig and a German edition of the last is announced; fortunately, I have just arrived in time to have some alterations made and to send the translator a copy of the last Edition." [E 99]

There is a radical difference between the attitude of Anna, the traveller in Italy, and Anna, the traveller in Germany, a difference which seems to reflect the prevailing attitude of the English. In Italy she was enchanted, but superior, a commentator on its art treasures, but never an intimate of its people; in Germany she finds a society which is intellectually and socially superior to her own, a society of which she stands in awe, and before which she is humble. She was not content to be a tourist looking at this society, separated effectively from a new culture by a language barrier. As in Italy, she set out at once to learn the language, terming herself "cribbed, cabined, confined" until she had done so. A month after her arrival she wrote of her excellent German tutor and of working four to six hours a day: "I am determined not to be repelled or diverted." [E 102]

She met Tieck of whom she had said ". . . instead of saying, like most people, 'I must learn German to read Schiller—to read Goethe,' I have always said, 'I must learn German to read Tieck.'" [M 66] They talked of Shakespeare, of the English stage, of Mrs. Siddons and the Kembles; Mrs. Jameson was present at two of his celebrated dramatic readings of Shakespeare, hearing *Julius Caesar* and a *Midsummer Night's Dream* and she had the opportunity of praising him for his recently finished translation of *Macbeth*.

At Bonn, Anna reports delightedly her meeting with August Wilhelm von Schlegel and, subsequently, her "conquest" of him:

There I became acquainted with the celebrated Schlegel, or, I should rather say, M. le Chevalier de Schlegel, for I believe his titles and his starry honours are not indifferent to him, and in truth he wears them very gracefully. I was rather surprised to find in this sublime and eloquent critic, this awful scholar, whose comprehensive mind has grasped the whole universe of Art, a most lively, agreeable, social being. [M 81]

The attentions paid her by Schlegel flattered Anna into a pleasant, bantering tone that is rare in her letters: "Pity I am married! for certainly his stars and his ribbons are very becoming, and as for his wig—I think he only wears one in imitation of his Jupiter. In short . . . I found him quite captivating." [E 107] He told her to speak whatever she might think when writing of her travels in Germany and she felt that she could never do otherwise than think and speak well of such an amiable people. One morning, as she looked at a red morocco edition of *Corinne*, a gift to Schlegel from Mme de Staël, he confessed himself "immortalized" in it, "the Prince Castel Forte, the faithful, humble, unaspiring friend of Corinne." [M 82]

At various points in the letters of this period the name of Mme de Staël is linked with her own. The correspondence in ability and in ambition was a fantasy which her family seem to have enjoyed and which, in her heart of hearts, Anna promoted. In a letter to her father and mother, written after she had been in Germany for a month, she remonstrated with her parents for their affectionate compliments on her success: "I am not Mme de Staël, but would be well content with half her greatness. I will confess, however, that though I have often dreamt of fame and sighed for it, I never knew before what it really is. . . . my name and the opinions and sentiments I advocate are well known even to those who have not read my little books; everywhere I find friends and people anxious to talk to me and to inform me on subjects of art and literature and to know in return what I think of them and their country." [E 103]

The romantic dream-come-true, of being likened to the astonishing Mme de Staël, of feeling herself the celebrated mistress of a salon, was satisfying, as were the gratifications of ambition realized. But any approach to such an identification, even if recognized as totally unrealistic and kept sanely tenuous in her mind, was a dubious foundation for a solid marriage, and such a taste of Continental fame was a radically wrong medicine for a woman whose lot would normally be an eventual sharing of her husband's residence in Toronto.

Anna's marriage brought her unhappiness as it must have done to Robert Jameson. From its earliest years, it had been an uneasy and unsatisfactory union; there are no letters recording a period of happiness and peace, even in courtship. Here in Germany in 1833, Anna Jameson found many compensations; she was soothed and flattered by all those she met and she made friends who became very important to her. More and more her intense friendships substituted for the married happiness she missed; more and more as she submerged herself in them, contentment in her marriage or the thought of residence in Upper Canada, became impossible to her.

Her family was always important to her. They were honestly proud of her, they leaned on her as the brilliant sister, and, shortly, as the supporter of father and mother. Denis Murphy had praised and pushed his eldest daughter and though he had not been averse to the marriage he is, in many letters, the sympathetic recipient of Anna's complaints about Robert. On her side, Anna never forsook the role of dutiful daughter; her care for her family was a constantly accepted duty, far outweighing any discernibly similar feelings toward Robert Jameson for whom exasperation and a determined forbearance seemed to be the best sentiments she could offer.

All the Murphys lived to some extent on the fame of the clever Anna. Charlotte, in a report from Bonn, introduces Goethe's daughter-in-law, Ottilie, her sister's most absorbing new friend, to the family at home:

The reception here has been quite delightful; Nina [Anna] has been received with open arms. Madame de Goethe, in particular, she is much charmed with; she is the daughter-in-law of the poet, a most lively and delightful person, so very delightful that she is the cause of our departure. We accompany her to Bonn, where it is Nina's present intention to stay for some time. . . . I feel such constant excitement that I find it quite impossible to fix my attention to write to you. [E 98]

Robert Noel's introduction of Anna Jameson to Ottilie von Goethe instituted for Anna an enduring and probably the most hectic alliance of her life.[4] In its beginnings, the friendship was a four-way affair, with Ottilie and her friends Adèle Schopenhauer and Sibylle Mertens equally involved in an often tense relationship with "die Jameson."[5] Ottilie, who before her marriage had been the Baroness Ottilie von Pogwisch, was the widow of Goethe's son August (d. 1830), and the mother of Walther (1819–85), Wolfgang (1820–83), and Alma (1827–44). Described with some condescension by Mrs. Jameson, shortly after their first meeting, as an "amusing, affectionate *little frisk*" [E 105] she shortly became "Die Frau vom Andern Stern"[6] to Anna and, as such, the object of a romantic attachment, a motherly devotion and a sisterly exasperation.

She was admittedly and demonstrably a wildly erratic, passionate and attractive woman, capable of extreme devotion to Goethe and also of extreme and capricious selfishness toward him. She had devotedly nursed him through his final illness, but at the same time had contemplated a runaway desertion with her current lover. Her life's story is a history of passionate attachments and just as passionate disappointments, and though her reckless abandon appalled Anna Jameson, it also fascinated her. A few months after their first meeting, Anna shrewdly assessed her friend's attraction for her:

I love you dear Ottilie for that *abandon*, and would almost add that inconsequence where yourself are concerned; I respect and esteem in you that delicacy towards your friends which I do not often meet in others. My own nature is so reserved, that discretion is in me scarce a virtue, for my mind and heart—though always full, too full—seldom overflow, but were

I to place confidence in anyone I would trust in you. . . . Torment your
lovers as you will—torment yourself, if you must—but spare your friends.
[E 110]

There were complications concerning Anna in the Ottilie-Adèle-
Sibylle friendship. Adèle, writing to Ottilie in December 1833, says:

. . . Die Jameson ist leidlich wohl abgereist—so lieb sie mir ist, so unendlich
ich sie beklage, frappirt mich doch sehr, wie sie zu mir und zur Mertens
stand denn jede glaubte mit ihr intimer zu sein und die Discretion mit
welcher die J[ameson] zu schweigen versteht, wenn einer von uns sagt, was
sie längst vom anderen weiss, ist selten—Wir in Weimar sind das nicht
gewöhnt, wir haben ein grossartigeres kühneres Vertrauen—doch hat die
Jameson klugerweise recht, Sybille hat sich gewaltig exaltirt und mich
sogar unfreundlich behandelt aus lauter Liebe zur Jameson, welche Sybillen
wie eine Todtkranke behandelt, und dieselbe stets schonende Klugheit
von mir verlangt.[7]

To Adèle's complaint, Ottilie answers as peacemaker and arbitrator:

Ich verstehe ganz Deinen Schmerz um Sybille, glaube mir ihr Hauptunglück
bestand darin keinen Mann geliebt zu haben, das gab ihr diese Wunder-
barkeit der Empfindung in der Freundschaft—denn diese Art ist zwischen
Frauen nicht natürlich. Sie hatte die Freundin als Surrogat des Geliebten,
—deshalb war sie so anfordernd, so leidenschaftlich. . . .[8]

It is wise to balance the reactions of astonishment and repugnance
which one feels on reading the protestations of devotion in Anna's
letters to Ottilie by a realization that she was initiated into this
hysterically emotional feminine society and was not its instigator. Her
letters redound with apologies for her constitutional reserve of
temperament. Although by our standards she was warmly affectionate,
perhaps over-eager in her courting of chosen friends, by the standards
of nineteenth-century correspondence, and particularly of the group
to which she now adhered, she was not radically effusive. Her obvious
eagerness and intensity of desire for Ottilie von Goethe's friendship
is again and again pathetic because it betrays so nakedly Anna
Jameson's combination of loneliness, Irish exaggeration and the tendency to invest all her own disappointed emotional stock in the lives
of a few chosen friends.

Anna's friendship, freely and fulsomely offered, was more than a
matter of words; she was ready and capable of extreme quixotic self-
sacrifice as she was to prove for the first time, but not for the last,
in the winter of 1834-5, when Ottilie had a child by an Englishman,
Charles Sterling. In these first months of their friendship, she was
constantly exhorting Ottilie to be cautious, to do what is right, to care
for her legitimate children.

Ottilie von Goethe flew from one infatuation to another with amazing speed; in the first year of this acquaintance we learn that she was compromised by letters to a Captain Storey and rumoured to be marrying him; she was interested enough in Robert Noel to question his relationship with Anna Jameson and hence to embarrass and trouble her new friend; she was willing to be romantically diverted from both these men by the arrival in Weimar of Abraham Hayward, English translator of *Faust*, against whose superficiality Anna warned her; finally, entranced by Charles Sterling, a poor theological student, son of the British Consul at Genoa, she became his mistress and bore his child. [N xvi]

Small wonder that Anna's letters are constantly admonitory, though the tone is that of the fascinated and doting rather than the sternly disapproving schoolmistress:

And then Noel writes to me in anger and in despair, and seems to think that I mean to give up all intercourse and friendship with him on your account. I had no such meaning. I love Noel truly and appreciate all his good qualities, but certainly if with your rashness and his irritability I am placed in a position which obliges me to choose whether I will remain *his* friend or *yours*—then I remain *yours.*—It is an inconsistency very consistent with your character, my dear Ottilie, that you at the same time hate to be deceived, and resent it beyond everything else—and yet can hardly bear the truth, and shrink from it painfully. These alone are worthy to hear and know the truth, who can really love it, and nobly endure it; and all my own experience tells me that the most fatal evils of life arise from want of courage to speak and hear the truth. If I had had the courage to tell you all the truth last year, which I knew of Noel's character and sentiments as they referred to you, we had been spared much pain since. My love for you, my fear of wounding you, prevailed over my sense of right. [N 12]

As early in their friendship as July, 1833, Ottilie had caused Anna some similar embarrassment about Noel: "From some parts of your letter and from some words dropt by your friend Adèle I see that you think Noel loves me.—I really blush while I write the last words, the thing is so *impossible*. Pray believe this. . . ." [N 4]

These tortuous, if stimulating relationships and the gratification of being "fêted, that is, welcomed like a princess," [M 83] ended abruptly in November, 1833, with the news of Denis Murphy's sudden and serious illness. With no hesitation, but with great disappointment because of her growing affection and concern for her friend, Anna Jameson returned to England. On her way home, she wrote to Robert Noel, then in Dresden, about her parting from her "dear Ottilie. . . . When I think of all that I have left, and all the consequences which may attend my precipitate return, I could sit and wring my hands; but as that will do no good, I think it better to use them to some purpose." [M 84]

Her father had suffered a stroke, and from her first news of it, she had prepared herself for his death. She found him considerably improved, his speech returned and some recovery discernible in the use of his arm, which had been paralysed. His physicians were hopeful of further recovery and Anna found a certain consolation for the interruption to her own life in his joy at seeing her: "my mother tells me so continually how he has been pining for my return, and how my presence will contribute to his recovery—I feel so convinced that I have done right in coming that I cannot repent it." [M 83]

9

Visits and Sketches at Home and Abroad

THE PUBLICATION in 1834 of a two-volume collection of Anna Jameson's work was a tribute to her growing reputation as a writer and to the success and prestige of her *Characteristics*. Her own reaction to it was wise, if somewhat over-timid:

I do not like the book which my publishers, rather than myself, *will* give to the world. This collection of all sorts of fugitive things never owned, and the *Ennuyée* included. I have also written some slight sketches of the comparative state of art in England and in Germany. Had I remained a month longer in Dresden, I would have made this better; but I have done what I could—thrown out a few thoughts which others must take up and improve. This book, about which I care little, will subject me more than any former one to angry criticism, because I see I have just attained that point of reputation which, by giving a certain weight to my opinions, will provoke contradiction. So be it! [M 92]

Part I, "Sketches of Art, Literature and Character," is a series of three dialogues between Alda and Medon, her now familiar introductory characters, in which Mrs. Jameson sets before her reader a *pot-pourri* of facts, history, moralizing, and opinion on Germany and its people. To unify this work, the second of her travel accounts, she substitutes these dialogues for the specious heroine of her first success, the *Diary of an Ennuyée*.

As in the *Characteristics of Women*, the adoption of *personae* allows the authoress a useful breadth and elasticity of expression. Alda and Medon can disagree and so present two sides of an argument, or they can agree and so emphasize their author's favourite point of view:

MEDON:—There are people who, when they travel, open their eyes and their ears (ay, and their mouths to some purpose), and shut up their hearts and souls. I have heard such persons make it their boast, that they have returned to Old England with all their old prejudices thick upon them; they have come back, to use their own phrase, "with no foreign ideas just the same as they went:" they are to be congratulated! I hope you are not one of these?

ALDA:—I hope not; it is this cold impervious pride which is the perdition of us English and of England. . . . [VS, I, 15]

She weaves the experiences of her 1829 and her 1833 trips together to make a stage-by-stage travelogue, giving details of interest *en route*, characterizations of people met, descriptions of galleries and collections visited, with historical background or anecdotes added for interest and variety.

Part of the charm of her work lies in its name dropping. In Germany her *entrée* into the high ranks of society and of the arts was made easy. The reporting of such cordial relations is constantly fascinating to the reading public and the market for chatty yet humble, impressed yet impressive memoirs of famous people is a constant quality, a balm to the nerves of publishers in any century. Consequently, Ottilie, a "literary princess" of the house of Goethe, is a fitting and a guaranteed successful subject for characterization:

Conceive a woman, a young, accomplished, enthusiastic woman, who had qualities to attach, talents to amuse, and capacity to appreciate Goethe; who, for fourteen or fifteen years, could exist in daily, hourly communication with that gigantic spirit, yet retain, from first to last, the most perfect simplicity of character, and this less from the strength than from the purity and delicacy of the original texture. . . . Sometimes there was a wild, artless fervour in her impulses and feelings which might have become a feather-cinctured Indian on her savannah; then, the next moment, her bearing reminded you of the court-bred lady of the bed-chamber. Quick in perception, yet femininely confiding, uniting a sort of restless vivacity with an indolent gracefulness, she appeared to me by far the most poetical and genuine being of my own sex I ever knew in highly-cultivated life. [VS I, 79]

Anna's reminiscences of Schlegel, largely identical with the letters she sent home, are combined with a lengthy and spirited defence of Mme de Staël against the neglect and calumny to which her name was then being subjected in Germany:

They forget, or do not know, what we know, that her *De l'Allemagne* was the first book which awakened in France and England a lively and general interest in German art and literature. It is now five and twenty years since it was published. The march of opinion and criticism, and knowledge of every kind has been so rapid that much has become old which then was new; but this does not detract from its merit. Once or twice I tried to convince my German friends that they were exceedingly ungrateful in abusing Madame de Staël, but it was all in vain; so I sat swelling with indignation to hear my idol traduced, and called—O profanation!—"cette Staël." [VS I, 36]

Anna's special interests are displayed at various points on her trip: a catalogue and description of the Prince of Orange's pictures and those of the Stadel Museum in Frankfurt; a lengthy appreciation of the present state of German sculpture, painting and drama and an enthusiastic account of her reception by Germany's principal artists. The studies of the sculptors, Schwarthaler and "the good and gifted old man," Dannecker, were opened to her; she persuaded Moritz Retzsch, the painter, to send her a selection of his *Fantasien*, drawings and moral musings, which she translated, introduced and negotiated for publication in England. Mme Schroeder-Devrient, the operatic *prima donna*, inspired her warm admiration, mixed with certain moral misgivings. To Noel she wrote, "do what you can to elevate and steady her mind." [M 90]

In a passage of discussion, Medon is given a spirited and informative argument for the reception of a new, an experimental, a "romantic" style in sculpture:

MEDON: . . . But I am an enemy to the inclusive in everything; and— pardon me—your worship of the Elgin marbles and the Niobe is, I think, a little too exclusive. All I ask is, that modern sculpture should be allowed, like painting and poetry, to have its romantic as well as its classical school.
Alda: It has been otherwise decided.
Medon: But it has not been otherwise proved. There has been much theoretical eloquence and criticism expended on the subject, but I deny that the experiment has been fairly and practically brought before us. . . . I contend, that to apply the forms suggested by the modern poetry demands a different spirit from that of classic art. . . . And why should we not have in sculpture a Lear as well as a Laocoon? a Constance as well as a Niobe? a Gismunda as well as a Cleopatra? . . .
For my own part, I look forward to a new era in sculpture. I believe that the purely natural and the purely ideal are one, and susceptible of forms and modifications as yet untried. [VS I, 75]

The final section of Part I is heavily weighted to the woman reader. It contains a catalogue of present German lady authors, introduced by a short essay on woman writers and their variety of motives, including the one which Anna Jameson undoubtedly attributed to herself:

Some, who are unhappy in their domestic relations, yet endowed with all that feminine craving after sympathy which was intended to be the charm of our sex, the blessing of yours, and somehow or other has been turned to the bane of both, look abroad for what they find not at home; fling into the wide world the irrepressible activity of an overflowing mind and heart, which can find no other unforbidden issue,—and to such "fame is love disguised." [VS I, 83]

In too tactful a way to incur censure as a crusading feminist, she also inserts a plea for women's rights commensurate with the ideal of chivalry to which men adhere, but for which they too often substitute practical benefits: "I speak thus, knowing that, however open to perversion these expressions may be, *you* will not misapprehend one; you know that I am no vulgar, vehement arguer about the 'rights of women'; and, from my habitual tone of feeling and thought, the last to covet any of your masculine privileges." [*VS* I, 83]

Once again she makes a strong plea for more sensible education for Englishwomen. Although she deplores an obsessive concern for housekeeping which she found in Germany, she finds German women of rank and fashion more useful and more genuinely accomplished than their English counterparts: "The wife of a state minister once excused herself from going with me to a picture gallery, because on that day she was obliged to reckon up the household linen; she was one of the most charming, truly elegant and accomplished women I ever met with." [*VS* I, 90] Moreover, German women were predisposed toward England; they preferred the study of English to that of French and considered Shakespeare "a species of household god, whose very name was breathed with reverence." [*VS* I, 91]

"Sketches of Art, Literature and Character," Part II, is of a less personal nature. The author loosely catalogues and comments on the holdings of the great German galleries in Munich, Nuremberg and Dresden. She recants her stated preference for Italian art and admits a glowing appreciation of the Flemish school:

Somebody calls the gallery at Munich the court of Rubens; and Sir Joshua Reynolds says that no one should judge of Rubens who has not studied him at Antwerp and Dusseldorf. I begin to feel the truth of this. My devoted worship of the Italian school of art rendered me long—I will not say *blind* to the merits of the Flemish painters—for that were to be "sans eyes, sans taste, sans every thing!" but in truth, without that full feeling of their power which I have since acquired. [*VS* I, 131]

Personal and subjective, her judgments remain stubbornly linked to the possible "moral influence of painting." Anna Jameson is an enthusiastic proselyte for art in all its forms; she cajoles, bludgeons and shames her readers into awareness and a sense of national responsibility:

The public—the national spirit is wanting; individual patronage is confined, is misdirected, is arbitrary, demanding of the artist anything rather than the highest and purest intellectual application of his Art, and affording neither space nor opportunity for him to address himself to the grand universal passions, principles, and interests of human nature! Suppose a

Michael Angelo to be born to us in England; we should not, perhaps, set him to make a statue of snow, but where or how would his gigantic genius, which revelled in the great deeps of passion and imagination, find scope for action? He would struggle and gasp like a stranded Leviathan! [VS I, 132]

In the early thirties, Carlyle was undertaking to promote popular awareness of Germany; *Sartor Resartus* appeared serially in *Fraser's* during 1833 and 1834 and his essay on the *Nibelungenlied* appeared in the *Westminster Review*, 1831. Included in Part II of *Visits and Sketches* are comments on and translations from the *Nibelungenlied*, as well as a compact summary of its plot. Anna was here, as always, both fortunate in assessing public taste and clever in taking advantage of it.

The final part of volume I and all of volume II constitute a mixed bag of her former productions. The sketch of Fanny Kemble is a farewell biography and critical tribute to her young friend, now about to leave the stage to become Mrs. Pierce Butler of Philadelphia. This is incorporated with her text to John Hayter's sketches of Fanny in the character of Juliet, originally written in 1830. The final pages of appreciation are distinguished by a plea for acting of the complete text of a Shakespeare play:

Had she [Fanny] remained on the stage, her fine taste and original and powerful mind would have carried the public with her in some things which she contemplated; for instance, she had an idea of restoring King Lear, as originally written by Shakespeare, and playing the *real* Cordelia to her father's Lear. . . .

At Dresden and Frankfort I saw the *Merchant of Venice* played as it stands in Shakespeare, with all the stately scenes between Portia and her suitors—the whole of the character of Jessica—the lovely moon-light dialogue between Jessica and Lorenzo, and the beautiful speeches given to Portia, all which, by sufferance of an English audience, are omitted on our stage. When I confessed to some of the great German critics, that the *Merchant of Venice, Romeo and Juliet, King Lear*, etc. were performed in England, not only with important omissions of the text, but with absolute alterations, affecting equally the truth of character and the constructions of the story, they looked at me, at first, as if half incredulous, and their perception of the barbarism, as well as the absurdity, was so forcibly expressed on their countenances, and their contempt so justifiable that I confess I felt ashamed for my countrymen. [VS I, 299 and note]

In Anna Jameson's day the reading of Shakespeare was a popular entertainment, untainted by any question of propriety such as adhered in some quarters to actual theatre-going. Anna had written a memoir of Mrs. Siddons for the *New Monthly Magazine* shortly after the death of the famous actress in June, 1831. [E 87] The story of her unsuccessful attempt to be Mrs. Siddons' biographer has already been told; in *Visits and Sketches* her tribute to the great lady of the stage is coloured by her own experience of the elderly Mrs. Siddons as a play-reader and not of the younger and palmier days of the actress. Her comments provide, as well, an entertaining sidelight on nineteenth-century taste:[1]

I am not old enough to remember Mrs. Siddons in her best days; but, judging from my own recollections, I should say that, to hear her *read* one of Shakespeare's plays, was a higher, a more complete gratification, and a more astonishing display of her powers, than her performance of any single character. On the stage she was the perfect actress; when she was reading Shakespeare, her profound enthusiastic admiration of the poet, and deep insight into his most hidden beauties, made her almost a poetess, or at least, like a priestess, full of the god of her idolatry. . . . When in reading Macbeth she said, "give me the daggers!" they gleamed before our eyes. When, in King John, she came to the passage beginning
"if the midnight bell,
Did with his iron tongue and brazen note," etc.
I remember I felt every drop of blood pause, and then run backwards through my veins an overpowering awe and horror. No scenic representation I ever witnessed produced the hundredth part of the effect of her reading Hamlet. This tragedy was the triumph of her art. . . . [VS I, 284]

Articles on the estates of Hardwicke and Althorpe are historically informative accounts of the founding families of two of England's stately homes, with emphasis on Anna's special interest, the private art collection in each mansion. The final portion of each is an informal cataloguing of pictures. Whether impressions are truly present on the canvas or not, Anna reads into the paintings what she knows of their subjects:[2]

Old Sarah (The Duchess of Marlborough) hangs near her. One would think that Kneller, in spite, had watched the moment to take a characteristic likeness, and catch, not the Cynthia, but the Fury of the minute; as, for instance, when she cut off her luxuriant tresses, so worshipped by her husband, and flung them in his face; for so she tosses back her disdainful head, and curls her lip like an insolent, pouting, spoiled, grown-up baby. . . .
And yet I suspect that the Duchess of Marlborough has never met with justice. History knows her only as Marlborough's wife, an intriguing dame d'honneur, and a cast-off favourite. Vituperated by Swift, satirized by Pope, ridiculed by Walpole—what angel could have stood such bedaubing and from such pens?
"O she has fallen into a pit of ink!"
But glorious talents she had, strength of mind, generosity, the power to feel and inspire the strongest attachment. . . . Imagine such a woman as the Duchess of Marlborough out-faced, out-plotted by that crowned cipher, that sceptred commonplace, Queen Anne. [VS I, 267]

Here, as always, she writes well as a partisan. Her willingness to take sides, to voice her opinions and to apply her excellent historical imagination, which clothed any character in lively flesh, be it poet's lady, Shakespeare's heroine, or painter's subject, is the most attractive attribute of her writing. It is not difficult to account for the popularity of such work: governed by the conventions of her day, Anna Jameson wrote her kind of biography for lady readers. In our day, working under a different set of conventions, which would encourage realism of portraiture instead of moral sentiment, Anna might well have become a superb historical biographer.

The three tales which are included in *Visits and Sketches*, volume II, do no more than confirm the wisdom of her subsequent abandonment of fiction as her *métier*. They are commonplace and weak in invention: "The False One" is a revision of her childhood romance of the East, "Faizy," and was first published in 1827; "Halloran the Pedlar," written in 1826, was published in 1827 in *The Bijou*, an annual.[3] Its plot was taken from an incident reported in the newspapers and later incorporated into Bainim's novel *The Newlans*. [VS II, 34] It relates a melodramatic Irish incident with the usual large measure of sentimental sympathy for the brave pure heroine, and with the self-conscious use of an occasional word of Irish dialect. "The Indian Mother," written in 1830, is a deliberately heart-tearing tale of a mother's devotion, distinctive only for its South American setting, and even this was arbitrarily chosen because it was remote and exotic. Mrs. Jameson's fiction inventions are always "stories told by a lady"; there is none of the warmth or the involvement of the author that one finds in her more successful biographical-historical sketches or in her travelogues.

Volume II also contains "Much Coin, Much Care, a Dramatic Proverb for Little Actors," written sometime during her tenure as the Littleton's governess, 1822–5. Its title indicates its nature: it is a moral little drama for her charges to perform and, like the three tales, it is undistinguished in invention and technique. These, with a republication of the *Diary of an Ennuyée*, make up volume II of *Visits and Sketches*.

Anna Jameson discarded this moralizing fiction early in her career in favour of the popular criticism of society, literature and art for which her talents were best suited. The compliment paid her in 1834 by the *Edinburgh Review* was well deserved: "In no point, we think, is Mrs. Jameson's talent more conspicuous than in her correct appreciation of the bent of her own powers, and the department in which they might most efficiently be exercised."[4]

The reviewer, in spite of his obvious preference for the *Characteristics of Women*, which he is discussing in the same article, found much to admire in *Visits and Sketches*. His disapproving remarks on the *Diary* are more than counterbalanced by his discriminating appreciation of the rest of the work:

The travelling "Sketches" which compose the rest of the publication, possess many of the merits of the "Characteristics,"—a delicate sensibility to beauty, whether in character, scenery, art or literature, and the same power of varied, discriminating, and eloquent expression. The authoress seems to have travelled under the most favourable circumstances; to have seen everything and everyone worth seeing and knowing; and to have enjoyed the intimate and familiar acquaintance of some, to whom our English travellers in general appear to be strangers. Her remarks on Tieck, on the German stage, and on the distinguished actors of Germany, are interesting; and she gives the best and most satisfactory account of modern German art, both in sculpture and painting, we have yet met with.[5]

This review gave great satisfaction to both Anna and to her family. She was in Vienna with Ottilie when she heard of it from her mother, and although in replying she discounted its importance in comparison with her mother's affection, she was sufficiently elated to make the review a subject of letter conversation between her German friends:

OTTILIE TO SIBYLLE: WIEN DEN 16 JANUAR 1835
In diesem Augenblick hat Anna die Freude, dass man ihr das Edinburgh Review schickt, wo ihre "Visits" angezeigt wurden; da Sie es wahrscheinlich gern sehen werden, sage ich Ihnen, dass es das Oktoberheft 1834 betrifft.[6]

Anna's first notice in the *Quarterly Review* came in 1837, with reference to *Visits and Sketches*. Her work is not the prime object of the reviewer, but in the course of dealing with other travel books on Germany he quotes from her descriptions of Tieck and Retzsch and adds:

The ordinary amusement at Tieck's soirées is a dramatic reading by himself— usually scenes from his own and Schlegel's admirable translation of Shakespeare: We had the good fortune to be present at one of his readings, and agree with Mrs. Jameson, that, with the exception of Mrs. Siddons, there has been nothing of the kind within living memory to be compared with them. This lady's description of the Dresden Gallery is also much the best we are acquainted with. . . .[7]

It was not until 1845 that her work received a full-scale review in the *Quarterly*. This brief notice, however, was a satisfying beginning, demonstrating her acceptance as a voice in the literary world.

10

Fame and Friendship

HER RETURN FROM GERMANY, early in 1834, marked Anna Jameson's entry into London society as a literary notable. From being protégé of a smaller group, whose centre was the Montagus and the Procters, she became a sought-after celebrity in a much wider society, an honour which, as described by the American author, Catherine Sedgwick, who subsequently became her friend, was undoubtedly a stimulating, but certainly a trying experience:

Oh, it is a horrible arena, where, like trained gladiators, each awaits his turn to spring into the place of action and display his strength, while others are breathlessly waiting to succeed him. It is a state of society that belongs to a high degree of civilization—but the civilization of savages. I would rather die at once than to struggle, as they do there to maintain an existence in "society". But these are only reflections afterwards; for the time, it was all delight, animation and fatigue. . . .[1]

Anna's letters to Noel and to Ottilie von Goethe abound in accounts of social gatherings which are rosters of names well known in nineteenth-century society and the arts. She reports that she is living "a life of laborious dissipation" and tells Noel of one particularly congenial friend, Sarah Austin, the daughter of John Taylor of Norwich and the wife of John Austin, a distinguished professor and writer on jurisprudence. Mrs. Austin came from a remarkable family, part of an influential intellectual and literary group with which Harriet Martineau's family, also of Norwich, was closely connected. This group was enthusiastic about German literature and responsible for some of its vogue and dissemination in England. Mrs. Austin's best known work is a translation and commentary, *Characteristics of Goethe*, but when Anna first met her and termed her "a remarkable woman," with "one of the largest and healthiest minds I ever met with in a person of my own sex," [M 80] she was translating Victor Cousin's reports on the system of public education in Prussia with the hope of spreading progressive educational ideas in England. Sarah Austin's friendship for Mrs. Jameson was no doubt cemented by their mutual interest in Germany, its arts and literature; it was to be a valuable and a lasting association.[2]

In this same year, Robert Noel introduced Anna Jameson to his cousin, Lady Byron. Anna's first impression was of "implacability," but she capitulated to the fascinating aura of mystery and suffering which enveloped Lady Byron and her daughter, Ada. In spite of the self-warnings which she writes to Ottilie, Anna denied her own wisdom and embarked on another intense and tortuous relationship with the Byrons:

I have seen a great deal of Lady Byron, who is certainly one of the most excellent beings in the world. Blasted as she has been, in life, heart, soul, health and all the promises of existence, she appears to have saved for herself a wreck of happiness, by devoting her mind earnestly to do good, and to the education of her daughter. Ada Byron is a singular girl, and one whom I could love exceedingly if we were more together; but my path in life being marked out for me and my future inevitable, I must not let my feelings and affections stray towards those, whom I must lose.   [N 21]

Anna introduced Lady Byron to Harriet Martineau whom she admired as a capable and intellectual author whose reputation was already secure. Lady Byron, in her turn, made Anna known to the gentle, aging and revered dramatist, Joanna Baillie. Through these months, Anna's initiation into the various echelons of nineteenth-century literary activity was more and more gratifying.

But always, through the various family, literary and social occupations, she was preoccupied with thoughts of Ottilie and of going back to Germany. Robert Noel is her confidant: "How I wish I could raise the mind of that sweet [Ottilie] prostrated as it now is, to look forward for herself and her fine children, particularly little Alma! If God had but given me children, I think I would have been blessed." As early as January, 1834, she had written to him of returning: [M 95]

Shall I whisper something to you? I indulge a hope of revisiting Germany in the spring. It depends on so many contingencies that I scarcely dare permit myself to dwell on it. But if my letters from Canada are definitive, if I can finish the printing of my book, if I can so arrange my money matters as to perform what is right to others and spare something for selfishness, then I shall spread my wings sometime in April or May, and you will see me alight on a spring morning among my dear German friends, like a bird escaped from its cage, with its plumage ruffled and torn with beating against the wires.   [M 90]

The trip was not possible as early as she had hoped, but in June, as she writes again to Noel, she is on the point of escaping from London where the whole period since her return has been one of "labour, distasteful dissipation and extreme sorrow. My poor father, though in no danger now, is a miserable wreck; all I could do for him in his present state is done, his affairs arranged and my mother's comfort provided for." She is about to "fly off to forget for a few months all this pain" and she consoles herself for the uncertainties of her future by the thought of her reunion with Noel: "Never mind, we shall have a ramble together, talk philosophy, enjoy the summer air—and then to work again." [M 97]

In the summer of 1834, Anna was able to leave her family and set out for Germany, for a stay which was to last almost two years. Her first letters home read like continuations of the triumphal social progress of her 1833 trip; in spite of all disclaimers she was delighted with her receptions, including one at a minor German court:

You must know that when the Grand Duchess [of Saxe-Weimar Eisenach] returned from Carlsbad, she sent me an *invitation* to appear at court. I did not ask to be presented, nor much *wish* it. I was afraid I should have been nervous; not from *mauvais honte* but because there was considerable curiosity excited on my account and several persons present who were fond of me and anxious I should please. . . . I said I understood her Imperial Highness spoke and understood English perfectly, but she said she would not venture English with me; she is rather deaf and speaks very quick and inarticulately, so that I was under much disadvantage. However, it seems I made a favourable impression; I was kept to dinner—the Grand Duchess seated me next herself and I did not find that this propinquity to an Imperial Highness took away my appetite for I was extremely hungry. . . . I was told afterwards that my French was particularly approved of . . .   [E 114]

However, her great preoccupation was Ottilie von Goethe, who was expecting Sterling's child in the winter or early spring of 1835. It speaks well for Anna's charity, as well as for her enthusiasm for her friend, that after her repeated warnings to Ottilie about her various infatuations, she was ready to give largely of all her resources in time and money, as well as in affectionate care. Between them, Anna and Sibylle Mertens undertook the care and support of Ottilie; Sibylle's role was largely advisory and financially supporting; Anna's was that of travelling companion, nurse, financial manager, and friend.[3]

The trio went to some odd extremes in their attempt to maintain secrecy about the scandal. Mentioned in letters throughout these months is "Octavia Jameson," a non-existent travelling companion of Anna and Ottilie as they went from Weimar to Vienna and settled down to await the baby's arrival. Sibylle Mertens wrote to "Octavia" and Ottilie from Bonn in April, 1835.[4] To add to this mystery, we have the record of still another name for Anna Jameson at this time. In October 1834, Ottilie wrote to Sibylle asking her to send mail to "Mrs. Azetti Jameson."[5] It seems unlikely that there was a third companion with the two in Vienna; certainly none of Anna Jameson's sisters was with her. The identity of "Octavia" must, therefore, remain mysterious, with the likeliest explanation being an expedient covering of tracks during these months of trying to mitigate the social effects of Ottilie's indiscretion.[6]

There is no doubt of Anna's true affection for Ottilie; at the same time there is no doubt that veneration of the great name of Goethe played its part. Anna Jameson was a very conventional being in her own life's affairs, but her imagination was highly romantic and dramatic; certainly unwilling herself to dare society's disapproval, she was concerned that her friend should avoid society's full penalty and that the name of Goethe should not be blemished by scandal. Her passion for the dramatic could and did expend itself vicariously in Ottilie's life, and both her undoubted kindness of heart and her training and tendency toward family management could find outlets in the service of her friend.

The letters of both Anna Jameson and Sibylle Mertens are warm testimony to feminine friendship, but it was evidently Anna who stepped forward as the social and moral monitress. She encouraged Ottilie von Goethe to return to Weimar shortly after the child's birth in March, 1835, refusing to join her there, but staying behind in Vienna where she could watch over the baby. She prudently counselled home and duty, "leaving no room for blind passion." "Be but true to yourself, dearest Ottilie, and firm, and we shall not have suffered and sacrificed in vain." [N 24] "While by your conduct you have shewn that you despise opinion, do not *brave* it. For God's sake do not enter into any impotent and degrading competition with Society. You have broken thro' its severe laws; take the consequences with gentleness and dignity, and you may keep your place." [N 26] Her advice was evidently taken and proved sound. On July 6, 1835, she writes to Ottilie in great relief:

It seems *too* great a happiness to dare to believe . . . that the past sufferings, pain, terror, shame, grief, suspense have not been in vain!

. . . I must be glad that I was not with you in Weimar . . . your own energy and power of will have supported you unassisted . . . without suffering [your] mind to wander after unhealthy and forbidden sources of excitement . . . [N 26]

The baby was called Anna Sibylle, with Anna Jameson the official godmother and both the friends concerned with paying for its care. In a letter from Bonn in April, Sibylle Mertens writes to "Octavia" and Ottilie that she has sent one instalment of the money she had offered to provide each quarter-year for the payment of Ottilie's and the baby's expenses. The next payment will follow at the end of May, "und wir sind dann auf einem Wege der geschäftsmässigen Ordnung. . . ."[7] There were others who befriended Ottilie: Dr. Seligmann of the medical staff of the University of Vienna looked after her and was a party to the conspiracy of silence:

[Seligmann met at the café the usual set,—Grillparzer, Bauerfeld, Witthauer and the others. They talked of the report concerning Ottilie as the most ridiculous thing in the world.] . . . He was really surprised to see how completely they were all convinced that the *truth* was a *falsehood*. [N 24]

Anna was always aware that circumstances could and would probably demand her departure for Canada and there was evidently some discussion of Ottilie joining her there. Sibylle Mertens resented Anna's influence over Ottilie, but her judgment on this proposition was surely sound: "Ihrer Idee, später nach Griechenland zu gehen, kann ich nicht beipflichten: wozu sich eine dauernde Qual schaffen, zu all den Qualen, die das Schicksal so reichlich schafft? Mit Anna und Anna nach Canada—das fasse ich eher: muss aber immer fragen: 'Und Alma?' "[8] Various plans were prepared to care for little Anna: Robert Noel suggested putting her to board with her nurse, and Sibylle suggested that Anna should bring the child to Genoa. The care of the baby was, however, a short-lived problem. She died very young, probably in the spring of 1836. [N xviii]

It is unlikely that the Murphys were aware of the primary purpose of Anna's lengthy residence in Vienna. Her letters home are very much in her usual travelogue style, although Ottilie complained to Sibylle that Anna was not going into society, that she would not use her letters of introduction or visit the people who would like to become acquainted with her.[9]

To her family, however, these months were meant to sound like another triumphal procession, a continuation of her last year's German visit. She wrote to them of her "many interesting acquaintances. You will perhaps be amused to hear that my most intimate friend is a sovereign princess—the princess of Hohenzollern." Carolyn von Pichler, an elderly and honoured German writer, was another of her circle, "so that I am in the very midst of all I want." She did admit to a lack of funds, however: "I feel like a sponge, drinking in all around me; the worst is, the want of money, or rather the want of *money enough*—a very general complaint. I have just enough to live and go into society and visit the galleries. . . . it is quite certain that in the midst of my travels and all the amusement and excitement I enjoy, I learn self-denial and many hard lessons beside." [E 118]

Their Christmas in Vienna in 1834 was celebrated in the German manner and reported with enthusiasm and detail by Anna. Either Ottilie von Goethe had her children with her, or the Murphys were to believe that they were present, for the family gathering is given in some detail:

The presents which Madame de Goethe had prepared for her children, family, servants on that evening cost her at least 150 or 200 florins. The custom is to display these gifts on an illuminated table, with the fir-tree planted in the middle, to which are suspended abundance of wax lights, sugar plums and little toys and trinkets. Noel, who was at Prince Metternichs that night, says that the presents etc. which covered the table were worth at least 10,000 florins. Madame de Goethe gave me a beautiful head of her father-in-law, engraved on a fine cornelian, which had been done from life and a gift from him to herself. [E 116]

By the summer of 1835 the strain and conspiracy had broken down Anna Jameson's health and she speaks to her father of "a relapse of those spasms which are now my horror." Probably suffering mainly from nervous reaction, she was ordered to the mountains for rest. Her accounts of this enforced holiday show it to have been one of the happiest and most pleasant episodes in her life. By her own nature and desires she was almost always deeply involved in the lives of others. Here, free for a few months, alone, independent, and glorying in it, she foreshadows the intrepid "Rambler" she later became in Upper Canada: "I came to Gmünden on the Gmünden See. . . . I am really living in a kind of earthly paradise for half a crown a day, all expenses included, except boating, in which I am rather extravagant. Just behind my cottage, which is on the very edge of the Lake, there is a little nook where I plunge every morning and frighten the fishes; I then take a little walk among the rocks and try to sketch now and then." [E 124]

On her way to her "exile," she had visited Robert Noel, who had recently married a German girl and was living at Rosawitz in Bohemia. To Ottilie, she wrote of his "sweet, excellent wife . . . he ought at least to be happy—and *is so.*" [N 27] Noel was still "a most kind and useful friend"; he and his wife remained in Anna's closest circle. He had provided her *entrée* into German society and he was obviously prized, besides, for intellectual fellow-feeling. His devotion had encouraged a sense of being the acclaimed and accepted mistress of a salon, a link with "Madame de Staël herself in all her glory" whose likeness in herself Anna always denied but never forgot. Once at Gmünden, she even allowed herself a note of romantic regret as she wrote to Noel: "You might be at Gmünden, at the little inn there, and we might have had some pleasures together. Fate owed it to us, and I did half hope it—but now it is too late." [M 102] To the incurably romantic and diversely involved Ottilie, she writes in November of the same year:

If ever, dear Ottilie, you indulged a feeling of jealousy about me and him, it is, I hope, all over. You must know that it is absurd as far as we are both concerned. Life has assumed to me too serious and fixed an aspect to allow *me* to trifle either with my own feelings or another's. He sees this, and he sees that I understand him perfectly. What other people may think or say I care not, but if *you* could suppose there was any sentimental nonsense between us, it would indeed give me pain. [N 30]

Noel was, to some extent, financially dependent on Lady Byron and in the spring and early summer of 1836 we find Mrs. Jameson interceding for him with his wealthy cousin who had heard some gossip concerning Noel, Ottilie and Anna. To Ottilie she reports at least a limited success in her mission:

I have had in these last two days two melancholy letters from poor Noel. In the latest, received yesterday, he begs of me to go to Lady Byron and speak to her. It appears from her letters to him that some scandal has reached her about you and Noel, and about the Zichy, and I fear about me too. . . .

June 1.   . . . I have not told you of my scene with Lady Byron. She sent her carriage for me and I went down to Fordhook, trusting in a good cause and a clear conscience. I cannot give you the details, but tho' I think she is inexorable about the money, I certainly softened her and set her right on other points. I left her less displeased with Noel. [N 43]

Anna's repeated embroilment in various touchy relationships can be seen as a lamentable weakness or as enviable strength. Sometimes, it seems rooted in nothing loftier than a desire always to be setting things right—in short, to be the dominant character. There is also a sincere desire to help all of her friends all of the time. If these involvements sometimes display the incorrigible "busyness" of the managing woman, the reasons for them are amply explained, both in her disposition and in her disappointed emotional life.

All work was not suspended during the months of strain with Ottilie and of recuperation afterwards. Her ignorance of German she termed "a daily and hourly torment" [N 29]. "I suffer at every moment . . . I am studying very hard." [N 24] By the fall of 1835 she was back in German society, reporting a meeting with von Humboldt, the traveller who "half turned my head" [M 30] and with John Kemble, Fanny's brother, a student of Old English who "ought to be bound up with an old Saxon manuscript, I am afraid he is good for nothing else." [N 29] She spoke of going to Dresden "to gain some information on subjects connected with my new book" and to Mrs. Procter of bringing home "a half-finished book, which I think will please you more than my last." [M 104] Finally, shortly before returning to England in the spring of 1836, she writes with a hearty reversal of her former extreme vulnerability to the charms of Weimar's ducal court: "You must know I am in great favour with both the Grand Duke and the Grand Duchess; but on the plea of my health, I accept about one invitation out of three, for I have something better to do than to stand dangling in a court circle talking nothings." [M 104]

Unless part or all of the material she mentions was incorporated into the "Winter Studies" section of her Canadian work, this "half-finished book" was not completed or published. On her return to London, Anna Jameson was immediately involved in plans for her long-deferred, but now necessary, departure for Upper Canada.

II

The Voyage to Canada

"PRAY MY DEAR FATHER, can you form the most distant guess at the reasons of Jameson's conduct? It is near three months since the date of his last letter!" [E 122] So wrote Anna Jameson from Vienna in the spring of 1835. The tone of exasperated mystification characterizes all the correspondence with and about Robert Jameson in these years. His recorded letters are invariably affectionate, however, and prejudice their reader against his wife as the guilty party in the estrangement. This letter, one of the few which remain, was dated October 30, 1834, some eighteen months after Jameson's departure for Upper Canada:

I have not yet acknowledged the receipt of your last letter, dated 4th of July, which duly arrived. The tone is more kind and cheering than some of its predecessors. I hope you have received the money safe. I shall send the second part of the bill on London to Henry [Henry Bate, Louisa's husband], perhaps by this packet. Dearest Anna, let me look forward to our meeting with hope. Let me not lose the privilege of loving you, and the hope of being loved by you. Let me come to my solitary home with the prospect that my daily labours shall, before any very lengthened day of trial, be rewarded by your presence and your most precious endearments. I have no single hope that does not depend on this one. Do not school your heart against me, and I will compel you to love me. I have been fencing in my nice little piece of ground on the banks of the lake, where I am promising myself the happiness of building you a pretty little villa after your own taste. I have set a man to plant some trees and shrubs also, for the place was quite denuded, though by far the finest situation in the town. I have ground enough for a pretty extensive garden, nearly three acres. [M 100]

The loving and wistful tone of this letter, as well as its demonstration of Jameson's practical concern for the support of his wife, is very persuasive. Another letter which has survived, written in the spring of 1835, has the same tone:

A feast followed by a long, long Lent, speaking of your intention to proceed to Vienna for the winter and probable return to England in the spring. Where you have since been, or where you are now, I know not, but I hope in England. Your letters, even more than usually delightful, glitter throughout with such bright names and proof of your high fame among your German admirers, that I sometimes despond for your poor North American savage . . . my hopes of receiving you in a house of your own have been for the present thwarted—I have not the requisite money. But I have the ground, which I trust I shall not be driven to sacrifice, because I should never meet with so pleasant a situation; and before long I trust still to have a nice cottage, at all events, upon it. And then what portion of happiness we enjoy in it depends upon you, dearest Anna; and I think you will not wilfully shut it out of doors, merely because it may be a better fate than I deserve. I have been planting trees, and, as I told you, potatoes, on a princely scale; and often when I can steal an hour, I go and exercise myself with my spade and pruning knife, and then I feed my fancy with the idea that you will, before the leaves disappear, be walking there by my side. [M 101]

The difficulties of patching a weak marriage or even of maintaining the structure of a strong one, with the wife in Germany and the husband in Upper Canada, are obvious. Distance and delay in communication each played its contributory part in the permanent estrangement of these two incompatible people. We see this demonstrated in a letter from Anna, dated Weimar, February, 1836, its tone and its text demonstrating her confusion and concern:[1]

MY DEAR ROBERT, . . . the feelings of perplexity and uncertainty into which I have been thrown by the whole course of our correspondence almost discouraged me from writing to you, and take from me all power to express myself with that flow and openness which were otherwise natural to me. From October 1834 down to this present February 1836, I have received from you *two letters* dated 12th of October, 1834 and 14th May, 1835, and these two letters contained no syllable which could give me the slightest idea of your social position in Canada; and though you express in the last letter a general wish that I should join you, very slightly and vaguely expressed (a *hope* rather than an intention or an expectation), there was not a word which I could interpret into any decision on the subject, no instructions as to my voyage, and no answer to the questions and inquiries with which my letters were filled. Between October 1834 and October 1835 I wrote you *eleven* letters. In August 1835 I received from you a bill of £ 100, and in January 1836 I received from Henry the intelligence that you had sent me a bill of £ 100, but *no letter for me*. I wrote immediately to beg for some information concerning you, and Henry by return of post sent me your letter to him. It is a letter of about two pages, in a jesting style, complaining that you never hear a word from me, but not saying that you have written, or giving the dates of any letters you have forwarded to me; not saying anything of your position in Canada, although the state of affairs there, as it is reported in all the papers, English and German, made me expect either the news of your return, or some intelligence from you that should tranquillize me about your situation and movements. [M 107]

Anna is franker and seems more sincere in this letter than in any other record. She offers definitely to come to Canada and to plan to stay there *if* Robert Jameson will be equally decided in the statement of his plans for her coming:

You say in the same letter that it is your intention to marry again immediately. My dear Robert, jesting apart, I wish it only depended upon me to give you that power. You might perhaps be happy with another woman—a union such as ours is, and has ever been, a real mockery of the laws of God and man. You have the power to dispose of our fate as far as it depends on each other. I placed that power in your hands in my letter written from England, and had you used that power in a decided manly spirit, whether to unite or to part us, I had respected you the more and would have arranged my life accordingly. But what an existence is this to which you have reduced us both! If you can make up your mind to live without me— if your vague letters signify a purpose of this kind—for God's sake speak the truth to me; but if, on the other hand, it is your purpose to remain in Canada, to settle there under any political change, and your real wish is to have me with you and make another trial for happiness, tell me so *distinctly* and *decidedly*—tell me at what time to leave England—tell me what things I ought to take with me, what furniture, books, etc., will be necessary or agreeable, what kind of life I shall live, that I may come prepared to render my own existence and yours as pleasant as possible. To the letter from England, written before my departure for Germany, containing my own wishes, and certain conditions, on the fulfillment of which I could be really *happy* to join you, I received no answer, though I have every reason to believe that you received that letter.

I came to Weimar completely broken down. I have since been staying with the Goethe family, who have nursed me like a pet sister, and the first physician here has done much for me. Since the beginning of January I have been recovering, and am in hopes that I shall be able to return to England in April or even sooner. There I shall await your next letter, and according to its contents I shall regulate my future plans. Farewell! I expect your answer in July next. [M 108]

There are passages in the foregoing letter which defy interpretation: the "power to dispose of our fate" placed in Jameson's hands by his wife and his "intention to marry again immediately." The only specific power which could have led to divorce and remarriage was proof of adultery. That Anna Jameson provided him with such proof and still contemplated life in Canada with the apparent sincerity of this letter, seems quite unlikely; that he had provided Anna with such proof would have made her trip to Canada unnecessary. It is more probable that she speaks here in a general way and that the power placed in his hands was the power of choice.

She seems here to wish, above all else, that Jameson would assert himself as a husband, that she would be the dominated and not the dominating party. This desire, always unfulfilled, may well have been the basis for the couple's incompatibility. In the early days of their courtship and marriage, Jameson seems to have looked upon his wife as a superior being; certainly she was capable of arranging things for herself and for others, as she had always done for her family and, of later years, for her friends. But her idea of a marriage required assertion by the male and Jameson was unwilling or unable to assert himself over her. Paradoxically, her mention of a certain letter, containing "my own wishes, and certain conditions," suggests that, while Robert Jameson was to seem to make the rules, Anna was, in fact, set in her ideas and determined to have marriage conform to her desires.

However we may assess Jameson's responsibility for the separation, it must be admitted in his favour that he did not tyrannize over his wife as he might legally have done. He could have claimed her earnings; instead he contributed, if meagrely, to her support.[2] His attitude toward Anna, as far as it is recorded in any way, was unfailingly courteous and correct; his wrongs toward her may have been hard to bear, but they were sins of omission rather than the more spectacular sins of commission for which it would be easy to damn him.

Anna Jameson had known from the time of her husband's departure for Canada of the difficult choice she had to make. In November, 1835, she writes of her decision to Ottilie:

Now with regard to Munich and myself. I will tell you in few words that my sentiments and feelings are not changed,—they *could* not unless my nature and my situation could alter. But my fluctuating resolutions are fixed immutably. I go to Canada. I see it must be so. I cannot brave the alternative. If, when we meet, you ask any questions about myself, I will answer them honestly. I have suffered much, but I have no reason to blush before any human being. I am not troubled with the *besoin de faire les confidences*; and with me, I know not why, sympathy adds to my suffering and does not console it. I have had a hard struggle of about 18 months duration, but it is passed; and having made my choice, shall I weakly sit down and wring my hands over the inevitable, the irremediable? Shall I give, unnecessarily, to any human being the right to look upon me with pity?—or to seek in my eyes or my countenance for feelings I do not choose to betray? I could not endure it. . . . [N 31]

In spite of these proud words, her friends and family were aware, and were made aware by her, of her unhappiness. To some extent she dramatized herself and her woes. To a considerable extent she was guilty of playing the Ennuyée all her life. Ironically, the role which had been chosen by her, partly in earnest, but chiefly as an interesting affectation on which she was willing to capitalize, now became her true role and one which she could not discard at will.

In the spring of 1836, Anna Jameson's letters to Ottilie were a compound of concern for Ottilie and for Ottilie's sister, Ulrica, who was living with Anna in London, of reports of an active social life, seeming to centre around Mrs. Austin and her numerous literary friends, and of a constant suspense about Canada.

No one need doubt that Mrs. Jameson was now accepted and sought after by the literary society of London:[3] "Last night there was a party at Mrs. Austin's. We met Rogers, Hallam, Sydney Smith, the sisters v. Raumer, Babbage, the Lockharts, Mrs. Marcet and other *stars* of the first magnitude, but they put out each other's light, and I came away tired." [N 42] On June 18, she writes about a meeting with Edward Trelawney, who had recently been in Canada:

Trelawney was with me on Sunday and staid from eight till past 12. He did not amuse me (as they say he does others) with a recital of his outrages and murders,—perhaps feeling that I am not an admirer of the *Brigand* style. . . . I think if he loves anyone it is Fanny Kemble, who appears to be his *ideal* of womankind. He gave me a horrid description of Canada,—I mean the inhabited part of it, and of Toronto especially. He was at Niagara Falls with my husband. Is it not most strange that I never heard from this man? It is now 13 months since the date of his last letter. I am meditating a step, which will require great courage to execute, but which will make me at ease and in some respect independent for the rest of my life. For your sake I will do it, if his next letter is not what I wish. . . . [N 46]

A week later, a Mr. Atkinson from Canada delivered to her Robert Jameson's reply to her letter. He urged, perhaps commanded her to join him; her letter to Ottilie voices both resolution and resignation: "It is right that I should go, not only right, but inevitable." The final decision was shattering to her nerves, however; eight days were spent prostrated on the sofa, with the painful necessity of informing her parents postponed, and with her friends assuring her of the efficacy of the sea voyage to restore health and nerves. Some portion of the debilitation she felt was perhaps a reaction after the departure of the foolish and meteoric Ulrica von Pogwisch who was much closer to involving herself and her hostess in scandal than Anna's conventional nature could easily bear. And of course the voyage to Canada meant a lengthy separation from Ottilie and from the excitement and affection which she aroused. Ottilie unfairly, and rather unkindly, urged Anna to pay her a farewell visit to Weimar, but Anna could afford neither the time nor the money for the three days she would have there: "I have not money enough, tho' indeed by giving up some part of my wardrobe and other things I might have scraped it together; but to spend from my father and mother 15 days at this time seemed too unkind." [N 50]

Anna was always short of money. She was, at this time, living in London with her brother-in-law, Henry Bate, at a cost of £150 a year; she was in debt to her booksellers who published her work and who must have given her certain advance payments. From experience she knew that money from Canada arrived both little and late: "I had to borrow from my brother and when Mr. J. sent me money at last, it was not enough to pay my debts; and that which he sent to me for express purposes, which he specified, I could not with good conscience apply to my own gratification." [N 55]

She had some thought of reconciliation with Jameson and a satisfactory life together, but she considered the Canadian venture with more dismay than hope. In a desperate searching for a remedy for her own loneliness, as well as in true concern for Ottilie's future, she threw out a truly hare-brained suggestion: "If I find that there is a possibility of living with content in that place, and if the world treats you hardly, if you find difficulties about your child, will you come to me there, if I can arrange the means and a home for you with me or near me?" [N 45] The chapter that might have been written had Ottilie von Goethe erupted into the conservative, provincial Upper Canadian society of the 1830s is a delirious speculation!

As she tried to prepare herself to sail, Anna was bedevilled by money worries and by Ulrica von Pogwisch's behaviour. Once again a good-natured involvement for the sake of a friend reacted on herself, causing her embarrassment and the considerable annoyance of having been deceived in her trust:

Your sister is returned safe and looking very well. . . . I see her playing over again here with Romilly the same desperate game I saw you play in Frankfort to end in the same perdition perhaps, for what woman can stop herself where she likes? . . . I am in despair, and my life is so distracted by suspense about Italy, suspense about Canada, and misery and suspense about you and business and people and cares overwhelming me that this additional daily anxiety and gene is too much to bear. [N 47]

On August 25, she reports another letter from Robert Jameson and her intention of sailing on the *Quebec*, September 20. Robert Jameson had been aroused to hope and to urgency in his wish for her company. From Toronto he had written on July 30:

Write to me immediately, and say what measure of good is reserved for me. If you come out alone, I will either meet you at New York or make such arrangements that you shall not feel yourself in the least a stranger on your landing in the Western world. Alma [John Lees Alma, a family friend] vows it is his right to go to New York and escort his patroness to Upper Canada. But it is very possible that it may neither be in the power of one or the other. It is, however, consolatory that the great steamboat communication up the Hudson and by Lake Ontario makes a journey from New York a very different thing from an inland journey of like extent. [M 110]

The decision to go to Canada, even if happiness had been assured her at the end of the journey, would not have been an easy one for Anna Jameson. To her husband she felt she owed a duty; to Ottilie von Goethe and to her parents, both love and duty. Besides the conflict between inclination and responsibility, she was beset by financial difficulties and by the necessity of engraving an entire new set of etchings for the *Characteristics*: "So I am up at 7 o'clock in the morning and work all day till my eyes are so weary and my fingers too, that I am obliged to stop and go to something else; and it is so tedious." [N 51] In answer to reproaches from Ottilie charging her, it would seem, with neglect and lack of confidence, she makes several rather pathetic efforts to explain her position: "I consider, dear Ottilie, that I am placed this moment between two *duties*. If I could make you happier and soothe your wounded and weary spirit I should think it as much my *duty* to go to you as to go to Canada, and God knows *far* more my inclination. . . ." [N 55]

The physical discomfort involved in an 1836 journey to Canada is something of which we need only to be reminded to reflect, chastened, that our forbears were of sterner stuff than we. Mrs. Jameson drew the line at sharing her cabin: "I believe I had rather make the voyage in a long boat." [N 56] The *Ontario*, on which she finally sailed, had as comfortable accommodation as she was likely to find on any ocean passenger vessel, with the usual immigrant families in the steerage:

There is a fine salon about as long as your corridor, and wider. On each side are 8 little cabins each containing 2 berths or beds and sufficient space for a chair, or portmanteau, and other things. I have, by good fortune, one cabin to myself. . . . There are 78 poor emigrants on board who pay only £4 (24 dollars) for their passage, find their own provisions, and are all put together in one large cabin in the steerage,—but not so ill off. Many of these are Irish families, I hear, and I think I shall make more friends among *them* than among my own company, among whom are several ladies, American and English. I pay for my passage to New York 35 guineas; but then everything is included,—wine, provisions, attendance. [N 56]

During a week's delay at Portsmouth, Anna was sorely tempted to return to her parents, but she writes to them with determination, good humour and gallantry:

To be thirty days (at best) with this society appears to me sometimes worse than seasickness, storms or anything in the world and to think that in 24 hours I could escape all this! and be with you safe and well! the temptation almost makes my head turn; yet why give myself airs with the people on whom I am to descend for any particle of comfort and sympathy I am to expect for the next six weeks? All treat me with civility and respect and with this I must be content: . . . [E 132]

Sometimes, she was cheered almost to the point of laughter by the ludicrous elements of her situation, as when Mrs. Solomon Moses and Miss Matilda Levy amused the company by playing on her guitar. This, no doubt, is the same guitar which Mrs. Jameson received from Thomas, the bookseller, as payment for *The Diary of an Ennuyée*— an awkward piece of luggage for a lady traveller to take to Toronto, but one which signals a triumphant insistence on the amenities of existence, no matter what the inconvenience.

Anna departed on October 8, 1836, after the sad excitement of farewell gift-receiving and leave-taking from her friends and family. She was pleased to record gifts from Lady Byron and Lady Hatherton, but her most prized and probably most useful mementos were from her German friends who, with true practicality, presented her with woollen quilts and a foot-muff. She also took a good supply of German books, because, gauging her own inclinations and her destination, she expected to have time for study and writing. Already, as she wrote to Ottilie, she had gloomy anticipations of the society and the climate which awaited her:[4]

I certainly did not send you the book about Canada to show you in dark colours the hardships of a settler's life—quite the contrary. The book interested me, and pleased me very much, and it is thought to give so favourable a view of things, that they say it has made many persons emigrate. I wish much that I were going to live such a life, instead of residing in a small, vulgar, factious city, where I shall be afraid to speak, almost to think, lest I should inadvertently hurt Mr. Jameson's interests, instead of assisting them. But at all events while I speak and do what is right and useful and proper, as the wife of his Majesty's Attorney General, I shall be working for you. . . . I shall probably write a great deal, for the Politics are so utterly repugnant to my taste (and my conscience also) that I believe the utmost I can do will be to remain passive. The winters are frightfully severe. The account in the book I sent you is enough to give one cold, only to read it.—It was the part I liked least, and I must say I shiver at the idea of my dressing-gown freezing to my skin and cracking when I take it off. [N 60]

At this stage in her life, Anna Jameson's letters to Ottilie von Goethe are more lively than those to her family. The following letter is a good sample of her best writing style and a fine, if chilling description of what must have been a run-of-the-mill Atlantic crossing.

I spent a melancholy week at Portsmouth, quite alone. The Ontario was delayed in the Downs by contrary winds. Oct. 7 The Ontario arrived and I went on board with the other passengers. I fainted away almost immediately on going down to my room and from this time remained invisible to all but suffering. I was in utter misery. The 8th, as I heard, we sailed, but met a dreadful gale, and after going down the channel we were driven up again and with some difficulty anchored again at Portsmouth on the 11th. In these storms several vessels were lost, and on the 11th the Clarendon, a fine ship, was wrecked about two leagues from us, and all perished except 2 sailors. This seemed an ominous beginning for us. The wind continued contrary till the 15th and we then sailed thro' the Needles. . . . 17th A dreadful storm, but we were now in the wide Atlantic, with *sea room*, as the sailors call it, and in a good ship. With a 2 or 3 hundred leagues of open sea all around, a storm or two is not minded; it is the proximity of land which makes it fearful. 18th rather calmer, 19th another rough gale. All was confusion. I can give you no idea of the Hurly-burly of the elements, the shrieking of the winds thro the rigging, the roaring of the waves which broke over the ship and poured into the cabin. I was nearly thrown out of my berth, and everything movable was flung from side to side with a crash. By this time I was nearly exhausted, half delirious for want of sleep, constantly sick and fainting and not a soul to help me or speak to me. . . . The table was well served. We had a cow on board, 12 sheep and 5 pigs, a quantity of ducks, geese and fowls, excellent wines, champagne twice a week, fresh bread and cakes every day, in short there was everything it was possible to call for as in a Hotel: but what availed it all when one could not eat! Oct. 23 we were in Latitude 47° 23′ and longitude 28° 5′. The weather was calmer. I tried to eat for the first time and for two or three days was laid on the deck every day and was able to converse a little with Mr. Forbes [an American clergyman and ship-board friend]. 26th, Latitude 45°–46′, Longitude 34° 40′, another storm, dreadfully ill again this day and the next. 28th I was seized with fainting fits and convulsions and began to think I was going to die. Life seemed also quite indifferent. . . . November 1, ill in bed, all day. 2d. This morning at nine o'clock, while lying in my bed, I heard a sound on deck which froze me with horror. I knew all the usual noises of a sea life, but this was different. There was a cry, then a trampling of many feet, a hurry, a confusion of voices. I heard the gentlemen rush from the breakfast table and Mrs. Solomon Moses began to faint and squalled out 'Pirates! Pirates'. At last I heard the words 'a man overboard!', the Captain's voice commanding silence. In a moment a boat was lowered with an officer and 4 men, the vessel stopped but everyone knew it was in vain, who had seen the accident. The poor wretch (one of the steerage passengers) was climbing up the rigging for a wager of 5 shillings, fell from the *fore top gallant*, pitched with his head on the fore yard (which was covered with his blood) and thence into the sea. He must have been dead before he reached it. Of course all efforts to save him were unavailing, he had sunk for ever! The boat returned, after an awful suspense and everyone looked pale in each other's faces. The man had a wife and children in England, but no one knew anything of them or him. 5 Ill all day, wind exactly contrary. We were now about 200 miles from New York. 24 hours of fair wind would have carried us into the harbour and we were motionless. 5 a dead calm.— we lay still and motionless on the beautiful quiet sea. I went on deck and called to Mr. Forbes and in the evening watched the beautiful phosphoric light breaking in flashes from every wave, till the sea looked like clusters of glow-worms floating by the vessel. 8. dead calm, no progress. Dined at table for first time. 9. The wind became fair and fresh. 10th. Early this morning land was in sight. All were joyful, and every eye looked brighter, except mine. I felt lonely and sad. [N 62–5]

At New York, she had no one to meet her, contrary to her husband's hopes, but she was not long without acquaintances. Once again, no doubt, the useful and ubiquitous letters of introduction did their work. The *Ontario* docked on the 10th or the 11th of November and by the 24th of the month Anna wrote to Ottilie of a full social schedule, including meetings with Washington Irving and John Jacob Astor:[5]

Au reste I can only speak of the general aspect of the society. The men are chiefly mercantile, and those with whom I have formed an acquaintance are much like other gentlemen at leisure. But the pressure and activity of business here can hardly be conceived. Even London does not give an idea of it; for here all are men of business, and all seem to have more to do than they can do. In going into a crowded room I am struck by the *posé* quiet looks of the married women and the particular beauty, delicacy, and elegant toilettes of the young women, who have a frank open expression, and look as if they had nothing in the world to do but enjoy themselves. They dress in the first style and have everything direct from Paris 4 times a month. It has been in the fashion to study German. . . . Yesterday dining with the widow of the celebrated Governor Clinton I suddenly opened a little case containing the silver jubilee medal of your father-in-law. . . . I have just had a long conversation with Washington Irving. His new book *Astoria* has excited great attention, and he has been talking to me a great deal about it. I have seen John Jacob Astor, who is a German from Heidelberg. He came here a poor adventurer without a dollar, he has now 15 millions and is a very extra-ordinary character. [N 67]

Anna Jameson's writing had been known and popular in America for some years. In 1833, Fanny Kemble had written to her from Philadelphia, sending her a message from a bookseller who wished Mrs. Jameson to know that her books were as highly regarded in America as in England. "He is so enthusiastic about you that I think he would willingly go over to England for the sole purpose of making your acquaintance." [K 579] Fanny identifies this gentleman as Mr. Carey, who did publish some American editions of Mrs. Jameson's work, and deplores, as she does intermittently throughout her *Records of Later Life*, the American copyright law which "rendered Mr. Carey's admiration of my friend and her works so barren of any useful result to her." [K 579][6] A new edition of a work, published *in* America was, however, a profitable venture for a writer. Anna Jameson had hoped to republish *Characteristics* there and immediately on landing she must have begun to negotiate with possible publishers. "I have made an agreement about a new edition of the *Characteristics* which is likely to produce 500 dollars; the two last copies which remained were sold by a bookseller here for 12 dollars each—3 times the original price." [E 134] A later reference from Toronto identifies the publisher with whom she came to terms as Frederick Saunders who engaged Mrs. Jameson to make ten new etchings for a planned one-volume edition; these were her first artistic undertakings in the new world.

One benefit which she could not possibly have foreseen did perhaps accrue to Anna Jameson from this trip. Her removal from the tightly-packed literary world of London could not have been more timely. The most cursory reading of her letters to Ottilie von Goethe reveals many interwoven threads of relationship—a tightrope-walk to be negotiated to avoid the touch of gossip. It is a marvel that Anna could have so involved herself with Ottilie's and Ulrica's affairs and still have remained, as one writer put it, "unimpeached and unimpeachable."[7] We realize, from her letters to Ottilie begging discretion and relating the successful turning aside of suspicion, that for a woman to whom reputation meant a great deal—and to Anna Jameson it did—the danger of defamation was real and it was always present.

Among her contemporaries, Letitia Landon had been cruelly attacked, unfortunately at the same time that her reputation as a writer was waning; Lady Caroline Norton was the *cause célèbre* of the decade and continued her marital struggle with the maximum of publicity for many years. The former was helpless under attack; the latter, because of birth, beauty, social position, and the involvement of politics, notably with Lord Melbourne's vindication by the courts, rose above or outfaced the imputations against her. There is no question as to the category in which Mrs. Jameson would have fallen had she been luckless enough to be seriously impugned. She was without any background of birth or wealth which might have allowed her to challenge her enemies.

She was disappointed in her plan to visit Fanny Kemble, now Mrs. Pierce Butler of Philadelphia, on her way to Toronto. She and her friend had passed on the Atlantic, Fanny having sailed for England on November 1st. Mrs. Jameson was obliged, therefore, to stay in New York to await her husband's instructions, which finally came on November 29, after she had been about four weeks in New York:

My Dearest Father, Mamma and Sisters All!
You will be surprised to find I am still here and yet more surprised to hear that I have no tidings of Jameson—not one word. I am—just as I was writing these lines in came a letter from Jameson, which had been sent to the British Consul; it is like all his letters, very well written, very plausible, very kind, agreeing to everything. I shall set off immediately and have a world of business and packing up to be done. . . . [E 134]

She was about to venture into a frontier society, where her husband and not herself was the principal member of their partnership, where politics and not literature or art were the common preoccupation and where, far from the respectful treatment to which she was accustomed, the women, as she later put it, "express, vulgarly enough, an extreme fear of the 'authoress' and I am anything but popular." [E 150] The confusion of her relation with her husband compounded these hazards. Only a strong combination of desperation to have her status clarified and an awareness of duty combined to push the trip to its completion.

12

Canada and the United States, 1836-1838

A little ill-built town on low land, at the bottom of a frozen bay, with one very ugly church, without tower or steeple; some government offices, built of staring red brick, in the most tasteless, vulgar style imaginable; three feet of snow all around; and the gray, sullen, wintry lake, and the dark gleam of the pine forest bounding the prospect; such seems Toronto to me now. I did not expect much; but for this I was not prepared. [WSSR I, 10]

This was Anna Jameson's bluntly honest impression of her new home, written on December 20, 1836, a few days after her arrival. It was unfortunate that for a venture where the cards were already stacked against success, weather had also to play its considerable part. Had she arrived in Upper Canada in the spring or the summer, the story of her reception and her reaction to it might well have been very different. As it was, she arrived at a time when Canada's appearance and climate were bound to make the worst possible impression.

Her report to her family of a winter journey from New York to Toronto is as graphically written and as worthy of quotation as was her earlier account of the Atlantic crossing.

I left New York on the 6th, very sad and with many misgivings, for Jameson remained still inexplicable and I had no letter in answer to mine written on my first arrival; but I also had no money left and I thought the letter had miscarried, so off I set, accompanied to the last moment by every kind attention and every mark of interest. I had a convoy of 6 friends to the Steamboat, lingering till the paddles began to splash and loading me with letters, advice, comforts and kind words; the enormous boat contained more than 400 passengers and the scene was very curious. Unfortunately there was no *day boat*. We set off after a glowing sunset and I sat or walked on deck as long as I could, to escape the stifling air of the ladies' cabin where 89 women were stuffed pell mell—some in berths, some on the ground, on chairs, and with children sprawling about. I threw myself on to my berth in despair and slept while we were passing, in the dark, through some of the grandest scenery in the world, the shores of the Hudson and the Catskill mountains. I had taken my passage to Albany, but the Captain had stuck up a notice that he would only go as far as the ice permitted. When we got a little beyond Catskill and about 6 miles below Hudson, we encountered ice in great quantities; it was now daylight, a bright but intensely cold morning. At length the expanse presented only an icy surface but the gigantic boat, armed for the purpose with an iron prow, kept on crashing her way through the ice which closed behind so as to scarcely leave a track a few yards from the stern; it was a strange and beautiful sight. We reached Hudson at 9 and there were obliged to stop as it was freezing powerfully and the captain feared being frozen up at Albany. We and our luggage were tossed out without ceremony and I joined a party in taking a carriage on to Albany with a waggon for my baggage; we jolted the 30 miles in about 8 hours, through a fine country, but wintry looking and thinly inhabited. [E 136]

The journey from New York to Toronto took about eight days. From Albany to Niagara there was variety in the conveyances, although all of them were uncomfortable. Anna's physical discomforts were mitigated, however, by the presence of an experienced young Canadian traveller who became her escort:[1]

At Albany I met a person known to Mr. Jameson, a Mr. Percival Ridout, some distant relation of the Mr. Ridout who married Mathilda Bramley [whether this meeting was by Jameson's arrangement or not we are not told]. This most goodnatured and goodlooking young man took me and my baggage under his protection and proved a most efficient Cavalier; he had not much cultivation or manners, but he had great activity and cheerfulness and was quite unassuming—though as for conversation there was none. From Albany to Utica we went by the rail road 90 miles in 6 hours, with 8 carriages each containing 24 persons. From Utica we came on to Rochester, in 36 hours. It was horrid travelling; the Canal was frozen, the stage coaches are the most extraordinary clumsy, ill looking, mean looking things you can imagine, holding 9 persons, 3 in a row—but the coaches suit the roads, on which certainly the 'Tally Ho' or the 'Brighton age' would have capsized in five minutes. Such a road I did never yet behold, or rather I was destined to see them before they were made. I recollect we were once 6 hours going 9 miles and with 4 horses, often for hours through half burnt forests, the blackened stumps of enormous trees just seen above the snow; a dismal prospect! . . . We did not sleep at Rochester, but hired a carriage and came on at once to Lewiston, 40 miles in 28 hours, crossed the Niagara in a Ferry in the dark and slept at Queenston, for I could go no further; I was quite ill and done up. The next morning (Monday 13) we got two spring carts of the country for selves and baggage and just reached the town of Niagara in time to go by the steam vessel—our good luck was the greater as it was the last trip of the season, the bays and harbours beginning to freeze. . . . From Niagara to Toronto by land is 100 miles and two days journey over horrid roads, by the lake 36 miles; the water was as rough as I have often seen it at sea. After an hour of very melancholy thoughts and feelings, I threw myself down quite exhausted and slept till I was told we were at Toronto. [E 139]

After such a trip, made in the dreariest time of year, Anna's unfavourable first impressions of Toronto are not surprising. Furthermore, she found no one at the dock to meet her, though Robert Jameson must have expected her arrival at any time. Young Mr. Ridout took her to her temporary home, a set of rooms on Brock Street, and there, "it was worse still; all looked cold, comfortless, the fires out, or nearly so, a bedroom had been half prepared for me, on the unmade bed things were piled. The servants looked half surprised, half alarmed and I felt as miserable as possible. I put, however, a good face on the matter and when J. returned he seemed at least glad to see me." [E 139]

Predictably, after her European successes, she found Society negligible; what there was of it was intolerably stiff and conservative for her tastes:

On my arrival the Governor [Sir Francis Bond Head] sent his secretary with a polite message of congratulation, expressing his regret that Etiquette did not allow him to visit *in person* the ladies of the place, but he hoped I would find some grievances to complain of or petition to present, and so be induced to visit *him*. I did not like this at all, for, as far as I can judge hitherto, the only man worth knowing in the place is himself. [E 40]

A little later in the winter she conceded the presence of one lively companion, Captain Fitzgibbon:[2]

As yet I have not found here a single person who interests me. There is a Captain Fitzgibbon, an Irishman, who began life as a common soldier and became from his own bravery and merit the Captain of his Regiment. He is now a proprietor of land and has a high civil office. He is quite an original, has a strong mind and a most excellent heart, with that overflow of animal spirits, that *superflu de vie*, which seems peculiar to my dear Countrymen. We have not yet absolutely sworn an eternal friendship, but I like him very much. The women I have seen are all *below par*. But I am a spoiled child, I must needs confess it. [N 74]

Her life with her husband is summed up on a note of melancholy resignation in a rare few lines of German to Ottilie: "All is just as I thought it would be, ich bin unglücklich, aber ich bete und arbeite—was kann man mehr? Ich lese alle Tage Deutsch und in meinem nächsten Briefe ich will dir alles sagen was ich studiert habe." [N 71] Undoubtedly, one major reason for Robert Jameson's desire to have his wife with him at this time was the imminence of his appointment as Vice-Chancellor of Upper Canada. Socially and officially, his position was such that the presence of a wife and the appearance of married stability would be powerful allies for him.

The history of the courts of Upper Canada is the story of a slow, gradual breakaway from complete dependence on the courts of England to a position of self-government and self-determination in the legal sphere. One such step along the road was taken in 1837, when a Court of Chancery was authorized in the province. The titular head of the court was the Lieutenant-Governor, but the local representative and chief legal officer of the Crown in the colony was to be appointed as Vice-Chancellor.[3] It was this appointment which Jameson as Attorney General, the present senior legal appointee of the Crown, anticipated and had every reason to expect. In February, Anna informs her family of the passing of the Bill and of the anticipated improvement in Mr. Jameson's income. She also commends her husband's fitness for the Chancellor's position, though his character assets seem negative, at best: "The Chancery Bill has passed and I am in hopes the appointment of Chancellor will follow quickly; the Salary of the Attorney General is 1200 a year including fees and contingencies—and the Salary of the Chancellor will be 1200 a year—*not* including fees, and so the income doubles or nearly so. Jameson will make an excellent Chancellor, he is just cut out for the office, so cautious, so inoffensive and so clever in Chancery practise." [E 144]

On March 15, she writes of the appointment to her family. There is satisfaction in her tone, but a certain shade of irony as she cites in his favour "his excessive reserve" which, in Canada, is counted "the greatest of possible virtues":

You will all be glad to hear that Jameson is appointed Chancellor *at last*. He is now at the top of the tree, and has no more to expect or to aspire to. . . . No one loves him, it is true; but everyone approves him, and his promotion has not caused a murmur. The Solicitor-General Hagerman is now Attorney-General, and Draper (the member for Toronto, and a friend of Trelawney's) is now Solicitor-General. The organization of the new Court of Equity, and the moving into his new residence, will occupy Mr. Jameson and me for a month or two. [M 125]

In May, a less kindly variation of the same opinions goes to Robert Noel, along with a damning analysis of her situation, both in her relation to Robert Jameson and to Toronto Society:

Your wish that I might find here a sphere of happiness and usefulness is not realized. I am in a small community of fourth-rate, half-educated, or uneducated people, where local politics of the meanest kind engross the men, and petty gossip and household cares the women. As I think differently from Mr. Jameson on every subject which can occupy a thinking mind, I keep clear of any expression (at least unnecessary expression) of my opinions. He is now Chancellor of the Province, and, having achieved the first judicial office, can go no higher; he has much power, and also luckily much discretion, and a very determined intention to keep well with all men, and lead a peaceful life. Is not this wisdom? It is not exactly my wisdom, but I shall not contend with what cannot be altered . . . one of the objects of my coming will be, I think, accomplished, and my future life more easy, and my conscience clear. [M 127]

Anna Jameson's summary of her husband's qualifications and probable conduct of the court was an astute one. Mr. Justice Read in his *Lives of the Judges* has recorded Jameson's dependence on precedents and his adherence to the examples set by Lord Eldon, his former patron and employer;[4] Sir George Arthur has termed him "an amiable, kind and inoffensive person."[5] Unfortunately for both his legal career and his personal life, the negative qualities of his nature outweighed any positive drive or ability for leadership which might have made him capable of filling his position with distinction or of holding his wife with decision.

The house which Robert Jameson was building when his wife arrived in Toronto was on the land of which he had written to her in 1834, with "ground enough for a pretty extensive garden, nearly three acres." It was pleasantly simple in design, without the elegance of the best examples of the earlier Loyalist-Regency style, but also without the pretentiousness which produced the later Victorian Gothic. Its best feature was its southern frontage where four large windows overlooked a pleasant lawn and Lake Ontario.[6]

One of Jameson's most tormenting characteristics, in his wife's opinion, was his indifference to friends and society. Soon after her arrival in Toronto she writes to her family of the pleasantness of the house which was annulled by Jameson's unsociability: "The new house which he is building, from the plans I have seen, must be a nice comfortable little place. I remarked that there was no arrangement made for a friend—no place to put Alma and Emily if they came over, or any friend who might stray this way, but I thought the omission characteristic." [E 139]

In a March letter to sister Charlotte, Anna speaks warmly of the possibilities of the house and grounds in spite of her personal unhappiness:

The house is very pretty and compact, and the garden will be beautiful, but I take no pleasure in anything. The place itself, the society, are so detestable to me, my own domestic position so painful and so without remedy or hope, that to remain here would be death to me. My plan is to help Jameson in arranging his house, and, when the spring is sufficiently advanced, to make a tour through the western districts up to Lake Huron. Towards the end of the year I trust by God's mercy to be in England. [M 125]

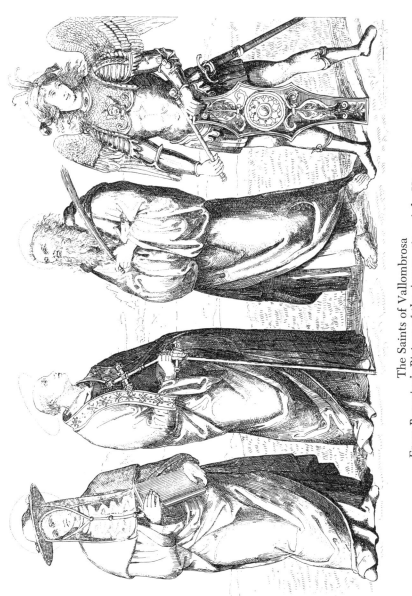

The Saints of Vallombrosa

From Perugino's Picture of the Assumption of the Virgin

Mrs. Jameson
From the lithograph by R. J. Lane
after the painting by H. P. Briggs, RA

Anna Brownell Murphy,
age sixteen
From a miniature by her father

Robert Sympson Jameson
by J. W. L. Forster
Courtesy Law Society of Upper Canada

Sault Ste. Marie to Manitoulin, July 1837
Pen and ink drawing by Anna Jameson. Royal Ontario Museum, University of Toronto

Winter journey to Niagara, by Lake Ontario, January 1837. *Pen and ink drawing by Anna Jameson. Royal Ontario Museum, University of Toronto*

By the end of April, she is writing decisively of her return, yet still with a tone of apology, as she describes her unhappiness to her father:

I hope to be with you about the end of the summer. I will not make you melancholy by telling you of what I have suffered in this long and most miserable winter. Mr. Jameson is just the same and I am just the same and therefore we are just as much and as hopelessly separated as ever; he has done nothing to make the time tolerable to me, but this not from absolute unkindness, but more absence of feeling; he has no associates here and does not require them. Another winter would, I think kill me—I do not say I should *die* literally, but my mind and all that is good in me would die; as it is, the hope of being emancipated sustains me and I am so far from giving way that I try, as far as it is possible, to amuse and occupy myself. [E 149]

Anna, the author, had not been quiescent long, even in these adverse conditions. On New Year's Day, 1837, she informs her parents of the writing and etching project undertaken for the American publisher, Mr. Saunders:

. . . he engaged me to make ten etchings for it that might be something peculiar. I brought the plates here to Toronto and set to work as soon as I was well enough and in 20 days finished eleven etchings—but behold there was no *press* to prove the plates and when I had finished all, as well as I could, with much trouble and anxiety, Saunders being in the greatest haste, I packed all up to go off to New York and then could find no conveyance which would be responsible for the safe carriage of the packet and no respectable person (who would take charge of them) was going—so the plates lie by me, the publication of the book is stopped. Saunders is in despair and the loss to him and to me will probably be considerable and all because through this half-settled, half-civilized country (I mean the neighbouring states), the roads, conveyances etc. are in a more barbarous condition than you can imagine. No sum that I could pay could ensure the safety of my packet, for, as they told me, nothing was certain but its *loss*; it is as if one was out of the world. [E 141]

In spite of the difficulties Anna found a courier for her plates and, by February 19th, she writes of the publication to Ottilie as an accomplished fact and anticipates being able to help her from the proceeds. [N 80–1] Mr. Forbes, the American clergyman whom she had met on shipboard and to whom she refers several times in her letter about the voyage, was instrumental in negotiating with the New York engraver. Anna writes him explicit directions to allow the engraver "only one plate at a time for fear of accidents," citing her own previous misfortunes at the hands of engravers. She complains to Forbes that "my fingers are so frozen that I can scarcely write," and assures him of her lasting esteem and gratitude for his help: "To whose artist-like feeling and nature could I trust but to yours?"[7]

As early as January 18, in an unusually jocular letter to Ottilie describing the doubtful delights of being wife to an Indian chief, Anna had announced her intention of an extended tour, a plan which may have been forming itself in her mind for months before her arrival in Canada:

If you would like an Indian chief for a husband, Ottilie, you have only to come here. Bring with you a few hatchets, a couple of brass Kettles and some strings of Beads. Add a Cask of Brandy, and with such a dowry, you may choose, I can promise you, an Indian Hunter, six feet high and very prettily tattoed, one side of his face covered with red paint and the other painted with soot and oil,—will you have him? You must know how to skin a Buffalo in five minutes, and cut him up, *artistement*, and how to knock a dog on the head and put him, half dead, into a pot for a stew, and dig Jams. But all this is very easy. And if your Indian is dissatisfied, he will not kick you above six times a day and then sell you to his comrade for a gun or a Brass Kettle. And if he is satisfied with you and loves you, he will give you what is left of his dinner, and be so kind as neither to beat you or sell you. There are some exceptions to this picture; but on the whole good husbands and faithful lovers are not *more* common in savage than in civilized life, as far as I can learn. But in summer when I go up the country I shall see and find out more, and judge as well as I can for myself. [N 73]

Finally, with spring came freedom, or at least a release from the uncongenial atmosphere in Toronto. There is a marked lightening of tone in Anna's letters as she embarks on her travels, a lifting of the spirit which she is honest enough to trace to moderation of the weather as well as to an escape from her husband and her Toronto surroundings. From Toronto, she went to Niagara-on-the-Lake where John Lees Alma lived with his wife Emily.[8] Most of the month of June she spent there: on June 1 her letter to Ottilie von Goethe is dated from Niagara and on June 21, 1837, she writes to her father, still from Niagara, of her relief at being away from Toronto:

I am staying here for some days previous to commencing a *little* tour which I have planned and shall execute if I have strength. At Toronto I was both ill and unhappy—every hour added to my aversion and my misery, without society or sympathy and always watching myself lest I should offend the people. I felt like one caged and fettered and quitted the place with a light heart. The same day I left, Jameson opened his Court as Chancellor and I hear there will be immense business.

The plan of her trip was now firmly outlined and she gave its route to her family, along with the assurance that she was still writing:

I have not absolutely given up all thoughts of writing and on the contrary, have a work in great forwardness; but at present I cannot apply myself to scribbling. There is so much to see and learn that I must seize the opportunity of appropriating knowledge to be digested and applied afterwards.

Now take your *Map* and lay it before you and trace my intended journey. I am going from this to Hamilton—near the west end of Lake Ontario— thence westward to Brantford on the Grand River and thence to Blandford, where I stay a day with Mrs. Arnold—thence to London, thence to Port Talbot where I shall spend a day with Colonel Talbot of Malahide—he settled in this country 30 years ago under strange circumstances and has a beautiful property on Lake Erie; there I embark for Detroit—where I hope to meet Mr. and Mrs. MacMurray and go with them to their settlement among the Indians at the very extremity of Lake Huron. I wish to see, with my own eyes, the condition of women in savage life. Thence I come round the north west shore of Lake Huron with an Indian escort and by the Manitoulin islands, Penetanguishene and Lake Simcoe back to Toronto; thence, after rest, down the St. Lawrence to Montreal and Quebec and then by Boston to New York—and thence Home to you. [E 153]

Anna Jameson accomplished her "little" tour—and more. Her one day with Colonel Talbot became six, a record, indeed a unique visit, for a woman to pay to that crotchety and autocratic misogynist. There are no letters of hers preserved which bear directly on the journey as it progressed. But we do have a vivid account of one impression the famous Mrs. Jameson made as she stopped briefly in Detroit. An enthusiastic young lady, Miss Emily Mason, wrote to her sister Kate, a student at the Female Seminary in Troy, New York, of her meeting with the author who was one of her "greatest admirations":

. . . I hinted that connected with Mrs. Jameson's visit here there was a story which I was dying to tell you, indeed my sanity will certainly cause some serious catastrophe until I unburthen myself—Pour commencer à la commencement—Last Sunday coming out of church I observed some *redhaired* ugly, *red faced* woman staring at me all the way down the aisle and said to John Sprague who was with me—"do look at that ugly old woman—she is desperately taken with either you or I—who can it be?"—Judge of my consternation when I saw someone go up to her and was presently informed it was—*Mrs. Jameson!* one of my greatest admirations—who would ever have supposed from her writings which are everything that is elegant and lady-like that *she* was *red haired* and *fat!* But this is merely an episode has nothing to do with my story—you will find directly that I had reason to think her everything that was charming and agreeable—After church she went to Col. Schwartz! (to whom she brought letters from his Brother in Vienna) to enquire who a *certain lady* was, whom she had seen at church— with whose appearance she had become *greatly struck*—In fine she *actually* said "she was the *handsomest American Lady*" she had ever seen and (as she is famous for interlarding her conversation with french phrases) said divers fine things about "les beaux yeux qui sont *ecraser* le monde", but said that "les beaux yeux" seemed evidently accustomed to that sort of admiration for they gazed on as long as she did—Hosts of other things of like nature were said both to the Schwartz's and Brush (to whom also she had letters) who you may be sure did not suffer them to get cold before he told me—I called

to see her—and accompanied her to the Boat the morning of her departure—
gave her a letter to Mrs. Chas. Stuart who is at Mackinaw where Mrs. J.
stays some time—The first thing she said after I was introduced was to
apologize for staring at me so in church—She said many very agreeable things
and I was delighted with her—talks just as she writes—and after listening a
short time I discovered that I had made a great mistake in considering her
ugly—she has a *charming countenance.* . . .[9]

On August 17th, Anna was safely back in Toronto and reporting
"mission accomplished" to her family:

I cannot squeeze into one or even 20 sheets of paper all I was about to
tell you; therefore for the present I will only say that I am just returned
from the wildest and most extraordinary tour you can imagine, and am
moreover the first Englishwoman—the first European female who ever
accomplished this journey. I have had *such* adventures and seen *such*
strange things as never yet were rehearsed in prose or verse, and, *for the
good of the public*, thinking it a shame to keep these wonders only to make
my own hair stand on end, I am just going to make a book and print it
forthwith. . . .
The people here are in great enthusiasm about me and stare at me as if I
had done some most wonderful thing; the most astonished of all is Mr.
Jameson. [E 157]

In September, Anna Jameson left Toronto forever. In a letter dated
September 21, 1837, probably written for her to carry with her as
kind of reference and safeguard to her good name, Robert Jameson
wrote:

MY DEAR ANNA,—In leaving Canada to reside among your friends in
England or elsewhere, you carry with you my most perfect respect and
esteem. My affection you will never cease to retain. Were it otherwise I
should feel less pain at consenting to an arrangement arising from no wish
of mine, but which I am compelled to believe is best calculated for your
happiness, and which therefore I cannot but approve. [M 133]

From New York Anna wrote to Ottilie:

I left Toronto in September, after making an arrangement with Mr. Jameson,
that I may for the future live where I please, and I came here on my
return to England intending to sail the end of this month. . . . Money
matters are not settled with Mr. Jameson, nor the payment of my allowance
fixed. I am now awaiting the arrival of the papers with his signature. [N 95]

Her leave-taking was in the nature of a triumph, a farewell to Toronto
in a very different frame of mind to that of her arrival day, when she
walked up from the ferry "half-blinded by the sleet driven into my
face and the tears which filled my eyes." [WSSR I, 16]

Henry Scadding, who was later to become Canon Scadding, eminently respected in Ontario as clergyman, literary enthusiast and
bibliophile, was at that time tutor to the sons of Sir John Colborne,

Commander-in-Chief of the forces in Canada, at his summer residence in Sorel, Quebec. His unpublished diary records the arrival of Mrs. Jameson and a brief visit, obviously as an honoured guest of the Colbournes, before she finally left Canada for the United States.[10] Many years later Canon Scadding wrote a pamphlet in which he discussed Anna Jameson's marginalia in her copy of Collier's *Emendations to Shakespeare* which he had acquired. In the process, he added a lengthy reminiscence of Anna as she presented herself to her public in 1837, secure at least in her public role of acclaimed author and traveller, whatever might be the personal qualms and disappointments underneath the facade:

... a good many years ago I was so fortunate as to become personally acquainted with that writer under very pleasant circumstances. ... I was thus brought under the spell, as it were, of that influence which she everywhere so remarkably exercised, and had many opportunities of enjoying her conversation which richly teemed with anecdotes and incidents connected with numberless distinguished persons of modern and earlier times; all most aptly and tastefully reproduced. ... On several occasions [I] had pleasant little interchanges of thought with her, finding her always very frank and ready, most usefully and with great tact to indicate the crudities and inaccuracies she might detect in any speaker. She exhibited a kindly inclination to make a special favourite of one of Sir John's daughters on account of her Shakespearean name—"Cordelia".[11]

Anna had sketched her way through her trip; she entertained her hosts with her etchings and water-colours and she was diverted by Mr. Scadding's learned banter:

Mrs. Jameson had with her numerous beautiful water-colour sketches taken during her late tour, together with many etchings by her own hands; for one of which, representing a child sleeping in the open air under the shadow of a tree in a wood, I remember I furnished a scrap from Horace to be appended to it as a kind of motto, which much pleased her, viz.: "non sine disanimosus infans"; as did also a certain trifling extract from Henry Cornelius Agrippa's "Vanity of the Sciences," proving that in his time (1486–1535) the charivari customs, common among the "habitans" of Lower Canada, were well known in Germany.[12]

Finally, we get from Mr. Scadding a series of personal impressions which, for sympathetic interest and keenness of observation, have not been surpassed:

Mrs. Jameson was a perfect proficient in music, vocal, and instrumental, with a voice gentle and soft, accompanying herself in a very quiet and simple manner. The hands of Mrs. Jameson were remarkably beautiful. How their extreme whiteness and delicacy were preserved during the unavoidable inconveniences and exposures of the recent extensive canoe trip was a mystery, but I think in relation to some allusion to this escape I overheard a strong hint given to one of her young lady friends, that never under any circumstances must the hands be ungloved for one moment in the out-of-door air, or sunlight, a precept enforced by a reiterated emphatic *never*. I also gathered that a Bible and Shakespeare were almost the sole literary companions of her voyage, and that a small stiletto or poignard was secretly carried for self-defence if there should be any need. And once I recollect in allusion to her safety in the journey just accomplished she good-humouredly repeated some lines from a familiar song of Dibdin's: "They say there's a Providence sits up aloft, to keep watch for the life of poor Jack."[13]

Mr. Scadding has also the most appreciative and complimentary remarks to make about Robert Jameson of any of those who ever wrote of him, designating him as "a man highly educated and possessing great taste, and even skill, in respect of art," "a connoisseur and collector of fine editions [whose] conversation was charged with reminiscences and anecdotes of the celebrated occupants of the lake district of Westmoreland, the Coleridges, Wordsworths and Southey, with all of whom he had been intimate in his youth."[14]

If Anna Jameson departed with regret at her finally broken marriage, that feeling was overcome to a very considerable extent by other considerations; she was free of an environment that she had tested and found completely lacking in warmth and in congeniality; she had never had very high hopes that the incompatibility between herself and her husband could be mended—a great part of her purpose in coming out had always been the winning of some degree of independence; finally, her conscience, a stickler for duty and responsibility, was eased.

The contrast between the Canada she left behind, and the United States to which she returned in the early fall of 1837, was in every way a welcome one to Anna Jameson. She forgot the cold and the cultural barrenness of Toronto as she thawed and revived in a warm welcome from a few friends and many admirers of her literary work. On October 20, writing to Ottilie, she ascribed her delay in America to work, visiting and, most of all, the necessity of waiting for legal papers from her husband:

But two reasons make my delay for three or four weeks:—first, the necessity of writing off my Indian notes where I can have authorities to refer to; and secondly, the wish to spend some days with my dear friend Mrs. Butler, who arrived yesterday from England. We have been separated for 5 years and may never meet again. . . . Money matters are not settled with Mr. Jameson, nor the payment of my allowance fixed. I am now awaiting the arrival of the papers with his signature. I then go to Boston to see Dr. Channing, then to Philadelphia to see Fanny Butler. [N 95]

Robert Jameson's despatch to his wife was considerably delayed, by design or by an accident of time. The first days of December, 1837, were the days of the Rebellion in Upper Canada and the Chancellor of the Province may be pardoned for a neglect of personal responsibilities at such a time. In December, Anna herself was inclined to this charitable explanation as she wrote: "I only wait the arrival of some papers from Toronto, retarded by the late events in Canada, to return to New York and embark for England." [M 137]

She commented on "the late events" to Mrs. Austin in terms only slightly more frank and decided than she was later to use in *Winter Studies*. Her sympathies were, on the whole, with the would-be reformers:

I left Toronto before the breaking out of the disturbances, luckily; for though I think the lamentable folly of the people in being led by a few men into premature resistance could end no otherwise, yet I have sympathies with them. There has been much error and misrule on the part of our Government, and the magnificent capabilities of Canada seem, as yet, little understood. If any one can do good, it will be Sir Francis Head, a truth-telling, large-minded, strong-headed man, the first, I apprehend, whom they have had in the Upper Country that united liberality and decision. Sir John Colborne, whom I also know, I admired as a fine, true-hearted soldier; as for Lord Gosford, I must own I rather wondered how the deuce he got there.[15]

Late in December she was still delayed in America because of an unsettling and disappointing development with regard to her separation papers:

I have received the papers from Mr. Jameson, and when examined by a competent person it was found that the deed of settlement was quite deficient and the papers were all sent back to Toronto to be revised and altered. I will not stir from this country till my fate is settled and my future life provided for and rendered independent of accident or chance (as far as that is possible); so this will cause a delay of six weeks before I can sail, and the voyage is worse every way in January than in November or December. But fears I have none, and have none for me! The American packets are the wonder of the world for their admirable management, and they have made the great dark roaring immensity of the Atlantic like a beaten path. [N 98]

While she waited, Anna Jameson picked up her friendship with Fanny Kemble Butler. Through the years between 1832 and 1837, Fanny had been involved in the excitement of stage success and marriage in America, but she had faithfully and cordially kept contact with her friend. It is probable that Anna owed her introduction to and subsequent friendship with Catherine Sedgwick, and also her treasured visit with William Ellery Channing, to letters of introduction from Fanny Butler.

In November, Mrs. Butler, just back from her holiday abroad and probably feeling let down after her gay social life in London, sent to Anna a rather grudging invitation to visit her in Philadelphia: ". . . and therefore (however uncomfortably), I shall be able to receive you there after the first of next month. If a half-furnished home and a broken-down household do not deter you, you will find me the same as you have known me."[16] Anna evidently replied with a certain sensitivity to the half-heartedness of this invitation and suggested a boarding-house nearby, for her friend's answer is a considerably warmer and more genial welcome: "All this, though, is for yourself to determine on; bed, board and welcome, we tender you freely; your room and the inkstand you desire in it shall be ready on the day you name; and we will joyfully meet you."[17]

Editing her own letters many years after Anna Jameson's death, Fanny added a note: "Mrs. Jameson paid us a short sad visit, and returned to Europe with the bitter disappointment of her early life confirmed, to resume her honorable and laborious career of literary industry. Her private loss was the public gain."[18] On Anna's part, the visit was all joy; she wrote of the Butlers to Ottilie with warm enthusiasm:[19]

I am staying for some days with Fanny Butler, whose wonderful gifts of mind are a continued source of interest to me. She has written another Tragedy and is brimful of genius, poetry and power and eloquence, yet is an excellent wife, an excellent mother, and an excellent manager of a household,—no easy matter in this country, where no one will *serve*, but, if well paid, may condescend to *help* you. . . . After the pain, suspense and absolute torture I have suffered in the settlement of my domestic affairs, these few days of peace and quietness in Fanny's country house have been elysium. I like Pierce Butler very much,—more than I expected. It was difficult to please me in a husband for Fanny. [N 100]

The friendship which developed with Catherine Sedgwick was very important to Anna; to her she looked for guidance and comfort: "Keep me a little wee corner in that good heart. . . . How crammed and crowded unless it has an India-rubber capacity of extension— has it? Put me somewhere, stick me behind the door, anywhere, but let me in." The Sedgwick home in Stockbridge was the centre of a large, intimate family group and Miss Sedgwick combined to a notable degree the virtues of housewifery and a maternal warmth for all those within her orbit with those of a busy literary woman of well-stocked and inquiring mind. Anna felt fully the spell of both: the busy days, full of family visits and a reassuring routine of housekeeping chores, the terrace breakfast parties, replete with good food and good conversation, at which Miss Sedgwick entertained, the general atmosphere of comfortable, but not plain, living and habitual high thinking. She characterized her new friend in glowing terms to Ottilie:

I came to Stockbridge to see Miss Sedgwick and spent with her a few days previous to joining Fanny Butler at Philadelphia. Miss Sedgwick is the first female writer of America. She writes like Miss Mitford, and as a moralist exercises a wide and powerful influence over American society. She is besides a very charming and amiable woman, and I love her for her gentle qualities and womanly tenderness as much as I revere her for the use to which she has directed her very high talents. She is the maiden Aunt of a very large family of nephews and nieces, who adore her and look up to her for much of their happiness. [N 97]

Many years later, Miss Sedgwick wrote to her niece describing her friendship with Anna Jameson and ranking her highly as having "a more general cultivation, a richer imagination" and "a more poetic" style than Harriet Martineau.[20] Miss Sedgwick, a modest person, always found Anna's protestations of gratitude baffling and almost embarrassing: "I could only infer that some chance seed in my writings might have fallen on good soil in her heart."[21] She recorded the mutual sympathy and attraction that had sprung up between Anna and her brother Robert who suffered a stroke the next year, an irrecoverable shattering of his health and his legal career. Anna reciprocated the hospitality she had found in America when, in 1839, the Sedgwicks went to Europe: "Mrs. Jameson received me with the warmth of a true friend."[22] The final paragraph of Miss Sedgwick's memoir is as notable for its insight into Anna's personality as for its honesty of physical description:

. . . She sent me her beautiful books, and from time to time love-tokens, which were taken impulsively from her room or table as she was parting from some friend coming here. . . . I mention this to you, Alice, to show the steadiness of her feeling for me. I cherish this remembrance, for the impression she made was of an impulsive person whose affections would be rather showers than fountains. . . . She had a pale, clear, intellectual blue eye, that could flash anger or jealousy or love; her hair was red, and her complexion very fair and of the hue of an irate temper. Her arms, neck and hands were beautiful, but her whole person wanted dignity; it was short and of those dimensions that to ears polite are *embonpoint*—to the vulgar, fat. . . .[23]

While in Massachusetts, Anna was received by Dr. William Ellery Channing, the sage and saint-like Unitarian clergyman of Boston. He was venerated as a prophet by many who sought introductions and conversations with him and his every word assumed a magnified importance to his hearers. Dr. Channing was, as was the Sedgwick

family, of the New England *élite*; he was a particular idol of Fanny
Kemble's and he received her friend, Mrs. Jameson, with the gentle
courtesy and wisdom that his callers prized. Anna probably did not
know that Dr. Channing had been doubtful about the moral influence
of *Characteristics*. In 1833 he had written,

I have not dared to recommend it for the moral lies too deep for most
readers. Most readers would gather from it that woman has no higher
vocation than to love; that absorption in this passion, at the expense of
every other sentiment and every other duty is innocent. . . . Mrs. J. discovers
in her introduction so just an appreciation of woman, that I wonder a
loftier, healthier tone does not decidedly characterize her book.[24]

She went to him in the spirit of a pilgrim and she reported charac-
teristically to Ottilie von Goethe:

Now I must tell you something of Dr. Channing. He is a very little man,
with a look of feebleness and ill health, with no beauty whatever except
a most beautiful expression which comes over his face when he is preach-
ing or speaking. I had much conversation with him, having dined with
him, spent three evenings in his society, having been alone with him for
some time. The impression made on my mind was that of a human being
more good, more wise, more pure than any other being I had ever
approached. [N 98]

   She also called upon Washington Allston, the painter and brother-
in-law of Dr. Channing; on Allston's first visit to Rome early in the
century he had become friendly with Coleridge of whom he had
painted three portraits. His studio in Boston, with its huge and
perpetually unfinished canvas of *Belshazzar's Feast*, was, for some
decades, the hub of art in America, a gathering place for aspirants in
painting, sculpture, and for elevated thinking and talking about all
the arts. Allston had been so charmed by a reading of *The Diary of
an Ennuyée*, which he termed one of the most beautiful books ever
written on Italy, that he had sent its unknown author a lengthy tribute
beginning,

> Sweet, gentle Sybil! would I had the charm
> E'en while the spell upon my heart is warm
> To waft my spirit to thy far-off dreams,
> That, giving form and melody to air,
> The long-sealed fountains of my youth might there
> Before thee shout, and toss their starry stream
> Flushed with the living light which youth alone
> Sheds like the flash from heaven—that straight is gone![25]

Anna found it possible to reciprocate his admiration. She concluded
a memoir, written after his death in 1843, with a grandiose tribute:
"What Washington was as a statesman, Channing as a moralist—*that*
was Allston as an artist." [*ME* 365]

Through all this time of waiting she was organizing her notes from the trip and getting her book in order. She also considered that she was learning to deal with publishers, and she acknowledges the help of Captain Marryat, writer and adventurer, in New York after his American and Canadian tour, whose book covered some of her ground and was published shortly after her own. In it he engaged in an acrimonious and widely publicized rebuttal of material found in Harriet Martineau's *Society in America*. Anna Jameson was much too clever and experienced in keeping her place to invite similar competition from Marryat; she gained, instead, his help:[26]

The refusal of Otley [Saunders and Otley, publishers] to honour my draft upon such an excuse, absolves me from the necessity of returning to them as my publishers, if I can find a better offer in ready money. Captain Marryat, has put me up to some of the publishing tricks—and shewn me on paper what I ought to have. . . . He is a strange rough fellow but good-natured and 'cute enough to match even a London bookseller. Keep up your spirits, therefore—I am not losing any time but writing away as fast as I can and I shall probably make a good bargain *here* for my next book by publishing it in this country. [E 159]

She prudently decided to avoid the pitfalls of controversy and resentment by refraining from writing on her stay in the United States. To Mrs. Austin, she confided the contents of the work in hand: "I have no idea myself of writing anything, except on the only subject I do understand, i.e. the state of art in this country, which is more interesting than you can imagine. This, and my tour among the Indians will be the subject of my next perpetration."[27] She changed her mind, however, for her next work was *Winter Studies and Summer Rambles in Canada*, and it contained nothing about American art.

Finally, Mrs. Jameson's affairs were settled to her satisfaction, her husband agreeing to allow her three hundred pounds a year and to make no objections to her living apart from him. In February, 1838, she sailed for home and in a journal entry dated March 1—part of a letter to Miss Sedgwick—she rejoiced in a safe passage with a measure of fun rarely found in her words:

God be praised! We are on the English shore but I am so ill yesterday and today I cannot go on deck. We have what is expressively called "English weather," That is, a dull leaden sky, a foggy atmosphere, and a drizzling rain. It reminds me of one of Marryat's stories of an old quartermaster, who, returning from a three years' voyage to the East Indies, and approaching the English shore in weather such as this, looked up into the dull sky and hazy atmosphere, and, sniffing up the damp air and buttoning his pea-jacket over his chest, exclaimed with exultation, 'Ay, this is something like—none of your d—d blue skies here!' [E 139]

13

Winter Studies and Summer Rambles
in Canada

> And over that same door was likewise writ,
> Be bold, Be bold, and everywhere Be bold;
> That much she mused, yet could not construe it
> By any riddling skill or common wit:
> At last she spied at that room's upper end
> Another iron door, on which was writ,
> Be not too bold.

This epigraph, from Book III of the *Faerie Queene*, was carried by the first three-volume edition of *Winter Studies and Summer Rambles in Canada*, published in London by Saunders and Otley, November, 1838. It was a particularly apt one, considering that the following text was a personal account of a stay in Upper Canada from December 1836 to late August or early September 1837 while the Rebellion was seething toward its December climax. Moreover, the account published was by the "Chancellor's lady," the courtesy address which Mrs. Jameson acknowledges with some satisfaction.

The line she had to take was a delicate one, therefore, between a frank, truthful, salable account and one which might have hurt her husband's reputation by its ill-considered remarks or, even more serious since she had given up her marriage, reflect upon her reputation by its bad taste. With the skill of one who was now a veteran in tactful writing, Anna Jameson managed to tread the line, producing a work which is completely personal, impressive for the frankness of its tone and the exactness of its detail and at the same time insisting on its author's complete responsibility for the opinions she expresses.

Much of the piquancy and charm to a reading audience by now accustomed to her combination of travel memoirs with social and literary criticism would lie in the fact that in this book, too, she contrived to use her familiar technique. The "Winter Studies" section is a journal of her winter stay in Toronto, interspersed with translations and commentaries from German works she was studying and with a new set of variations on her old theme: the character, position and necessary education of women. "Summer Rambles," the account of an impressive and unprecedented tour of the Province, is also spiced with carefully chosen and well-authenticated Indian lore and, again, with a constant stress on the position of women among whites and Indians.

In "Winter Studies" particularly, the juxtaposition of her own cold and unhappy present surroundings with her German studies, an outgrowth of the cosmopolitan European civilization to which she was accustomed, keeps the author emphatically centre stage—an Ennuyée again, but this time with an engaging gallantry which insists on her own ideals of culture and learning even with the temperature at twelve below zero and the ink frozen in her inkwell. Similarly, though the "Summer Rambles" section contains much that is interesting and informative, it is the author, as heroine, that gives the work its form and is its chief attraction, in her day and in ours.[1]

The Preface begins, as usual, with a general apologia. Assuming a becoming modesty, the author addresses the book to her own sex, on whose mercy she throws herself:

This little book, the mere result of much thoughtful idleness and many an idle thought, has grown up insensibly out of an accidental promise. It never was intended to go before the world in its present crude and desultory form. . . .
My intention was to have given the result of what I had seen, and the reflections and comparisons excited by so much novel experience, in quite a different form—and one less obtrusive; but owing to the intervention of various circumstances, and occupation of graver import, I found myself reduced to the alternative of either publishing the book as it now stands, or of suppressing it altogether. [WSSR I, iv]

In a letter to Robert Noel, Anna confessed that her depressed and hopeless state of mind had had its effect on the book; she judges her work on Germany in every way inferior to that of her admired predecessor, Mme de Staël:

My intention was to have used these notes only as *material,* but I have been persuaded to print the diary in its original state, only with a few omissions; and after a little struggle with myself, I acquiesced. The truth is, I have not time, courage, heart, or spirits to write a sensible, well-digested book; so they may just take my scraps of thought, and make the best or worst of them. How contemptible, frivolous, old-fashioned, superficial, it will appear to your deep-thinking Germans—they who thought De Staël commonplace and superficial—and what am I to her? Well, never mind, it must go. [M 140]

It would seem that she is personally apologizing for the German "Winter Studies"; certainly this is the only reasonable explanation for her words, short of calling them a calculated falsehood, or, at best, a considerable quibble with the truth. From her first weeks in Canada, she had recorded her intention of travelling to the west and of writing a book, and in her letters home during her several months' wait in America she gave plentiful evidence of work in progress. About her German scholarship she did, no doubt, feel hesitant; what she said about Canada, she wanted to say. Further, Anna Jameson and her publishers would be well aware of the salability of an informal, candid, peep-over-the-shoulder memoir, particularly in 1838, when Lord Durham's conduct of the post-Rebellion difficulties made the Canadas especially newsworthy.

However sincere the apology of her introduction, her reputation as a popular writer was strong enough to sustain the risk she took, and the book's interest to the English public outweighed any errors or weakness either in German scholarship or in good taste. To Noel she writes in late autumn of 1838 that "My book . . . is out this month, and, I am glad to say, my success is entire, and I have never been so popular as now." [M 149]

Mr. Jameson, however, was not among the enthusiasts. "He is evidently much displeased by the extracts from my book which have appeared in the American papers. The book itself had not reached him." [N 109] Mr. Jameson's displeasure should certainly have been anticipated by his wife; after all, he was a permanent resident of the colony about whose society she had been far from complimentary. Although the Preface states that she has "abstained generally from politics and personalities," her text belies her words by such passages as this, on the pettiness and pretentiousness of the governing class:

I did not expect to find here in this new capital of a new country, with the boundless forest within half a mile of us on almost every side—concentrated as it were the worst evils of our old and most artificial social system at home, with none of its *agrémens*, and none of its advantages. Toronto is like a fourth or fifth rate provincial town, with the pretensions of a capital city. We have here a petty colonial oligarchy, a self-constituted aristocracy, based upon nothing real, nor even upon anything imaginary; and we have all the mutual jealousy and fear, and petty gossip, and mutual meddling and mean rivalship, which are common in a small society of which the members are well known to each other. [WSSR I, 74]

Even the conclusion of the passage, considered by Mrs. Jameson as a compensating ray of hope in the wilderness, would scarcely mollify the Toronto society so indicated: "Yet, in the midst of all this, I cannot but see that good spirits and corrective principles are at work; that progress is making: though the march of intellect be not here in double quick time, as in Europe, it does not absolutely stand stock still." [*WSSR* I, 74] She demonstrates a keen and ultimately optimistic observation of Canada though its "hateful factious spirit in political matters" offends her. "Canada is a colony, not a *country*; it is not yet identified with the dearest affections and associations, remembrances, and hopes of its inhabitants: it is to them an adopted, not a real mother. Their love, their pride, are not for poor Canada, but for high and happy England; but a few more generations must change all this." [*WSSR* I, 75]

Nor does she abstain wholly from political discussion, though here she is cautious, ranging herself with some timidity on the side of a union of Upper and Lower Canada, a measure soon to be advocated in Lord Durham's Report:

It seems, on looking over the map of this vast and magnificent country, and reading its whole history, that the political division into five provinces, each with its independent governor and legislature, its separate correspondence with the Colonial-Office, its local laws, and local taxation, must certainly add to the amount of colonial patronage, and perhaps render more secure the subjection of the whole to the British crown; but may it not also have perpetuated local distinctions and jealousies—kept alive divided interests, narrowed the resources, and prevented the improvement of the country on a large and general scale? [*WSSR* I, 77]

Mr. Jameson's displeasure had a variety of causes: he could turn from his wife's general condemnation of his neighbours to her indictment of the colonial policy and the Colonial Office to which he owed his appointment. In a particular fine flourish of self-contradiction, Anna Jameson says that her notes "have little reference to the politics and statistics of that unhappy and mismanaged, but most magnificent country"; she then produces a very precise summary of her opinions on the government of Upper Canada:

I saw of course something of the state of feeling on both sides, but not enough to venture a word on the subject. Upper Canada appeared to me loyal in spirit, but resentful and repining under the sense of injury, and suffering from the total absence of all sympathy on the part of the English government with the condition, the wants, the feelings, the capabilities of the people and the country. I do not mean to say that this want of sympathy *now* exists to the same extent as formerly; it has been abruptly and painfully awakened, but it has too long existed. . . . Add a system of mistakes and mal-administration not chargeable to any one individual, or any one measure, but to the whole tendency of our colonial government; the perpetual change of officials and change of measures; the fluctuation of principles destroying all public confidence, and a degree of ignorance relative to the country itself, not credible except to those who may have visited it; add these three things together, the want of knowledge, the want of judgment, the want of sympathy, on the part of the government, how can we be surprised at the strangely anomalous condition of the governed? [WSSR I, v–viii]

Her feelings about Toronto's people moderated with the weather; the spring and early summer provide several favourable impressions which might soften but would certainly not erase the effects of her first strong judgments: "It would be pleasant, verily, if, after all my ill-humored and impertinent tirades against Toronto, I were doomed to leave it with regret; yet such is likely to be the case. There are some most kind-hearted and agreeable people here, who look upon me with more friendliness than at first, and are winning fast upon my feelings, if not on my sympathies." [WSSR I, 221]

As she takes leave of Toronto for the trip west, she records, with gratitude, the friendly interest shown in her project: "In these latter days I have lived in friendly communion with so many excellent people, that my departure from Toronto was not what I anticipated—an escape on one side, or a riddance on the other. . . . The Chief Justice in particular, John Beverley Robinson, sent me a whole sheet of instructions, and several letters of introduction to settlers along my line of route." [WSSR I, 240]

Much of the attraction of "Winter Studies" lies in the variety of its contents. Notes on the frigidity, both of weather and of society, are interspersed with lively characterizations of those few who took her fancy, among them Colonel Fitzgibbon, the Irish soldier of fortune whom she describes at length and whom, she had boasted to Ottilie soon after her arrival in Canada, "loves me with all his honest heart." [N 85] White Deer, the Chippewa chief who with his two friends was brought to see her by Colonel Givins, the Indian agent, engaged both her sympathy and her reportorial eye at its keenest.[2]

The German studies which she undertook during the winter, and for which she apologized to Robert Noel, were, avowedly, an instrument to defeat despair and loneliness: "I must try all mechanical means to maintain the balance of my mind, and the unimpaired use of my faculties, for they will be needed. There is no rescue but in occupation; serious and useful occupation if I can make or find it—

trivial occupation when I can not. . . . To use my Lord Byron's phrase, I must get *'a file for the serpent.'* " [WSSR I, 124]

Two days later, she records the finding of "a file, or what I will use as such. I shall take to translating." [WSSR I, 124] This is Mrs. Jameson's introduction to her musings on Dr. Eckermann's *Gespräche mit Goethe*, which she studied and translated during her Toronto stay. Her remarks are prefaced by a sketch of Eckermann the biographer, and they are punctuated by her reminiscences of Goethe's home and family by which she introduces chatty domestic detail about the great man and his surroundings, somewhat in the manner of popular women's magazine writing of our own day:

When Goethe was more than eighty, he purchased for the first time, an easy chair. His indifference, and even contempt, for the most ordinary comforts of life and luxuries of this kind, were amusing. . . . But his drawing-room was elegant—I remember two very large frames, in which he was accustomed to dispose a variety of original drawings by the old masters, perhaps eight or ten in each. When they had hung some time, he changed them for another set. These were *his* luxuries: the set of drawings which he last selected, remain hanging in the room. [WSSR I, 171]

No one reading the "Winter Studies" would gain a scholarly or a deep and coherent critique of Eckermann's work, or indeed of any of the variety of German literature over which Anna ranges. Of this, she was perfectly aware; as she had written apologetically to Robert Noel, so she writes to Ottilie:

As to my own book, it is not a *brochure*, but in 3 vols. It will contain some German Criticism—for I have been working hard at my German—but such criticism as must appear to you Germans ten times more impertinent than anything of Madame de Staël; for surely I am not to be compared to her! But I do not care for that. I write for Englishwomen and to tell them some things *they* do not know. [N 101]

Within this limitation the "Winter Studies" would achieve their purpose. An Englishwoman would, of necessity, rise from her reading better informed on a variety of German topics: some criticism of Goethe's *Tasso, Iphigenia* and *Clavigo* as well as of Eckermann's work and of Grillparzer's *Sappho* and *Medea*; contemporary comments on the German stage and its actresses and a slight but shrewd comparison between German and English social customs over a wide-ranging area. The English reader would have every opportunity of being "improved and informed" as Mrs. Jameson intended she should be. Women would also be attracted by the novel circumstances of the author as she wrote. Finally, they would receive the intended beneficial lesson on the strengthening of moral fibre by the example of the author in her alien surroundings, who writes of these studies to Ottilie with a firmness we cannot doubt: "Decided, determined occupation and hard study I have found the best thing to keep the mind from wasting itself away and being weakened and disordered with the struggle of inward passion and vain regret." [N 88]

The "Summer Rambles" begin with her removal from Toronto to Niagara between the 10th and the 13th of June, 1837. They end with her return to Toronto on or about August 13: "At three o'clock in the morning, just as the moon was setting in Lake Ontario, I arrived at the door of my own house in Toronto, having been absent on this wild expedition just two months." [WSSR II, 339]

In the first month she went from Toronto to Niagara, Hamilton, Brantford, Woodstock, London, St. Thomas, Port Talbot, Chatham, and Detroit; though arduous, this could not be classed as a "wild expedition" in the way that her second month's travels could. Leaving Detroit on July 19, she went by the steamer *Jefferson* to Mackinaw, still well within reach of any eager traveller. From there, however, she travelled ninety-four miles to the Sault by *bateau*, a small boat which held at most fifteen persons and which was rowed by five French-Canadian voyageurs. Arriving there on July 29, she was off again on August 1, again in a *bateau*, for the annual Indian conclave at Manitoulin Island, a journey down Lake Huron of four days and three nights. On the 6th of August, she continued by canoe to Penetang, by canoe and portage to Lake Simcoe, thence to Toronto. This latter half of her travels may indeed be dignified by the name of a "wild expedition" and in its successful completion Anna Jameson took a justifiable pride.

There were several factors contributing to the trip's success and the most important of these are to be found in her own nature. She was an inveterate traveller, of long experience in Europe, accustomed to varying degrees of discomfort *en route*; in any case her Atlantic passage and subsequent winter journey to Toronto had provided a recent toughening beside which anything to be encountered in summer might seem a trivial inconvenience. As "the Chancellor's lady," provided with letters of introduction by Chief Justice Robinson, as an English lady with the unassailable confidence in her nationality which was a part of her time and as a genuinely interested and sympathetic author, Anna Jameson was triply protected. Her personality, however, played the most positive role in her success. She was obviously able, when travelling, to adapt herself to new environments quickly, to make the most of chance meetings and to sympathize and to engage sympathy easily. At every stage along her route she found someone ready, or at least persuadable, to help her on her next stage. With some of these persons—the McMurrays of St. Marys, Mrs. Johnston of the Sault and the Schoolcrafts of Mackinaw—she remained on the friendliest of terms.

Mr. McMurray, who had been Anglican missionary stationed at St. Marys since 1832, was married to Charlotte Johnston, whose mother, a full-blooded Chippewa Indian, lived across the river from the McMurrays on the American side of the Sault. Mrs. McMurray's sister was the wife of Henry Schoolcraft, American Indian agent at Mackinaw, an early and deservedly renowned authority on the Indians. Anna describes her meeting with the McMurrays as a happy accident, engineered by Dr. Rees of Toronto, in the last moments of her stay there:

I must confess that the specimens of Indian squaws and half-cast women I had met with, had in no wise prepared me for what I found in Mrs. McMurray. . . . In two minutes I was seated by her—my hand kindly folded in hers—and we were talking over the possibility of my plans. It seems there is some chance of my reaching the Island of Michilimackinac, but of the Sault Ste. Marie, I dare hardly think as yet—it looms in my imagination dimly described in far space, a kind of Ultima Thule. . . . To her own far-off home at the Sault Ste. Marie, between Lake Huron and Lake Superior, she warmly invited me—without, however, being able to point out any conveyance or mode of travel thither that could be depended on—only a possible chance of such. [WSSR I, 240]

Her interest in the northern reaches of Lake Huron had already been awakened by *The Travels and Adventures of Alexander Henry*, the fur-trader, which had been lent to her in Toronto. This interest was quickened by her meeting with the McMurrays and she did reach her Ultima Thule, gaining on her way and during her stay there most of the Indian material for her book.

With all of the interrelated Schoolcraft-McMurray group, Mrs. Jameson quickly became intimate, so much so that when she had successfully navigated the St. Marys' rapids in a ten-foot canoe, with an Indian steersman and George Johnston, a brother of Mrs. Schoolcraft and Mrs. McMurray, she was made an adopted daughter of the family:

. . . . they told me I was the first European female who had ever performed it [the shooting of the rapids], and assuredly I shall not be the last. I recommend it as an exercise before breakfast. Two glasses of champagne could not have made me more tipsy and more self-complacent . . . in compliment to my successful achievement, Mrs. Johnston bestowed this new appellation ["Wah, sah, ge, wah, no, qua"] which I much prefer. It signifies *the bright foam,* or more properly, with the feminine adjunct *qua, the woman of the bright foam;* and by this same name I am henceforth to be known among the Chippewas. [WSSR II, 235]

Henry Schoolcraft recorded in his diary his wife's account of her trip with Anna Jameson from Michilimackinac to the Sault:

Aug. 5th. Mrs. Schoolcraft writes from the Sault, that Mrs. Jameson and the children suffered much on the trip to that place from mosquitoes, but by dint of a douceur of 5 dollars extra to the men, which Mrs. Jameson made to the crew, they rowed all night, from Sailor's encampment, and reached the Sault at 6 o'clock in the morning. "I feel delighted," she says, "at my having come with Mrs. J., as I found she did not know how to get along at all, at all. . . . Poor Mrs. J. cried heartily when she parted with me and my children; she is indeed a woman in a thousand. While here, George came down the rapids with her in fine style and spirits. She insisted on being baptized and named in Indian after her sail down the falls."[3]

After her safe return to Toronto, Anna wrote to Mrs. Schoolcraft with affection and gratitude, although she feels that she has "but imperfectly achieved the object of my journey" and that she still knows far too little of the Indian women particularly:

As long as I live, the impression of your kindness and of your character altogether, remains with me; your image will often come back to me and I dare to hope that you will not forget me quite. . . . Mrs. MacMurray has told you the incidents of our voyage to the Manitoulin Island, from thence to Toronto; it was all so delightful; the most extraordinary scenery I ever beheld, the wildest! I recall it as a dream. I arrived at my own house at 3 o'clock in the morning of the 13th, tired and much eaten by those abominable mosquitoes, but otherwise better in health than I have been for many months.[4]

Henry Schoolcraft's *Memoirs* contain several passages relating to Mrs. Jameson and her trip which are complimentary to her. She had, he says, "none of the supercilious and conceited airs which I had noticed in some of her travelling country women of the class of authors." He rates her highest in accuracy of observation among his author-visitors to Michilimackinac, although she too suffered from the limitations of all of his visitors, including Captain Marryat and Miss Martineau:

It seems to me that Englishmen and Englishwomen, for I have had a good many of both sexes to visit me recently, look on America very much as one does when he peeps through a magnifying glass on pictures of foreign scenes, and the picturesque ruins of old cities and the like. They are really very fine, but it is difficult to realize that such things are. It is all an optical deception.

It was clearly so with Marryat, a very superficial observer; Miss Martineau who was in search of something ultra and elementary, and even Mrs.

Jameson, who had the most accurate and artistic eye of all, but who, with the exception of some bits of womanly heart, appeared to regard our vast woods, and wilds, and lakes, as a magnificent panorama, a painting in oil. . . . It has appeared to me to be very much the same with the Austrian and Italian functionaries who have wandered as far as Michilimackinac.[5]

Mr. Schoolcraft's account of Anna's visit is testimony to her individuality, her adaptability and her talent. He remembers her as an "eminent landscape painter, or rather, sketcher in crayon" who "had her portfolio ever in hand." Several times she came into his office to hear the Indians speaking and from the piazza she watched "the wild Indians dancing; she evidently looked on with the eyes of a Claude Lorraine or a Michael Angelo." He admired Anna's independence, her freedom of movement and especially her warmth of personality: "This freedom from restraint in her motions was an agreeable trait in a person of her literary taste and abilities. . . . Notwithstanding her strong author-like traits and peculiarities, we thought her a woman of hearty and warm affections and attachments; the want of which in her friends, we think she would exquisitely feel."[6]

Anna's chance meetings meant more to her than opportunities for grasping likely material for her pen. In 1839, in the name of Mrs. Jameson, Catherine Sedgwick visited Mrs. Schoolcraft who was then in New York, and in 1842 Henry Schoolcraft visited Anna in England: "He tells me that his wife still loves me *as a sister* and all the Indians remember me and count my visit to them an event." [N 137]

Henry Schoolcraft had been, for many years, engaged in the collection of a group of oral tales which were published in the spring of 1839. He had obviously talked of the project with Mrs. Jameson for he reports her advice on January 18, 1839:

The next letter I opened was from Mrs. Jameson of London, who writes that her plan of publication is, to divide the profits with the publishers, and, as these are honest men and gentlemen, she has found this the best way. She advises me to adopt the same course with my Indian legends (I followed this advice but fell into the hands of the Philistines).

"I published," she says, "in my little journal, one or two legends which Mrs. Schoolcraft gave me, and they have excited very great interest. The more exactly you can (in translation) adhere to the style of the language of Indian nations, instead of emulating a fine and correct English style—the more characteristic in all respects—the more original—the more interesting your work will be."[7]

Anna's feeling and desire for authentic information is demonstrated in a letter to Mr. McMurray dated Feb. 1, 1838, just before her departure from New York:

Mrs. Schoolcraft told me that it was when 11 or 12 years old that the Indian girls were sent apart to dream *for a guardian spirit*—you say in your letter *five* years old, which is a mistake, I presume—perhaps my mistake, the word not being clear—I should like to know by what title in their own language the Indians would address the Queen of England, their great Mother. I shall certainly see her Majesty on my return to England and wish I had something very elegant to present from your Indians—Catlin [the well-known painter of Indians] is here, with the most superb collection of Indian pipes, implements, weapons and curiosities of every kind, I ever beheld—he was seven years in the North West—did you ever see him? he has portraits and pictures from the Sault Ste. Marie—things which I envied and coveted—I think you will be pleased with what I have written of the Indians—I have not gone into any disputed points of religion or politics as I never meddle with such. I have told simply what I felt and saw and you and Mrs. MacMurray and your family must of necessity figure in my picture, but you know you gave me *carte blanche* on the point and I will be the most discreet of friends—in fact what need of much discretion where all I saw inspired feelings of good will and the most animated pleasures which novelty of scene and kindness of heart would bestow?—You must be content to be *immortalized* in my fashion. I like the song very much, but lament that I cannot have the music of the other—nor the *name* of the chief who composed the song you sent— small particulars which appear to you trivial and unnecessary are important to a narrator, like touches in a picture and . . . and new to English ears. Will you give my kind love to all my relations—how is Waitsky and his wife and children—do they live in the same lodge this cold weather? How is George Johnston who went down the falls with me so gallantly—and his daughter Louisa and how is my little sister Eliza with her dark clustering hair? And how is your little darling son. I have reason to complain that you do not mention each individually—for I do not forget any of you—Adieu dear Sir. . . .[8]

The letter is of interest beyond its demonstration of a scholar's curiosity and a friend's interest. In its words speaks Anna Jameson, the confident author, who for all her sincerely meant protestations of friendship says, and means: "You must be content to be *immortalized* in my fashion." Her anticipation of her audience with Queen Victoria, of whose accession to the throne she had learned as her *bateau* passed within hailing distance of another among the islands of northern Lake Huron, was not quite justified. She did pay a call to Windsor Castle, however, where she was cordially received by the Honourable Miss Murray, a lady-in-waiting, and warmly complimented on her Canadian book by Lord Melbourne; whether or not Mr. McMurray had supplied the Indian gifts so blatantly desired is not on record.

By now we recognize in Anna Jameson's writing method a three-part scheme. She read before travelling, in this case Alexander Henry in particular. This gave some basis of interest and comparison with her own experiences and some idea of a desirable route. She took notes and kept journals while travelling, these forming the core and the personalized part of her work. Finally, she edited and judiciously added supplementary material, as exact as possible in its detail.

A typical insertion of material may be seen in her histories of Pontiac; even more interesting is her discussion of the work of the Moravian missionaries among the Indians. The story of Brother Zeisberger, the missionary, and Wangeman, the Indian chief, follows her report of a conversation between herself and a pious, honest, but narrow Moravian missionary. The Zeisberger story is a paraphrase of the anecdote to be found in George Henry Loskiel's *History of the Mission of the United Brethren among the Indians of North America.*[9] Mrs. Jameson acknowledges this text, but does not give the author; nor does she make it known that the story she reports took place some fifty years previous to her conversation with the missionary.

There is no imputation of her scholarly method intended; she was bound by no method and none was expected or demanded of her. Such an example does, however, reveal that her procedures were a combination of careful research and astute book-making, not exact scholarship as we know it today, but work which was documented and authenticated beyond the demands of either the critics or the public of her day. I can find no instance of a reviewer encouraging a more exact reference method by commenting on its absence, though, commonly, the reviews about Anna Jameson's work were complimentary to the exactness and apparent validity of observation.

Reviewers in both the *Westminster* and the *British and Foreign Quarterly* were to find this work laden with the "Rights of Woman" question. As usual with this facet of Mrs. Jameson's work, a reader of today finds her remonstrances reasonable and even conservative: ". . . the true importance and real dignity of woman is everywhere, in savage and civilized communities, regulated by her capacity of being useful; or, in other words, that her condition is decided by the share she takes in providing for her own subsistence and the well-being of society as a productive labourer." [WSSR II, 310] Her strictures against the education of women are applied in a new area: the fate of a young lady who is obviously and disastrously ill-equipped to be a settler's wife: "I have not often in my life met with contented and cheerful-minded women, but I never met with so many repining and discontented women as in Canada." [WSSR I, 108] Her inquiry into the position of Indian women leads her to a comparison, favourable and unfavourable, with the status of European women:

Where, then, the whole duty and labour of providing the means of subsistence, ennobled by danger and courage, falls upon the man, the woman naturally sinks in importance, and is a dependent drudge. But she is not therefore, I suppose, so *very* miserable, nor, relatively, so very abject; she is sure of protection; sure of maintenance, at least while the man has it; sure of kind treatment; sure that she will never have her children taken from her but by death; sees none better off than herself, and has no conception of a superior destiny; and it is evident that in such a state the appointed and necessary share of the woman is the household work, and all other domestic labour.

Hence, however hard the lot of woman, she is in no *false* position. The two sexes are in their natural and true position relatively to the state of society and the means of subsistence. [*WSSR* II, 304]

Anna Jameson's attitude to the Indians is an admixture of a romantic conception of the "Noble Savage," a fatalistic conviction that nothing can be done to halt the progress of their destruction, and a schoolmistress' admonitory revealing of the unvarnished truth:

The attempts of a noble and a fated race, to oppose, or even to delay for a time, the rolling westward of the great tide of civilization, are like efforts to dam up the rapids of Niagara. The moral world has its laws, fixed as those of physical nature. The hunter must make way before the agriculturalist, and the Indian must learn to take the bit between his teeth, and set his hand to the ploughshare, or *perish*. [*WSSR* II, 38]

As she travelled through Canada she recorded her impressions in sketches as well as in written notes. These pencil drawings, some forty in number, are part of a collection of about seventy sketches which illustrate her trip, beginning at Portsmouth and including American as well as Canadian scenes. They were advertised after her death, by Christie, Manson and Woods, as "A Voyage to America," a misleading title since the group also includes a number of sketches of Italian and Austrian scenes. The considerable number which do illustrate the Canadian trip have the liveliness and the precision of description of Anna Jameson's best writing. In some cases she has judiciously added colour to the pencil drawings; her sketches of the dancing Indians at Mackinaw are particularly striking for this reason. All of the sketches are notable for the vignettes they provide of Upper Canada in 1837; they are especially interesting when considered as a stage-by-stage accompaniment to her trip.

For *Characteristics of Women, A Commonplace Book* and *Sacred and Legendary Art*, Anna sketched her own illustrations to the text and laboriously prepared etchings of them for the printer. Unfortunately, whether by her own or her publisher's decision, her Canadian sketches were not used, nor have they ever been used, to illustrate **Winter Studies and Summer Rambles in Canada.** They are, however, a remarkable collection, providing abundant proof of the "accurate eye" ascribed to her by Henry Schoolcraft.[10]

In December, 1838, shortly after the London publication of *Winter Studies*, Anna wrote to Catherine Sedgwick: "At this moment I have fame and praise, for my name is in every newspaper." Various comments record the praise that she gathered from friends and from associates in the ranks of lady-authors. Harriet Martineau wrote, quite without the drop of acid which often characterized her nature: "I feel so deeply the support and delight of your sympathy, as shown in your Canada book, that I acknowledge your right to all my thoughts on that set of subjects. I am always recurring in thought to that book." [M 149] The venerable and admired dramatist, Joanna Baillie, added her own praise and that of her sister: "But I may at any rate thank you for the agreeable amusement of the curious and interesting information we have received from it. You make the reader, both as to your internal world and external, live along with yourself, and an excellent companion we find you." [M 150]

Lady Byron, of whom Anna was still in awe, and whose commendation she accordingly valued very highly, also approved. Anna writes of her: "She was more than kind, and her approbation of my views and efforts on some moral points she expressed in a manner that went very near my heart." [M 155] In June of 1839, shortly after the New York publication of *Winter Studies*, Anna relayed to Ottilie von Goethe a report from Miss Sedgwick: "She says my book is the most popular book which has come out 'for many a day.'" [N 109]

The periodicals which reviewed the book leave us in no doubt as to the interest it aroused, or to the acceptance of Anna Jameson as a competent and continuing writer. They do not, however, give *Winter Studies* unqualified approval; the tone is one of careful and sometimes admonitory consideration. The *British and Foreign Review*, a publication devoted chiefly to geographical or political works with some notice taken of important literary productions, gives *Winter Studies and Summer Rambles* lengthy consideration. Its editor at this time was John Kemble, Fanny's brother, but in this case at least the influence of friendship did not secure for Mrs. Jameson a completely laudatory article. The introduction generously acknowledges both her reputation and her writing ability:

She has always stood alone among the parti-coloured crowd of authoresses, but her fate is, in one respect, singular. Unlike the generality of those enjoying a solitary and select reputation, she has hitherto passed along her literary career unscathed by contemporary petulance or ill-will. For the credit of human and literary nature, let it be hoped that one cause of an exemption so rare in these days of slander and acrimonious personality, lies in the sincerity of mind and purpose everywhere visible throughout her works. Though sometimes a passing affectation of style is permitted to creep in—though sometimes an ecstasy or a lamentation, artificially exaggerated, cannot but draw the reader down from the heightened contemplation of the enthusiast to the trivial unimportant personalities of the woman; none of Mrs. Jameson's writings display the task-work of the manufacturers. . . .

Besides so sterling an attraction as this earnestness of purpose, Mrs. Jameson possesses a large measure of elegance of taste and fineness of perception. To the plain speaker's convincing utterance, she adds the poet's genial imagination.[11]

This passage serves as a mollifying introduction to the reviewer's stern rebuke administered to the author for "a misjudging purpose to disturb the mutual existing relations between man and womankind":

No one reading these "Winter Studies and Summer Rambles" can possibly disentangle the outbreakings of the journalist's disappointed hopes and wounded feelings,—yet more precisely and poignantly stated than the interpolated and assumed heart-sorrows of the Ennuyée,—from the enthusiast's constant resolution to represent any arrangement of the position and duties of her sex whatsoever,—even that where the Squaw is the Red Man's drudge in field and wigwam . . . as more equitable and to be desired than that existing according to the present system of European civilization. Mrs. Jameson has thus rendered it impossible for anyone answering her in her capacity of advocate, to refrain from also inquiring into her personal stake in the cause she pleads so warmly. Courtesy forbid that we should do this!— though justice to ourselves and the public render it impossible for us to pass over so salient a feature in her writing—above all in this present book— without a general protest of grave and entire disapproval.[12]

Strong as is his disapproval of her position on the "Woman Question," the reviewer gives Anna Jameson full approval for her "Summer Rambles" section, including congratulations for the honesty of her reaction to Niagara Falls: "We cannot recollect another traveller honest enough to record the disappointment, which, being self-engendered by immoderate anticipation, some hundreds must have felt on viewing this marvel of the Western World."[13]

The comparison of Mrs. Jameson with other lady-travellers is complimentary, bearing out Henry Schoolcraft's praise of her and also unwittingly giving weight to his assessment of the attitude of all his visitors to the wilderness.

It is this blending of thought—earnest and sincere even when it wanders wild—with graphic power, which distinguishes her from other lady travellers with whom we have recently dealt, from the Mrs. Trollopes and the Miss Pardoes—the false and the flippant,—who return from foreign parts yet more self-complacent in their ignorance than when they left their own firesides. Many of Mrs. Jameson's descriptions of scenery remind us of those in Mary Wollstonecraft's "Letters from Norway"; there is a pensive mellowness of colouring in both, which recalls to us the tone of certain leafy forest-landscapes, by Gaspard Poussin, where a chastened sadness and splendour brood over pellucid skies and silent waters. But our contemporary is a more thorough mistress of her art than was her predecessor. . . .[14]

The reviewer continues with a reminder of the forbearance he has chosen to show the author on her treatment of the condition of women and closes with a defence of her meagre information on the Canadian political scene:

The "Chancellor's Lady" could hardly, without serious breach of confidence, have discussed the administration of colonial government . . . it must be added, in answer to some who have accused our authoress of withholding from the public the information it had a right to expect at her hands,— Mrs. Jameson left Toronto sometime before the first insurrection.[15]

It is obvious from this review that Mrs. Jameson has, finally, over-stepped the fine-drawn line between permissible criticisms of the education of and role assigned to her sex and the highly suspect field of feminist propaganda. Her writings on the "Woman Question" had formerly been prettily disguised as light reading for ladies; now, she was frankly speaking of and for her own sex—*women*, not ladies. Furthermore, she had dared to compare the lot of the European and the savage woman and to find the latter, in some cases, occupying the more honest and honoured position. Such radicalism could not be ignored.

This misdemeanour was probably the occasion for Thackeray's sup-posed attack on her, which he describes in a letter to Mrs. Procter:

I stop the pens to ask if you have seen an attack on Mrs. Jameson in the *Times* this morning. I am the author of course: as of the article on Procter— in this last one against poor Mrs. J. I think I have been as disgustingly offensive, vulgar and impertinent and cowardly as I ever was in my life. I really don't think I ever matched it.[16]

The "attack" is not to be found either in *The Times* or in any other publication. Mrs. Jameson may have been protected by her friend Henry Reeve, Mrs. Austin's nephew, who was at this time on *The Times*'s staff; she may even, as the "Chancellor's Lady," have had the much more influential protection of some highly placed political figure such as the Whig leader, Lord Brougham.

Reviewers' displeasure brought her strong support from the same friend to whom Thackeray wrote of this "attack": "Mrs. Procter writes me that the book is universally relished, and says 'a fig for reviewers.' 'The men,' she says, 'are much alarmed by certain speculations about women; and,' she adds, 'well they may be, for when the horse and ass begin to think and argue, adieu to riding and driving.'" [M 150]

To a twentieth-century reader Anna Jameson's dissatisfaction with women's lot is evident much earlier than *Winter Studies and Summer Rambles*, as is an increasing boldness in her indictments of society. One must conclude that a combination of sincere admiration for her work, particularly for *Characteristics of Women*, together with a condescending sense of their harmlessness, long since demonstrated by "Christopher North," had until now lulled her male censors. At any rate, her feminism had become sufficiently radical to warrant her favourable notice by the *Westminster Review*. In an article which uses several works as a launching platform for its programme of reform in women's position, the *Westminster* casts a sceptical and knowing glance on Anna Jameson's work:

This lady seems fond of giving her readers surprises. With the view, as she tells us, "to show that the education of women, as at present conducted, is founded on mistaken principles," she made some very charming criticisms on the female characters in Shakespeare, which she chose to call "Characteristics of Women"; showing, at any rate, that she herself possessed something of a kindred genius. In a later publication which led us to expect some account of Canada—she has done more to accomplish her design; her winter studies and summer rambles there having the same object—the nature and situation of women.[17]

By the standards of the avowedly radical *Westminster*, she is still a fledgling, sound but timid:

Many of her thoughts, although set down in the most desultory and hasty manner, and taking often a very fanciful shape, are acute and profound, displaying an intimate acquaintance with life (ladies' life especially), and a pretty exact appreciation of the point that society has attained in refinement, conventional or real. . . . Mrs. J. is rather in advance of most other writers, in the degree of latitude and freedom she bespeaks for the exertion of the "sisterhood," as she loves to name them, while the reference with which she sets out to what may be called the salic law of nature, is sufficient, we should think, to calm the greatest alarmist for petticoat invasion.[18]

Though the recognition that Mrs. Jameson was a deliberate exponent of the rights of women brought her critical disapproval, it also ensured her an audience, not only among women but among the general reading public and the critics. She had become an author whose works demanded to be dealt with, sometimes by the critical weapon of polite ridicule, very close to "Christopher North's" early tone toward her works, sometimes by the mollifying method of praise for her style. This combination is very evident in her first lengthy considera- tion by the *Quarterly*, which, though it did not come until 1845, considered several of her works in their "Women's Position" aspect. With reference to certain of her arguments, the reviewer comments:

It is characteristic of woman's sanguine and somewhat arbitrary disposition to hope and believe that almost every object of human desire may be attained by a simple exercise of authority; thus we hear so often that men should make a law against so-and-so, without much regard to the practical difficulties impeding legislation. Mrs. Jameson, for instance, is absolutely solemn in her denunciation of the Parliament for its remissness in not providing against the evil of falling in love unexpectedly.[19]

The ironic comment is balanced by a praise of her writing ability which one now recognizes as a usual reaction among all her critics:

Mrs. Jameson's ability as a writer is unquestionable. She is fond of pro- pounding odd views upon all kinds of subjects, but this perpetual oppug- nancy is delightfully contrasted by the elegance of her style—an elegance not resulting from mere fastidiousness in the avoidance of faults, but from the vigor of the writer's mind and her strong poetic feeling. Her pages, moreover, are rich with the fruits of good reading, and although the sub- jects which she chooses are often such as might easily draw her on to the utterance of many inanities, she guards herself so effectively against this worst of literary sins as to be never at all insipid.[20]

Finally Anna Jameson had achieved recognition by all of the major reviews of her time. Condescending consideration of her work, first shown by *Blackwood's* in its review of *Loves of the Poets*, had ripened to praise, in which the *Edinburgh* shared, for her *Characteristics of Women* and *Visits and Sketches*. The *Westminster's* recognition of *Winter Studies* acknowledged her presence, however timid, in the reformers' camp; and at last, the *Quarterly*, with an avuncular tone reminiscent of *Blackwood's* early reviews, both admonished and admired her. Thus, some ten years after "Christopher North" called the "Royal Reviews" to task for their neglect, Anna Jameson's repu- tation as a writer had finally been established.[21]

14

Love and Work Enough

ON HER RETURN FROM AMERICA IN 1838, Anna Jameson settled for a time in London with her sister, Louisa Bate. Though assured of both reputation and income, her letters for 1838 and 1839 carry a constant burden of unhappiness and difficulty in adjustment, a distress which was less a matter of personal regret at the loss of Robert Jameson than a superficial but nonetheless painful wound to her pride and her conventionality. She was now in a position to enjoy her recognition—the English equivalent of her German triumph—had she been in a state of mind or health to do so. Samuel Rogers begged for her presence at his breakfasts, Edward Trelawney, heartily cordial, invited her to visit, assuring her that she "will be received triumphantly and will find nothing but good men and true." [E 165] Mrs. Austin, Mrs. Grote, Mary Mitford and Lady Byron were all on hand to welcome and to flatter the returned traveller, but to Catherine Sedgwick Anna confided: "as they say the little cat that has been scalded dreads fire and water, so I dreaded, with an absolutely morbid terror, any new interest, any new *object* and any new liaison." [M 145]

It is also possible that the death of a friend, Henry Behnes Burlowe, in the summer of 1837 may have been a more important cause of her grief. Of his death Anna writes to Ottilie:

I defer weakly to tell what I can scarcely bear to write, it is so very painful.—Dearest Ottilie, my life has been darkened since I wrote to you last and I am suffering from a heavy blow. I have lost my best friend, the dearest to me on earth. The Cholera was raging around him. He refused to fly, but remained to give aid and comfort to others, and so he perished.— I neither repine at the will of God nor give way to tumultuous despair; but all my past, present and future are discoloured and darkened, and nothing can ever be the same to me as it *has been*. Remember, dear Ottilie, that I ask no sympathy and can endure no words of consolation from anyone on earth,—not even from *you*. I know you will feel for me and with me, but under the degree of pain I now suffer and must suffer for a long time, perhaps always, only *one* voice could speak comfort to me, and that voice I shall hear no more. So let it rest between myself and the God who made me what I am, to endure silently and sternly what must be endured. [N 101]

Nowhere else in Anna's records are we given indication of a special friendship with Henry Burlowe, though we are told that it was he who introduced her to Robert Noel. The very omission of letters recording the friendship may well be significant; certainly the depth of grief expressed in this letter to Ottilie suggests a close and an important relationship.

Henry Burlowe was the younger brother of William Behnes, the sculptor. Because of confusion between the two brothers, both sculptors, and particularly in repudiation of his brother's notorious social irregularities, Henry changed his name to Burlowe. He was not as talented as William, but he exhibited at the Academy in 1831, 32 and 33 and afterwards lived in Rome where he was employed modelling portrait busts. He is said to have been a person of "sterling character and generous impulses . . . everyway superior to his brother as a man."[1]

Anna Jameson's long-proven capacity for self-dramatization and self-pity accounted, no doubt, for some of this period's uncertainty and mental stress: "I find it difficult to get my mind together for a continuous effort. . . . I am living on quietly; as yet it requires an effort—a strong and painful effort—to go into society." [M 141] Burlowe may well have meant a good deal to her; if so, such statements as the following, and there were many such at this time, demand to be read with sympathy in the light of his death.

After my return I was ill for some weeks; I am now as much recovered as I can hope to be, but my existence is no more the same. Not that I mean to sit down and despair, but there is nothing left to think about, or hope for, or care for as regards myself; however, I *must* care for my sisters and help to support my father and mother, so I work. [M 139]

The most engrossing social event of the summer of 1838 was the Coronation of Queen Victoria. Anna was not so fortunate as to have a ticket to the Abbey, but her letters to her friends speak of her enthusiastic participation in an event which even the crotchety Carlyle found moving. To Catherine Sedgwick she wrote:

I have seen several Americans within these two days, and am much amused by their remarks on the coronation of our young Queen. The deportment of the people, the excellent order, the good feeling prevalent everywhere seem to have struck your countrymen; the police, as vigilant as good-humoured, were present to protect, not to coerce, and the military added to the splendour of the spectacle without infringing on the liberty of the people. My heart was with the mob all day. As to the Queen, poor child, she went through her part beautifully; and when she returned, looking pale and tremulous, crowned and holding her sceptre in a manner and attitude which said "I have it, and none shall wrest it from me!" even Carlyle, who was standing near me, uttered with emotion a blessing on her head, and *he,* you know, thinks kings and queens rather superfluous. [M 143]

Miss Sedgwick played an important role during these months, receiving her confidences and exhorting her to overcome her despondency. To one such homily Anna replied that she could achieve no philosophical acceptance, but at best only a "submission to bitter necessity":

I have a dear family who truly love me, and some excellent friends and a list of acquaintance anyone might envy; but in the whole wide world I have no companion. The two or three with whom I might have *companionship* are removed far from me. All that I do, think, feel, plan, or endure, it is *alone.* Now this unhealthy craving after sympathy, with a fastidiousness which makes me shut up from all sympathy which is not precisely that which I like and wish for, is, after all, one of the phases of disease, and as such I must treat it. You think I am not religious enough. I fear you are right; for, if I were, God would be to me all I want. . . . [M 152]

From London, Anna "cut her tether" and went to Windsor where she took a lodging on the verge of the Great Park. There she could see "the pretty young Queen with all her courtly suite, pouring out of the great gates of the castle on most beautiful horses, and sweeping through the avenues and glades of the forest here." [M 146]. From Windsor she wrote to Catherine Sedgwick of the first improvement in her state of mind: "In London, with a large and brilliant circle of acquaintances, I led a distracted heartless life. I thought it right to go on trying to keep up certain social interests and tastes, and I tried in vain . . . here I dwell, work, write, speculate and am better certainly than at any time since my arrival." [M 145]

The need of her family for her services, both personal and financial, was at this time a therapeutic agent given its due by Miss Sedgwick after her visit to England in 1839–40: "Our friend Mrs. Jameson I found much quieter and happier than when she was in America—as she should be, when, instead of fighting against the demons of ennui, she is quietly doing womanly domestic duties. What a safety valve they are."[2]

In the future, as in the past, Anna Jameson was to find the dependence of her mother, her father (invalided from 1833 until his death
in 1842) and her two unmarried sisters, Charlotte and Eliza, a burden;
in the year that followed her return from Canada it was she who
depended on their need of her to give her the motivation for action
which she would not have had without them. In the spring of 1840,
she could write with comparative cheerfulness: "[I] do not see that
I can leave my mother while my poor father exists, and how long
he is to linger thus is doubtful. . . . Meantime, though there is much
to be done and endured, I cannot say I am unhappy: my mind is very
serene, and I am so engrossed by the affairs, and interest, and sufferings of others, I have no time to think about myself." [M 165]

During this period, in spite of depression and the predominance of
family cares, the desire to travel, so constant a part of her nature, was
as strong as ever. Early in 1839, she planned a short winter trip to
Germany to see her friends, in particular Ottilie von Goethe who was
at this time passionately attached to Gustav Kühne, a writer of historical novels. Anna was distressed by the dangers of this new liaison
as her letters to Madame von Pogwisch, Ottilie's mother, to Ottilie
and to Robert Noel show. To Noel she confides her despair of effecting
any real change in Ottilie's nature or way of life: "I can never do any
good for my poor [Ottilie], but I may prevent some evil perhaps. It
is quite a hopeless affair, but even for that reason I cannot, and must
not, and will not give her up." [M 158] Her letters to Ottilie are
compounded of motherly concern for the children, anxiety for Ottilie's
happiness, reputation and financial situation, and amazement at her
friend's capacity for emotional involvement: "You are after all the
most strange piece of womankind I ever encountered. You outlive
things which would have killed me dead, long ago." [N 107]

The two women had nevertheless a wide-ranging community of
interests representing a considerable cultural exchange between England and Germany, one which was dispersed into the stream of contemporary thought by Anna's social contacts and her various writings.
Ottilie was often called upon to comment upon specific German
customs: "Pray, my dear Ottilie, what are the ceremonies of a
"Verlobung"? In what does it differ from a marriage?" [N 114]
Or, after considerable urging, she furnished a copy of Sir Walter
Scott's letter to Goethe which Anna gave to Mr. Lockhart to
eliminate an impression of animosity between the two. Lockhart
acknowledged her help, inserting the letter in later editions of his
Life of Scott. [N 103] In general, Ottilie kept her friend informed of

activities in the arts, literature and the hectic society of which she
was a member; Anna transmitted to Ottilie an astonishing variety of
information and commentary on the English social and artistic scene.

In the late winter and spring of 1839, Anna visited Germany for a
few weeks, partly to counsel reason and moderation to her impassioned
friend, partly for a change for herself into a social climate which she
found more congenial than England's. While there, she received word
of the financial failure of her brother-in-law, Henry Bate, the father
of Gerardine, for whom Anna was to make herself financially responsible from this time onward. It is unlikely that she legally adopted the
child; it is certain, however, that she undertook to educate her and
that she looked upon her, from this time forward, as a daughter-
companion. To a heavy responsibility towards the support of an
invalided father, an elderly mother and two unmarried sisters was
added the total support of a teenage niece.

Louisa and Henry Bate were in no position to state their own terms;
their financial situation was desperate and they were forced to be
grateful for any help. That Anna was the one to step forward—the
only one of the family able to offer assistance—is more dramatically
satisfying than humanly reassuring, particularly since her new responsibilities were undertaken with a certain condescension and conscious
superiority: "How far Henry's fate and imprudence may have injured
others I have yet to learn." [N 109] She suffered "a martyrdom of
vexation and care" on account of her family—"the exertions and the
sacrifices I must make to bring all right again exceed anything I
could have anticipated." [M 159]

During her absence in Germany, her family moved from their home
in St. John's Wood to a house in what was then a new district of
London, Notting Hill. On her return, Anna made this her home, with
many rueful comments in her letters testifying to the smallness of her
quarters. Her unmarried sisters, Charlotte and Eliza, were trying without much success to start a school. Charlotte's health was not good;
Eliza seems to have been, to her sister Anna at least, of a difficult
temperament. In this project, as in all family matters, Anna's influence
was paramount. In the spring of 1841, she writes of the school to
Lady Byron; the pupil she speaks of had come by courtesy of the
Littletons who had valued Anna as governess and continued to value
her as friend:

We have here a new pupil, a little nephew of Lord Cavan sent to us by
Hyacinthe Littleton—if we had but three more, the current expenses of
the house would be covered—but till that is done I must not think of

stirring or forming any plan for myself. However, we have got over this tedious & expensive winter & kept our heads above water—which is a comfort to me—and I have got some good port wine for my sister Charlotte —& some rose-trees for Mamma's Garden & two loads of gravel & there she is, dear woman, walking about *"superintending her improvements."*[3]

Another trip to the Continent in the spring of 1840 was cut short by a crisis in her father's illness. After a tantalizingly short stay in Paris—"I did not see George Sand . . . my stay was too short" [N 121] —she was called home as she had been in 1833. Once again Denis Murphy rallied, though he was increasingly helpless:

I am here, like a bird tied to a perch. I have not even a home,—only one very little room which scarce holds myself and my books, where I am not for a moment free from interruption, never independent, and Charlotte, the only one of my sisters who sympathizes with me, the one I love most, is always separated from me. I scarcely see her once in the day. . . . My poor father becomes every day more feeble and this severe weather makes him suffer much; he is almost always either drowsy or irritable. [N 133]

Through these years, Anna Jameson looked to Germany as a land of heart's desire. She longed to be near her friends there. To Robert Noel and his wife she voiced her dissatisfaction with England: "England does not suit me, or more properly the way of life to which I must submit in England. The circumstances with which I am surrounded do not suit me, are all against the wants of my individual nature. . . . I wish myself back in Germany with all my heart. Here I have no leisure to think." [M 160]   To Ottilie she wrote of her financial responsibilities and of her plans for going to Germany for a long period with Gerardine, to whom she now refers as "my child." At one time the plans included her sister Charlotte and another child, probably Gerardine's younger sister Camilla, for whom the family was assuming responsibility. There was a suggestion that the party might settle in the Goethe house with Ottilie and her family, sharing the burden of expense which was proving too heavy for Ottilie. In August, 1841, Anna sent Ottilie a rather detailed statement of her financial situation and her plans:

When I leave my house with all debts paid and 100£ . . . in the bank, to be for my father and Mother in any emergency, I shall think I am *free* so far that my duty to my little girl will then be my *first* duty. I cannot have Gerardine with me in this house. . . . She is growing a great tall, wild girl, and requires good discipline.—*Now* I am poor, but after Christmas I shall have 200£. Half of this I will leave with my sisters or for their use, and the other half I take with me to Germany. Part of the year I should stay with you at Weimar . . . and the other part with the

Noels at Rosewitz. . . . I should be able to spend 1200 dollars a year in Germany and to send you besides 50 dollars to make any preparation for me. . . . I could fix next April [1842] for putting this plan in execution. I dare not speak with certainty, . . . but this is what I am now revolving in my mind. . . . My father (if he lives so long) will then have every want provided for, and my sisters beyond the reach of anxiety. It has cost me a great deal to do this, but by steady determination I have done it. I have worked very hard all this year and am very tired and languid. The walls of my room seem to crush me. I long to breathe another air, and my conscience suffers on account of my child; but if I bear this patiently for six or seven months more and practice the greatest economy I can do what I wish. . . . The expenses of this menage cost me this year 2800 dollars in your money. [N 130]

These plans did not work out as Anna hoped; it was some six years before she managed to take Gerardine away for the Continental "finishing" of her education, and then it was to Italy and not Germany that they went. However, she did spend several weeks in Paris in the autumn of 1841, a research and not a social mission, with the Louvre and the Bibliothèque Royal National the centres of her orbit. During this trip, in a letter to Robert Noel, the note of confidence and decision, missing since her return from Canada, sounds again in her words. In a style full of her old vigour, she indicates that the most difficult problems of adjustment are over, and she confirms for the future the choice that she has made: "I do not like new things of any kind, not even a new gown, far less a new acquaintance, therefore make as few as possible; one can but have one's heart and hands full, and mine are. I have love and work enough to last me the rest of my life." [M 177]

In March of 1842, after nine years of invalidism, Denis Murphy died. Throughout the long period of paralysis and discomfort to himself, and of constant care and concern to his wife and the three daughters who were at home, he had remained very much the centre of the family. He was given his due as father and as head of the family long after he had lost the capacity to expect, enjoy or recognize the role.

Victorian family piety and the concern to make of death an important ritual of dignity and remembrance, no matter how excruciating the process and how exhausting the effort, are impressively and painfully recorded in Anna's various letters at this time: "There was terrible previous suffering, a long, gradual agony; but the last few hours were peaceful and without pain. He was conscious, and his mind and affections alive, till within twenty-four hours of his death." [M 183]

The recompense for filial devotion is simply stated: "It is a great comfort to have a father's and mother's blessing and to know we have done our best for them." [N 135]

The core of integrity in Anna's character resided in her sense of family duty. It is true that being the clever daughter and the leading sister was a role which she had assumed early in life and had maintained and enjoyed: it is more significant that for a lifetime she accepted and discharged the heavy responsibilities that accompanied the role. It is possible to analyse Anna Jameson's attitude to her family and its effects on her relationships with others into a tangle of psychological complexity; the terms "duty" and "affection" are the only ones by which she herself would describe or understand her own motivations as she planned the future for her mother, two sisters and her niece: "Only two things seem clear and certain,—the light that is above us, and the straight path of duty before us." [N 128]

15

Lady Byron

THE DECADES of the thirties and the forties, when Anna Jameson was between thirty-five and fifty-five, were the years of her widest activities. It is too easy and quite a mistake to picture her as overwhelmed by family cares, by laborious writing and engraving projects or by her friends and their problems. In truth, in these years she dealt competently with all of these: her interests were as wide as the western world, her friendships were warm on two continents and she combined a busy career of writing with a satisfying amount of domesticity, including the complete responsibility for her niece Gerardine's education for several years. She was a busy and, on the whole, a contented woman with an assured place in literary society and, through her continuing friendship for the family of Lord Hatherton, an *entrée* also into aristocratic country-house life. The two most absorbing friendships of these years were with Lady Byron and Elizabeth and Robert Browning.

Anna Jameson had said long before that her first impression of Annabella, Lady Byron, was one of "implacability." That impression, influenced though it may have been by a romantic attachment to the legend of Lord Byron, could not have been a truer omen of what was to come: the friendship between the two ladies ended in 1852 with hurt and bitterness on both sides. Its course was strange and hectic, analogous in emotional temperatures to the early days of the Anna-Ottilie relationship, but having this difference: Anna looked upon Ottilie as a charming, fascinating, but fractious child; she looked up to Lady Byron, as to Catherine Sedgwick, as a guide and mentor. She writes to Miss Sedgwick: "One of the persons I have seen most of since you left me has been Lady Byron, whose fine and truly noble character improves and opens upon me. I feel as if I could love her very much; but it were a bad calculation, for our paths in life are so very different."

[M 161] To de dominated, to play the child instead of the mother must have been attractive to Anna, who both by nature and by circumstances had assumed the dominant role so often.

Catherine Sedgwick was a gentle and a loving person whose influence was calming and softening, but diffused by the breadth of the Atlantic between them. Lady Byron was a very different sort of person—rich, lonely, compelling, and egocentric, her obsessive doing of good works often dominating, morally and financially, those who were drawn into her circle.[1]

The initial attraction for Anna was certainly the glamour of the Byron name, as with Ottilie the name of Goethe had exercised its magic. Subordinate, but important, was the interest in the "Woman Question" which she shared with Lady Byron. A sense of injury stemmed in part, no doubt, from their unhappy (in Lady Byron's case, calamitous) marital experiences, but their feminist zeal was given strength and purpose by Anna's years as a governess and as a writer for and about women, and by Lady Byron's restless drive to justify herself to the world, to reform and to dominate through various philanthropies. Lady Byron craved the warmth of affection and the unstinted admiration which Anna was so ready to bring to her friendships; moreover, she was flattered to be a part, even at second hand, of the literary circles in which Anna moved. In November of 1839 she was still occupying a pleasurable pedestal in Anna's affections:

Lady Byron I have seen frequently, and the more I know her the more I admire her, and would, I think, love her much, for she has a rare heart and mind. But it would not do; a new friend to me is not a new possession, but a new pang, a new separation. May God only spare to me what I have left, and may I not pass my whole life in *absence*, for that seems my fate. My friends, in the proper sense of the word, are very few, and I am doomed to live in separation from them. [M 163]

By July of 1840, the friendship had ripened, on Anna's side, into eagerness for participation in Lady Byron's affairs: ". . . find something for me to do—think of me as being literally *yours to* command besides being your grateful and affectionate Anna."[2]

At just this time, Lady Byron was involved in one of the strangest chapters of her own story, the attempt to befriend, but also to reform and control Elizabeth Medora Leigh, purportedly the daughter of Byron and his half-sister, Augusta Leigh. Medora was now about twenty-five years old and her life and loves had been as lurid as her supposed father's. It is said that she was seduced, if not with her mother's knowledge at least partly by reason of Augusta's extreme stupidity, by the husband of her sister Georgiana and had borne this man, Henry Trevanion, three children, of whom one, Marie, survived.[3] The most improbable Gothic novel could not out-do the various episodes in this sordid and painful shambles: Medora victimized by the unscrupulous villain Trevanion, using his own wife as a procuress; Medora's accusations of profligacy against her mother, including the accusation that she, too, had been Trevanion's mistress; Medora held prisoner in a lonely *château* by Trevanion and another mistress and made to work as their servant; and finally Medora, ill and desperate, appealing for help to her aunt, to her mother and then, through a solicitor, to Lady Byron. In 1840, Lady Byron met Medora and her child in France and brought them back to England with her, throwing herself into this philanthropy with the righteous zeal she had brought to the reform of Byron himself—and with just as spectacular a lack of success.[4]

In various episodes of this strange, brief protectorate—Medora left England in 1842, amid scenes of bitter rebellion and recrimination—Anna Jameson acted as Lady Byron's agent and as a deputized guardian for Medora, both thankless tasks which earned for her the epithet of "Turnkey" from her charge. Anna's first letters after Medora's arrival in England assured Lady Byron of what she wished to believe —that Elizabeth, as Medora was always called by her protectress, could improve herself, could forget the past, that her childish nature could still be redeemed. It is to the credit of Anna's common sense, however, that the bulk of the letters about Medora demonstrate her recognition of the facts of the case: "I have the thought that perhaps I am doing some little good here—but nothing permanent—for as it seems to me there is nothing permanent to work on."[5]

She managed to retain both dedication to Lady Byron's reforming zeal and some measure of sympathy for Elizabeth, though she speedily decided that in all the protestations of gratitude, the storms of remorse and the tantrums of rage, there was one purpose, and one only—"the purpose to get as much money out of her protectress as possible":

I wish to retain the power of helping her and of being of use to her at some future period. At present this is impossible. The character stands before me in the clear light—she can never again deceive me or give me pain—but I have pity for her—such as one has for a wilful child—one thing in her character has struck me very often, she cannot rise to the comprehension of anything superior to herself.[6]

Lady Byron and some of her advisor-friends tried to convince themselves that Elizabeth was insane and that Lady Byron should therefore be her legally appointed guardian and keeper. Anna argued against such self-delusion with blunt common sense and in evident dread of a possible repetition of a futile and damaging episode in the Byron family's lurid history. She was convinced that Elizabeth was pursuing a selfish end by the most foolish means, taking false views of her own false position, but *not* deranged:

As to taking charge of her [Medora]—you might as well catch the unstable waters in your hand—and to leave her,—while you extend to her money and protection,—the power to do as she likes is to make yourself responsible for her *écarts*—that will not do—your friend, I think, should have no scruples in obtaining for you the whole truth as to her inventions about you and your "debt of gratitude to her" and how far she has imposed on her servants and they on you—know all that you *can*, let nothing have to come out afterwards, if possible—there is such a strange confusion and perversion in her mind that if I did not know her I might believe the brain turned.[7]

This period in the spring and early summer of 1842 was so soon after the death of Mr. Murphy that only a strange complexity of character in Anna would lead her to protest her grief and exhaustion, her commitment to family cares and almost simultaneously allow herself—probably even offer—to become involved in this saga of hysteria, recriminations and doubtful motives on both sides.

In July, she was Lady Byron's agent, taking money to Elizabeth and to her maid Natalie, for their journey to the Continent. It is impossible to read of the transaction with Natalie and not conclude that Lady Byron was, in effect, paying the maid to spy on her mistress: when Anna Jameson gave her the money she impressed on Natalie that she should let Lady Byron know "if E. was ill—or *anything* happened which it was proper for you to know."[8] The gifts of money were hedged with restrictions that angered Medora and produced the tempers which caused Anna to write ruefully, "you know dear Lady Byron that there blow no trade winds here."[9]

Sometimes, in the midst of a progress report to Lady Byron, Anna would be called upon to calm Elizabeth, to persuade her that once as far as Marseilles, Natalie would release the £40 given for her trip by Lady Byron. After such an emotional crisis the letter would be resumed, its very transferring of the storm to paper obviously a useful therapy for its writer: " . . . such instability of purpose, such impotence of mind, such furious excitability of temper—forgive me dear Lady Byron—these are hard words—I hope you will think I have done my best—and ever *the best* that could be done—I think, I hope I have—I can add no more."[10]

Here, once again, Anna Jameson was living vicariously the kind of hectic and passionate emotional life to which she had become accustomed during her early friendship for Ottilie, particularly during the days in Vienna when Sterling's child was born. In Medora's case, however, Anna was not a friend, but an unwanted governess-guardian. Though it is difficult to sympathize with her willingness to be used as agent in a most unpleasant business, the combination of motivations which attracted her can be understood. Her considerable propensities for dominating any situation, especially when her activities could legitimately be called efforts toward moral reform of the weak and fallen, were encouraged by Lady Byron's constant manoeuvres—and then there was as added fillip, the romance of the Byron name and scandal, the "wickedness" whose attraction breathes from such a letter as the following:

> . . . any excess of wickedness in my own sex—even that a mother should conspire against the virtue and chastity of her own child; that she should corrupt the one and sell the other—this even I know to be possible but have always regarded it as the last,—lowest, worst degree of depravity— can it have been in that case—or have I mistook . . . .[11]

Anna also acted as Lady Bryon's agent in the service of her many philanthropies. She went to a meeting of an Italian school to which Lady Byron had sent a donation:

> . . . and Mazzini came up to me with his fine face lighted up and gave me such an *intense* grasp of the hand!—I wish I could transmit it to you herewith—for it was expressive of gratitude to you—and so he said—he it was who first projected the school—his whole demeanour last night everything he said—I though perfect in feeling and in taste.[12]

She acted as intermediary between a master, with ideas of his own, and Lady Byron, in a school which the latter financed, speaking with a sympathy that must have come from her own youthful experiences as governess: "I think his rather pompous manner arises from his having been made a teacher very young and obliged to *assume a manner*—or rather fancying it necessary with boys perhaps not much younger than himself."[13]

Disturbing though it may be to follow Anna's path through this period of subservience to Lady Byron's interests, the attractiveness of such service to her is readily understood. Her sphere of importance widened; she could hope and expect to influence her patroness who wielded the power of her name and her large fortune in her various philanthropic schemes. By no means all of her friends approved. Sarah Austin writes: "All the business of *women's work* seems to me in a strange state and quite out of joint. They cannot and will not do their own work and they want to do other people's. Why is this? And it is true of all classes." [E 168] Harriet Grote, wife of George Grote, the historian, was distinctly disgruntled as she wrote later in a memoir of her "Ancient Relations with Mrs. Jameson" that, "Mrs. Jameson became intimately connected with the late Lady Byron, and was so engrossed with that lady's family and concerns that she ceased to maintain several of her old social connections for some years." [M 172]

She did not lose her identity completely, however, but considered her various commissions from Lady Byron as avocation only, writing gaily to her friend of the unfamiliar fields in which she finds herself: "'Lady Blarney' has for the present forgotten her vocation and instead of 'pictures [,] taste, Shakespeare and the musical glasses' is deep in factory-statistics—allotments, and *Pedagogie*. . . ."[14] She does, also, have the confidence to plead certain pedagogical ideas to Lady Byron. Like so many of the aristocratic benefactors of her time, Lady Byron had no training and no practical experience in the areas in which she wielded influence. Anna had both of these and, when she writes of the education of women, her words have common sense and conviction:

When out with Mrs. Bracebridge [who kept a school and looked after various working-class projects for Lady Byron] we had a long talk about the education of girls—her own experience is not encouraging—and some things she told me were too shocking to repeat—yet she is hopeful of the results of a school in which the girls should be boarded and removed entirely from evil influences—I think it would be possible to define clearly the objects to be kept in view—and the objects to be overcome in such an undertaking. . . . I know you *do* think of it—but I mean as a purpose to be achieved—is not the Hofwyl system applicable in its spirit to the training of women for their especial duties?—this reminds me of the question at issue between H. Martineau and myself, she insists that there is no sexual distinction in mind—I think there is—is mind altogether independent of organisation? . . .[15]

The *Report of the Royal Commission on the Employment of Women and Young People in Mines* had appeared in 1842. In 1843 a series of three articles commenting on the shocking findings of the Commission was published in the *Athenaeum*. Anna Jameson wrote the third of these in which she summed up the *Report* and commented on its findings. She demanded that public opinion and public support come to the aid of working women and provide increased educational facilities for all women. This was her first overt pamphleteering for an improvement in women's rights, though her work had always been suffused with her interest in the subject and her Canadian book, at least, had been criticized for its feminism. She was put in an embarrassing position, however, by her masquerading as a male in this *Athenaeum* article: Lady Byron was hurt that she had not been taken into Anna's confidence and both of them feared that their mutual friend, Harriet Martineau, would be annoyed at the deception, particularly since she had commented favourably on the article and would feel herself duped by her friend. The letters of this March record a ridiculous storm in this teacup world of brittle feminine friendships.

Never again, as far as we know, did Anna mask herself as a male; the timidity and caution which were partly temperamental, partly expedient in a contentious "cause" were discarded. From this time forth, what she had to say about the position of women she said in her own name, finally confident that she would be protected by her reputation or, at least, that it would withstand temporary censure. Further, the climate of "Women's Rights" had altered. Where in 1832, she had been a ladylike pioneer and in 1838 a radical thinker, she was now with the current of a popular movement, both shocked at conditions for the woman labourer and concerned for their amelioration.[16]

While Lady Byron received Anna's slightly sycophantic adulation for her "moral elevation," Anna was praised and flattered by Lady Byron and her circle for literary and critical abilities. From time to time she received poetic effusions from Lady Byron for her criticism. Although she was linked in the earliest one of these to "the poet souls of every age," Anna's critical sense was not entirely etherized by fulsome praise: "Your sonnets contain some of the best—the most nervous and poetical lines of yours I have seen . . . — the weakest lines in yours are precisely those which ought to have been the strongest—the 2 last lines of the 2d sonnet—I do not like 'spirit-bondship'."[17] She was capable of judging the verses of a mutual friend, Miss Taylor, "better than yours," though she softened the blow somewhat by adding, "but the thought in yours is the most beautiful—it is very beautiful and practical!—but as usual you almost strangle it in the expression."[18] The publication of Elizabeth Barrett's poems in 1844 occasioned an accolade, which was certainly flattering to Lady Byron however doubtful a tribute to Miss Barrett: "the sonnets remind me of some of yours—because the beauty of the thought is greater than the force of the expression and she ends the thing carelessly and with an anticlimax."[19]

Anna Jameson and Lady Byron shared both admiration and concern for Harriet Martineau who, in the early forties, was bedridden and considered to be hopelessly ill. In 1842, seemingly at Lady Byron's instigation, Anna visited the invalid at Tynemouth. Her quick sympathies were totally engaged by Miss Martineau and her letters to Lady Byron and Ottilie are full of praise for Harriet's intellect and for her fortitude of body and of spirit:

She is as she described herself, "poor, hopelessly sick, banished from society, unable to follow her usual pursuits and perfectly happy." I found her lying on a couch, without hope of recovery, protracted suffering and a painful death before her. I found her not only cheerful but gay, full of interest about everything in the world, full of passionate gratitude to heaven and to her friends, occupying herself with needlework in which she excels, now and then writing letters, always receiving them with delight. . . . She was ever bright and cheerful while I was with her, and her conversation rich with amusement and entertainment. [N 141]

Harriet Martineau provided society of the forties with a continuing *cause célèbre*; her alleged cure from hopeless invalidism by mesmerism, then her unorthodox views on Christianity and the after life and, finally, her belief in her own gift of prophecy.[20]

Anna was not as radical in her beliefs or in her actions as Miss Martineau dared to be. She was always reticent about her religious persuasions, and when pressed to commit herself, as she was by Lady Byron, she vouchsafed statements of impeccable and non-committal tact: "I am afraid you think I have but little faith—and yet I have some —else should I be *here*? I have faith in God—and I have faith, consequently, in the reality of virtue—in the immutability of truth—in the possibility of happiness—and I have faith in you my dear dear friend— and in your love for me and I have faith in myself—without which could I have faith in you or anything?"[21]

Miss Martineau, on the contrary, was an adept in the philosophies of all religions; she had grown up in a kind of intellectual atmosphere which Anna's home had lacked; she was constantly engaged in religious dialectic and in voicing each further stage of her own enlightenment. Anna was intrigued and stimulated by the strange, opinionated, energetic, and deaf woman whom she visited much as a disciple might visit a seer, and whom she later described, after her cure at her home near Ambleside, as "looking wonderfully well, alert, full of life and spirits, walking seven or eight miles a day, and most enthusiastic about mesmerism." [M 209]

Neither Anna's social nor her family life suffered total eclipse during the years of intimacy with Lady Byron. Among the Lovelace papers as elsewhere in Anna's correspondence are lively descriptions of various gatherings: Mrs. Jameson had *entrée* to a wide range of social groups. One evening in 1842 she was one of a party, which included the

Proctors, Mendelssohn and James Field, the American publisher of the
Atlantic Monthly, at the home of Adelaide Kemble, now Mrs. Edward
Sartoris. Both Anna and Mr. Field report this evening as having a
grand climax, the singing of "We were two daughters of one race" by
their hostess. "Her attitude was quite worthy of the niece of Mrs.
Siddons. . . . Mrs. Jameson bent forward to watch every motion of her
idol, looking applause at every noble passage."[22] On another party-
occasion, Anna tells Lady Byron of engaging in "perfectly beautiful"
tableaux with Lord Lansdowne, the Milmans, Harness, Kenyon, the
Landseers, Procters, "Some agreeable foreigners," and, again, Adelaide
Sartoris, who quoted Sydney Smith's *bon mot* on Paradise: "eating
pâtés de Foie gras with an accompaniment of trumpets."[23]

She attended Samuel Rogers' breakfast parties, attracted by Mr.
Rogers' art collection and his knowledge of the field which interested
her most and by his large circle of friends whose connections with and
reminiscences of a vanishing world of great literary figures intrigued
her: "While at Breakfast with Mr. Rogers this morning the news came
of Southey's death—and Rogers pronounced his funeral oration, avec
beaucoup d'action—I read the letter describing his death—which was
described to Wordsworth—he died quite calmly. The letter reflects
severely on Mrs. Southey—but of this family quarrel I do not pretend
to judge."[24]

Anna's relationship with the Carlyles was a friendlier one than might
have been prognosticated by the first impression she had made; certainly her sympathy for Jane and her awe of Thomas are evident as
she tells Lady Byron of an especially lively visit with them:

> I spent great part of yesterday and today with the Carlyles—last night
> Carlyle was *great!*—thundering away about Oliver Cromwell—of whom he
> thinks "as of a man sent from God"—Even his horrible Butcheries in Ireland
> he called "doing his appointed work" which he "*could not but do*"—as an
> instrument of Gods Justice, and so forth pouring out such a strain of
> eloquence and big emphatic epithets—It was like standing a battery of great
> guns—and this morning he talked all breakfast time in defence of Slavery—
> and called the abolition movement "Twaddle!"—in such grandiloquent
> phrases of Scorn mingled with grim laughter that I stood aghast . . . will
> you believe that I had the audacity to fight him—absolutely to contradict
> Carlyle?—
>   His wife sat by laughing and amused and I left her better—but the life
> she leads, is (for her nature) neither a healthy nor a happy life—married to
> a man of genius "with the Devil in his liver" (to use his own words)! it must
> be something next worse to being married to Satan himself.[25]

In November of 1842 Anna, her mother and sisters had moved to
Ealing, then a small village well away from London. She always

describes their cottage as excessively small—"a kind of amusing and lovable dolls' house"—its largest room being about twelve feet square:

You would smile if you could glance at our little domicile here—I came down on Monday with all my goods and chattels—and the wee cottage contains twice as many persons and ten times as many things as it was ever meant to contain—but much may be done by order and good-will—and tho our intérieur reminds me of the cabins on board of an American packet-ship —we do very well—the arrangement is like an Indian wigwam—we each have our own corner—our own chair—our own drawer—our own peg—our own half of a toilet table—every article, however trifling, has its own place— and all difficulties and discomforts are by some alchemy of good humour converted into a source of diversion—our wants make us witty—our dilemmas are delightful—even poor dear Charlotte has smiled—and she insists that the cottage ought to be called Caoutchouc cottage—because it is so *elastic*—and serves so many purposes—

Yesterday we had not room to move—to turn—as to sitting down to write to you—it was impossible—there was not space to stir my elbow—I stood and worked from 10 to 3—and then from five to 9—today we revel in space and repose and I write to you from my own domain—a corner about 3 feet square. . . .[26]

For the next ten years at least the cottage at Ealing was home to her. Though away from it a good deal, on working and social expeditions, she regarded it as her base and she kept her possessions there. However imperious the demands of a friendship such as Lady Byron's, Anna's sisters and her mother were her primary responsibility and more important, her emotional anchor: "I came back to my little den—quite wearied and exhausted in body and mind and spirits—to find my dear Minnie [an affectionate name for her mother] in her arm chair—the cat minking and blinking on the rug—the kettle singing on the hob—Tea on the table—and all things breathing peace and quiet."[27]

In the summer of 1845, Anna went abroad for a short period, the main reason being the death of Ottilie's young daughter, Alma, and her wish to see and to comfort her friend. Ottilie's letters to Anna, heavy with her sorrow and full of entreaties to her to come and to bring Gerardine, who was just of Alma's age, are sad to read. Some combination of reasons, among them good sense, which rejected the notion of making one teen-age girl a kind of proxy for another one, recently deceased, prompted Anna to go by herself. She and Ottilie visited Nuremberg together and then went on to Venice, Anna returning to England in the autumn after about two months away, ecstatic in her reaction to the charm of Venice and firm in her confirmation of the ties of her old friendship: "When I parted from you, dearest Ottilie, I felt more deeply than I had ever felt before how much I really love you." [N 153]

16

Works, 1840-1846

IN THE YEARS dating from 1840, Anna Jameson began the compiling and editing of works which prompted Henry Crabb Robinson's remark: "She makes books for the great publishers, and having taste and a knowledge of the market is able to edit and be well paid for editing works of taste or commenting on pictures, etc."[1]

In 1840 her translations of the dramas of Princess Amalie of Saxony appeared, a collection which, in keeping with her firm but usually tactful feminism as well as with her policy of red-herring titles, was called *Social Life in Germany*. This book, like *Characteristics* and *Visits and Sketches*, is prefaced by an Alda-Medon dialogue which sets forth a variety of male and female points of view. During its preparation she had consulted Ottilie on many points of German custom and etiquette; the finished work is a product of her interest in German literature, and, even more, of her interest in the comparative status and training of English and German women. She may also have hoped for stage production; Macready, the actor-producer, records Mrs. Jameson's making an appointment to read a play to him and her subsequent visit: "February 14th [1839]: . . . Mrs. Jameson called and read the greater part of her MS.—a translation from a German play by the Princess Amelia of Saxony. There was much to praise in it. Acted Claude Melnotte rather wearily. Mrs. Jameson's visit had knocked me up."[2]

If Anna was disappointed in her hopes for the dramas, she does not show it, exulting instead in "ten reviews of it, and all most favourable." [N 121] Two other books were germinating in her mind and of both of them she wrote enthusiastically to Ottilie. One was to be a history of female artists, a three-volume series on all the women who had made their livings by the "public exercise of their talents," [N 131] whether as musicians, singers and dancers or actresses, and a discussion of their situation and influence on society in the past, the present and the probable future. The other work, in which Ottilie was urged to participate, was to be a series of dialogues between persons, some real, some imaginary, discussing a wide variety of questions on art, literature and morals. Neither of these works came to fruition, though an article on Adelaide Kemble's musical and artistic success, which appeared in *Memoirs and Essays* [1846], may indicate the form the collection would have taken. The dialogues would probably not have differed significantly from the Alda-Medon Introductions to *Characteristics* and *Visits and Sketches*; the "Celebrated Female" compendium might well have been an addition to Anna's works and its stifling is regrettable.

What she did instead of either of these was to undertake the cataloguing of the private and the public art galleries in and near London. Her negotiations with John Murray about the publication of the first of these two "Companions" were satisfactorily completed, but the process affords us a rare picture of author and publisher, horns locked in disagreement, as Mr. Murray declines to alter his accustomed practices to suit Mrs. Jameson:

MY DEAR MADAM:

It is with unfeigned regret that I perceive that you and I are not likely to understand each other. The change from a Publisher, to whose mode of conducting business you are accustomed, to another of whom you have heard merely good reports, operates something like second marriages, in which whatever occurs that is different from that which was experienced in the first, is always considered wrong by the party who has married a second time. If, for a particular case, you have been induced to change your physician, you should not take offence, or feel even surprise, at a different mode of treatment.

My rule is, never to engage in the publication of any work of which I have not been allowed to form a judgment of its merits and chances of success, by having the MSS. left with me a reasonable time, in order to form such an opinion; and from this habit of many years' exercise, I confess to you that it will not, even upon the present occasion, suit me to deviate.

I am well aware that you would not wish to publish anything derogatory to the high reputation which you have so deservedly acquired, but Shakespeare, Byron and Scott have written works that do not sell; and, as you expect money for the work which you wish to allow me the honour of publishing, how am I to judge of its value if I am not previously allowed to read it?[3]

Anna capitulated. The work involved was tedious, but the payment was handsome by the standards of the 1840s and from a letter to Robert Noel one infers her satisfaction at being chosen for the work, although she protests that Dr. Waagen, head of the Berlin gallery, would have been a better choice:

I believe I told you that I had undertaken a new book called a 'Companion to the Galleries of Art.' It has proved a most laborious affair; the research and accuracy required have almost beaten me, and I am not easily beaten. It is a sort of thing which ought to have fallen into the hands of Dr. Waagen, or some such bigwig, instead of poor little me. And that being at some distance from town, and without any near assistance, sympathy, or companionship, my difficulties have been much increased by circumstances. I am to receive 300 £ for it (one volume), and I expect it will be finished by next February. The printing has begun, and what with preparing MS., hunting dates and names through musty ponderous authorities, travelling to the British Museum, wearing out my eyes over manuscript or ill-printed catalogues, and correcting the press to keep up with the printers, the most irritating thing possible, I have never one moment of leisure in the week. [M 172]

The publication of the two catalogues—the *Handbook to the Public Galleries of Art in or near London* (National Gallery, Windsor Castle, Hampton Court, Dulwich Gallery, Soane's Museum, Barry's Pictures) [1842] and the *Companion to Private Galleries of Art in London* (Buckingham Palace, Bridgewater, Sutherland, Grosvenor, Lansdowne, Sir Robert Peel's, Samuel Rogers') [1844],—indicates a growing public interest in and a market for works on art. After them she began to specialize in the field of art, where she was to become one of the arbiters of public taste both in Victorian England and in America. The Queen herself was pleased to receive a presentation copy of the first handbook. The Hon. Amelia Murray, the same lady-in-waiting who had presented Anna's *Winter Studies* to the Queen, wrote: "I was gratified to see that your catalogue elicited one of her beaming smiles, such as are rarely bestowed save upon her own husband. Few are yet sensible what a fascinating creature she is."[M 168]

In February of 1842 the *Athenaeum* dedicated its leading article to a favourable review of the first catalogue, describing it as "one of the best executed works which has been turned out in these days of broken literary promises and unfulfilled literary duties."[4] Harriet Martineau echoed public with personal approval as she wrote: "How pleased I was to see the 'Athenaeum' notice of it and some others! It must be about as difficult a work to do well as one could set himself to, requiring a variety of powers of knowledge, and thoroughly good judges seem to think you have done it." [M 182]

During the preparation of the second catalogue, Anna was given access to the private collection of Sir Robert Peel. The British Museum preserves an interchange of letters between them, fulsomely flattering on her part, models of polite courtesy on his, as he graciously accepts the dedication of the completed volume: "I assure you with perfect truth that I consider myself amply repaid for any information which I had it in my power to give you by the opportunity of making your personal acquaintance."[5]

A work which was a mark both of Anna's friendship with Robert Noel and her admiration of Dr. Waagen, the Director of the Berlin Gallery, the admired "bigwig," as they called him, of the German art world, had appeared in 1840. The publication of *Rubens: His Life and Genius*, translated from the German of Dr. Waagen, with an Introduction by Mrs. Jameson, had been negotiated by Anna. Robert Noel was the translator, to whom she relayed the publishers' proposals: "Saunders and Otley will, if you like it, publish the paper on Rubens . . . in a series of articles . . . they will subsequently publish the whole at their own risk, dividing the profits, if any, fairly with you. I would look over it and correct it for the press." [M 149]

Neither Anna's concern for her friends nor her industry can ever be questioned. During the early forties she was a close friend of Harriet Grote, whose letters were the liveliest, next to Fanny Kemble's, of all Anna's correspondence. Mrs. Grote was an outspoken, witty, eccentric Victorian "blue-stocking," though, to quote John Steegman, she "habitually wore red ones."[6] Her letters to Anna are markedly about *her* affairs, in particular her hopeless and, in retrospect, amusing efforts to bring some semblance of respectability to the life and social career of her protégé, the dancer Fanny Ellsler. Anna refused to be drawn far into the Grote-Ellsler orbit; she could, upon occasion, restrain her managing tendencies in favour of circumspect non-intervention. Mrs. Grote bombarded her with horrified but enthralled accounts of Fanny's peccadilloes, but obviously bore her no grudge for declining close association. [E IX]

Through her social connections, she helped Anna in her study of art history and literature. In 1840 the two ladies made a tour whose ultimate goal was a visit with Sydney Smith in Somersetshire. *En route*, however, Mrs. Grote introduced Anna to several of the finest private collections in England—Lady Pembroke's at Wilton, Sir Richard Colt Hoare's at Stowhead, Mr. Mile's at Leigh Court, and the Marquis of Lansdowne's at Bowood: "The visit afforded Mrs. Jameson, as well as myself, great pleasure and instruction." [M 171]

In 1841 Anna wrote a series of articles on the early Italian painters for the *Penny Magazine*. These were successful for both author and publisher; the circulation of the magazine increased and in 1845 the series was collected under the title *Memoirs of Italian Painters*. It was commended in the *Athenaeum* of August 16 for its price (one shilling) and for its purpose—"the artistical education of the masses." [M 174] This collection, like *Characteristics of Women*, was reprinted many times in England and America; twelve editions are listed in the Library of Congress and British Museum catalogues. In 1862 it was translated into French, with a Preface which was a fair enough assessment of Anna's talents and influence as an art critic:

Mrs. Jameson parle des arts en Anglaise qui examine tout avec scrupule, en femme qui aime passionnément la peinture, en touriste qui, ayant beaucoup vu et beaucoup voyagé, n'est nullement exclusive; en erudite qui, ayant immensément lu, compare les opinions de tous avant de faire valoir les siennes. Cependant la réunion de ces différentes qualités ne ferait pas encore du livre de Mrs. Jameson un livre d'une lecture facile et agréable, commode à consulter dans un salon, tel enfin que bon nombre de personnes qui, sans être artistes, aiment cependant les arts sans trop vouloir les approfondir, avaient le droit de l'exiger, si Mrs. Jameson n'avait été avant tout un écrivain d'un tact exquis, d'un goût parfait, qui juge les peintres en véritable connaisseur et en parle en femme de monde. [M 174]

Anna's comments to Lady Byron on the success of this effort show her both pleasurably flattered and naïvely impressed by the amount and quality of the attention she was getting: "My essays have been successful if I may trust the letters I receive—one of eight pages last week from Mr. Oldfield, Fellow of Oxford—but with *Latin* quotations—enough to make me desperate."[7]

Howard Mumford Jones speaks of the *Memoirs* as the beginning of Anna's "enormous appeal" in America and of the "innumerable reprints" of her works there.[8] Certainly these early art works, easily readable and cheaply available, at once fostered and answered a growing public taste and demand. Art was moving away from its former position as the prerogative, the hobby and amusement of the aristocracy, a few of whose members had commissioned and collected with informed taste, more of whom had collected and preserved as a decorative accessory or a form of family-ancestor reverence. Masses of people now wished to be informed; many were caught in the age-old snob appeal of being in tune with the intelligentsia, but many others had an eagerness to be taught and to appreciate aesthetic values which must be respected, though it is often deplored as producing a narrow didacticism in art criticism and a lamentable vulgarity in public taste.

Some of the fruits of Anna's quick trip to Italy, in 1845, may be seen in her compilation *Memoirs and Essays*, published in 1846. In particular, her enthusiasm for Venice and its art and architecture—an enthusiasm which was to be voiced more influentially by her younger contemporary, John Ruskin—is as evident in "The House of Titian" as it is in her letters during this trip: "Did you [C. Sedgwick] visit Venice? I forget. In the world there is nothing like it. It seems to me that we can find a similitude for everything else, but Venice is like nothing else—Venice the beautiful, the wonderful!" [M 171] "The House of Titian" expressed certain ideas which were important in the thought of the 19th century. If one takes its motto,

> 'For the painter
> Is not the painter only, but the man;
> And to unfold the human into beauty
> That also is art.'

and the contention, expressed in the essay, that art is not the medium of expression for the present age (about which Elizabeth Barrett records her disapproval), the step is a small one and a logical one to the influential strictures which Ruskin pronounced two years later in his "Nature of Gothic." This is not to say that John Ruskin's genius found its genesis in the work of Anna Jameson; it *is* to say, however, that certain ideas were current and operative at that time and that Ruskin found a public already prepared and disposed to listen to him directing such ideas into powerful dogma.[9]

Memoirs and Essays is a mixed bag of themes. An article on Adelaide Kemble, containing some comments on women artists, is the only surviving, and probably the only finished, portion of the work on female artists that Anna Jameson had planned in the thirties. The biography and appreciation of Washington Allston, American painter, is similar—and the only published part of her projected work on the arts in America. Her essay on Allston is a tribute to the gentle wisdom she found in the man, to his pervasive influence on the Boston *literati* of his day and to her own bent toward sentimental biography.

For the rest, the essay on the Xanthian marbles is distinguished by two translations by Elizabeth Barrett Browning, one in blank verse and one, less felicitously, in hexameter couplets, of the story of the daughters of Pandarus from the *Odyssey*. The two "Rights of Women" pieces, "Women's Mission and Women's Position" and the "Relative Position of Mothers and Governesses," were expansions of earlier works. The first of these had been the *Athenaeum* article of 1842 on the Royal Commission *Report*; the second had been first undertaken as a pamphlet to draw the attention of the public to the wretched lot of most governesses and, in particular, to bring support to the Governesses'

Benevolent Association."[10] The conclusion of the collection is indicative of her attitude toward the whole "Women's Rights" movement: ". . . there is no remedy to be looked for but in the general advance of society through the influence of enlightened Christianity . . . there is no amelioration to be hoped for but in individual efforts, and in bringing as much as possible of conscience and benevolence to bear upon it on both sides." [*ME* 298]

Memoirs and Essays fits her own description of the earlier *Visits and Sketches*—"a collection of fugitive pieces." Its very collection and publication provides further evidence of the stability of her reputation and the popularity of her work with the reading public of her day.

Through the forties, her serious professional interests were directed more and more towards the history of art and of artists. In a sense, she was serving a second apprenticeship as a writer, this time in the field which had always been her major interest.

17

The Brownings and Italy

THE PLAIN-LIVING and high-thinking gloom which surrounded Lady Byron and all those who entered her orbit is dispelled by many vignettes of brightness in the friendships of Anna Jameson, among them none more shining than her association with Elizabeth and Robert Browning. She was introduced to Miss Barrett by John Kenyon in 1844, shortly after Browning himself met the invalid poetess. Mrs. Jameson did not immediately make a good impression, but when her interest was involved Anna was nothing if not persistent in her attentions, and soon Miss Barrett began to warm toward the visitor; throughout the days and months of the Brownings' courtship there are many references in letters to the opinions and general good offices of Mrs. Jameson who, for some time at the beginning of the friendship, lived with a friend, Caroline Kindersley, at 51 Wimpole Street, almost on Elizabeth's doorstep.[1]

Anna Jameson, Mr. Kenyon, Miss Mitford and Robert Browning were the only visitors sure of admittance to Elizabeth's presence, and Anna was quick to observe the growing devotion between the two poets. As plans for their marriage and elopement were formed, one of the considerations of the lovers was whether or not to tell Mrs. Jameson, who had been "so kind," who had urged, and was still urging, Elizabeth to accompany her to the Continent for her health's sake. Robert Browning, though he encouraged his "dearest Ba" to do as she wished in the matter, plainly preferred that the secret remain theirs. Elizabeth felt herself pressed by Anna's kindness and concern for her recovery and avowed that, though she would not go to the Continent under Mrs. Jameson's care, she would do so soon and with efficient arrangements made for her health's sake.[2]

With so much admitted, one would have to be far less acute and much less curious than Anna Jameson to miss the air of excitement and secrecy which must have pervaded the invalid's presence. She was certainly unaware of details of the elopement however; moreover, she admirably kept to herself whatever suspicions she had of such an event. She went on with arrangements to take Gerardine to the Continent, a project which she had planned since before Mr. Murphy's death in 1842, but which had been postponed repeatedly for one responsibility after another. She urged Elizabeth Barrett to accompany them right up until the time of her departure in the second week of September, 1846, and Elizabeth and Robert did seriously consider travelling with Mrs. Jameson. In fact, they arrived in Paris shortly after Anna had established herself there with her niece. The "surprise," which Gerardine reports as her aunt's reaction, was "something almost comical, so startling and unexpected was the news" and may well have been superficial only, the conventionally correct response on such an occasion.

Until recently, it has been all too easy to see Anna as a busybody and a tiresome interloper on the honeymoon of the most celebrated lovers of the nineteenth century: "Mrs. Jameson lost no time in going to the hotel where her friends were staying, and induced them to come at once to the quiet *pension* in the Rue Ville l'Evêque, where she herself was living. The result of all which was that, after about a fortnight spent together in Paris, the whole party travelled leisurely south to the Brownings' destination, Pisa." [M 231] In fact, however, as attested by the warmth of their future friendship for Anna, as well as by Gardner Taplin and Dorothy Hewlett, the two most recent and definitive of Mrs. Browning's biographers, the eloping couple were delighted to rest upon the advice of one who was both a veteran traveller and a kind friend. Elizabeth Browning was exhausted with the excitement of the elopement and the fatigue of travel by the time she reached Paris. Anna's sympathy and dismay sound equally heartfelt as she writes of her new charges: "I have also here a poet and a poetess—two celebrities who have run away and married under circumstances peculiarly interesting, and such as render imprudence the height of prudence. Both excellent, but God help them! for I know not how the two poet heads and poet hearts will get on through this prosaic world. I think it possible I may go on to Italy with them." [M 229] The four did travel together to Pisa. The journey was one of intense romantic delight to the sixteen-year-old Gerardine, its highlight a pilgrimage to Vaucluse, where Robert Browning "took his wife up in his arms, and, carrying her across through the shallow curling waters, seated her on a rock that rose throne-like in the middle of the stream. Thus love and poetry took a new possession of the spot immortalised by Petrarch's loving fancy." [M 232]

For Anna, whose travelling acumen and sense of responsibility were both in full play, the journey had many tensions and was "in some respects a happy one, in others most anxious and tedious. My poor invalid friend suffered much from fatigue; and, considering that she had passed seven years without ever leaving her room, you can imagine what it was to convey her from Paris to Pisa." [M 234] From daily observation she became increasingly optimistic about the Brownings' practicality, and therefore about their chances for happiness in marriage. Elizabeth she called at the end of six weeks "rather transformed than improved" in health. She wrote to Lady Byron from Pisa:

. . . we are in no haste to part from our friends. They have settled themselves in a comfortable lodging—and all their arrangements are as sensible as if they had never spoken anything but prose in their lives and they are so happy!—and the *quality* of the happiness is so rare and so fine:—O if it may but last! I have a letter from Kenyon today in which he tells me that he had considered her—with all her fine qualities of mind and heart as doomed to end her days in her sick room . . . what would he say if he saw B—carrying his wife up and down two flights of stairs—hanging over her as if she were something spared to him for a while out of heaven! . . . we are together every day and sometimes for nearly the whole day—never weary as it should seem of each other—and if I talk of going on to Florence,—such a shade comes over the countenance of both—I cannot but feel it—and Gerardine!—she will certainly be improved by all she hears—I would desire nothing better or higher for her just at this period of her life—[3]

After three weeks in Pisa, Mrs. Jameson and Gerardine left the Brownings comfortably established and went on to Florence: "I left Pisa with exceeding regret—or rather our friends there—the attachment on all sides seemed to gather strength daily and it was time to part—since our existence was to be of necessity divided. Not often have four persons so different in age, in pursuits—and under such peculiar circumstances been so happy together."[4] Many letters to her from Elizabeth and Robert Browning demonstrate the quality of the friendship that had been cemented by travel and that remained close until Anna's death. She had become "Aunt Nina" or "Moña Nina" to them and her departure for Florence was followed by messages of most obvious warmth: "Kind dearest friend, keep on making me happy by such letters with good news of yourself. . . . Good, best bye, Dear Aunt and Dear Geddie—RB."[5]

The sensitive kindness and the intelligence which emanated from the Brownings bathed in a gracious light themselves and all their relationships. The many letter records of their long friendship with Anna Jameson are no exception. They show Anna at her most appealing, as a wise and sought-after friend whose welfare and opinions were cherished equally: "So we shall be arrived six days before you,—and the good seventh, blessed in all ways, will bring you to us. . . . Do you think we would let you leave Italy without seeing us?"—And as for seeing anybody else, you *cannot* . . . for our current of talk will hold out two mortal days and then be unexhausted, be sure![6]

Arriving in Florence in November, Anna and her niece stayed briefly at the home of Sir Charles Herbert whose wife had been a girlhood friend of Mrs. Murphy, and whose daughters spoke Italian well and were pleasant companions for a sixteen-year-old. Then they moved to lodgings which Anna describes as spacious, with "an ante-room, sitting-room, and two bed-rooms, all large handsome rooms! [at 15 piastres a month]—and this sum includes linen, plate and service. Our expenses of living I calculate at thirty-five piastres—about 12£ English money per month altogether." [M 234]

The trip was designed to provide a kind of finishing school for Gerardine's education—polite society, the accomplishment of languages, training in art appreciation and, more than that, an apprenticeship to her aunt's sketching and engraving labours were all on the list of requirements. In a letter to Lady Byron Anna, whose penchant for the improving of others was insatiable, sounds regrettably like that lady herself: "I have to contend with some bad habits and some hereditary faults but the sweetness of the temper and the exceeding quickness of perception render her a charming companion. I am a little afraid of her being led into some dissipation here—of course it depends on myself how far I shall allow it—and I will do my best for her."[7] Gerardine's own account of life with her aunt reflects nothing but pleasure and gratitude and the "improvement" which Anna so zealously cultivated for her. In Rome, where they settled for the winter, she writes that her aunt is a considerable figure in Anglo-Italian society, exerting the influence of a kind of artistic duenna from her residence overlooking the Spanish Steps:

Our rooms were over Spithover's shop [Piazza di Spagna], with little balconied windows looking out over all the amusing scenes in the Piazza, the sparkling of the great fountain, and the picturesque figures, models, and contadini, that group themselves upon the Spanish steps, so familiar to all visitors of Rome. We had a large old-fashioned drawing-room, hung with dim long mirrors, that gave a shadowy unreality to everything they reflected. . . . Here my aunt sat, always with a certain gentle dignity; for though she was not fond of being looked on as a lion, she was far from being destitute of a sense of her own well-won honours, and felt the social homage she received in her own house to be her due. [M 242]

Rome in this particular winter was crowded with visitors who came seeking sunshine and culture, and these at reasonable rates. "Father Prout," the correspondent for the *London Daily News*, announced Anna's arrival as an addition to the congregation of "the female literary celebrities" present, and his or other correspondents' despatches must have sparked this letter to mother and sisters at home:

You amuse me with the newspaper accounts of my doings. I have very pleasant *soirées* on Sunday evenings, which are liked; but my room is so small that I cannot have above twenty people, and I give them only tea, at the dispensing of which Gerardine officiates very prettily. I never go out, because if I went to one place I must go to another. I let Gerardine go out occasionally with dear Mrs. Reid, but seldom, for the little head cannot stand it. [M 238]

The days were spent in studying masterpieces of painting and sculpture with the minutest care, in sketching paintings, particularly their details of composition, and in training Gerardine to be as meticulous in her cataloguing and sketching as Anna was herself. She and her niece sketched hundreds of outlines, made hundreds of tracings and transferred these to drawings on wood plates to be sent home to be engraved for the many illustrations which her work in progress required.

The atmosphere of her aunt's celebrity and unremitting industry was a somewhat rarefied one for an impressionable sixteen-year-old, recently within the aura of the Brownings' romance and herself considerably fêted among the English circle of Rome for her own attractive youthfulness. She was dazzled by the talent and the glamour which she associated with the habitual visitors to Anna's Sunday evening "at homes":

John Gibson, the sculptor, modest and quaint and homely, not yet quite so great a man as he afterwards became; Frances Sylvester O'Mahoney (Father Prout), wearing an ineradicable air of the priest and seminarist in strange combination with his frank Bohemianism; Charles Hemans, gentle, correct, and bland, at the very opposite height of scrupulous respectability. . . . Mme de Goethe came, surrounded by her own little train of enthusiastic friends from Germany, filling the little Roman salon with a perfume of court atmosphere, true *grande dame jusqu' au bout des ongles* that she was. Mr. and Mrs. Cobden—English of the English, in strongest contrast to the brilliant and sentimental Germans—were very constant during their stay in Rome; and we had occasionally Lord Compton and Lord Walpole, then leading artist lives amid the artist studios in Via Margutta. . . . And when all had left, the half-hour spent in discussing the talk and the talkers. . . . What half-hours ever passed so quickly as these? [M 240]

Such an amalgam soon produced its inevitable result, a romance; its hero, Robert Macpherson, was a poor art student, unsuitable to Anna's eyes in every way, considerably older than Gerardine and, seemingly most ominous of all, a Roman Catholic. This was by no means a surprising outcome of Anna's undertaking for her niece, but judging from the many statements of regret and frustration in Anna's letters she suffered all the disappointment of a wish-dream for a child of her own, one whose life she wished to govern and whom she could not bear to set free.

Gerardine and Robert Macpherson were married in due course with considerable laceration of the feelings of all the adults involved: Anna Jameson and Gerardine's parents, Louisa and Henry Bate. Anna had considered Gerardine her adopted daughter for some half-dozen years and had supported her for much of that time, but how far the Bates had concurred in resigning their daughter to Anna's foster parenthood is doubtful. In 1849, when the Brownings received a wedding announcement, they expressed surprise that Gerardine's name had not been Jameson, for she had evidently travelled with her aunt as Gerardine Jameson.[8] Some years passed before Anna's resentment of Robert Macpherson subsided and she was able to reassume a close but radically altered relationship with the niece who had been, for a time, a surrogate daughter.

Elizabeth Browning, who had come to know Gerardine well in the course of their travelling together, was sympathetic, but also a wise and just friend to Anna throughout this crisis. Her letters, while comforting, do not encourage the indulgence in self-pity of which Anna's Irish nature was all too capable:

With the most earnest sympathy I read what you wrote of Dear Gerardine and yourself, and understanding your feeling in writing it, in all its painfulness and tenderness, I understand besides that she *could not* choose as you would choose for her (—the thing is not possible—) and that she has a right to choose, if it is once granted that she is old enough to marry— therefore and whatever your regret and grief my be, there is not room for blame.[9]

And after the marriage she wrote, with a characteristic combination of wisdom and sympathy:

In respect to her [Gerardine], I am very sorry,—I feel a perfect sympathy in all your regrets,—. . . Still we must hope the best for our dear Gerardine, and I am very glad to understand from you that she talks of herself as happy. Life has a great many colours, we should remember, and each is suited best to some particular pair of eyes. Your blue is not like Gerardine's pink, but Gerardine's pink may do excellently for Gerardine notwithstanding— Ah, but I am sorry that it isn't Gerardine's blue instead—very sorry I am, both for her and for you.[10]

Because of the sudden flowering of Gerardine's romance, the stay in Europe, which was to have been of two years' duration, was cut short in the autumn of 1847. The travellers returned to England, Gerardine to her parents' home, where a waiting period was imposed on herself and Robert Macpherson, and Anna to her mother and sisters at Ealing. There was always both welcome and need for her there—and work enough indeed, in the preparation of her next book, the first two of the volumes that Howard Munford Jones calls her "mighty triptych" on the history of art.[11]

18

Sacred and Legendary Art

THE TWO VOLUMES published by Longmans in 1848 as *The Poetry of Sacred and Legendary Art* mark a new level in Anna Jameson's literary career. With their successors, *Legends of the Monastic Orders* (1850), *Legends of the Madonna* (1852) and *History of Our Lord*, the last a two-volume edition finished and printed in 1864 after Anna's death, they formed the series now known as *Sacred and Legendary Art*, which was reissued again and again in England and in the United States and which provided popular reading for the cultivated tourist who required just such a well-bred, informative and impeccably correct guide to the development of artistic appreciation. "Poor Mr. Babcock," wrote Henry James in *The American*, "was extremely fond of pictures and churches, and carried Mrs. Jameson's works about in his trunk; he delighted in aesthetic analysis, and received peculiar impressions from everything he saw."[1]

So soon after Anna's time was a reaction to set in against the taste of the Victorian middle-class, and so sweeping did that reaction become as it gathered intellectual and then popular momentum that James's needle-thrust would seem to have been the pattern of all the commentary upon her work. This is far from the case—in the decade when the first of these volumes was printed, "Art for morality's sake" was the accepted tenet and Anna in her introduction decries "mere connoisseurship" with its stress on Taste, the Sublime, the naming and dating of painters and schools at the expense of "the true spirit and significance of works of Art, as connected with the history of Religion and Civilisation."

Such a publication as this one was a step, and a fairly significant one, in informing the nineteenth century's great and growing reading public. The demand for knowledge and for cultivation of taste spread rapidly in the wake of the financial rewards of the Industrial Revolution. From the few cultivated milords who were the eighteenth century's art patrons to the wives and daughters of the John Bull manufacturers of the nineteenth century was a giant step toward a mass audience, inevitably carrying with it a trend to conformity, timidity and a worship of the genteel. But for this market all of Anna's works had been designed—and now with a certain knowledge of its needs and desires, made the more forceful because they were sincerely her own, she spoke to her public on art.

Anna had undergone continuous self-education in the knowledge and appreciation of art since her first travels and the publication of the *Diary*, but she had found support and a direction for her beliefs and predilections about art in Alexis François Rio's *De l'art chrétien*, called in translation *The Poetry of Christian Art*. In 1841 her meeting with Rio in Paris she called "the great event of my life" [M 176] and on her subsequent visits to the Louvre with Rio "at my elbow" she "profited accordingly" from her guide's knowledge and instruction. She was sympathetic to Rio's passionate defence of the early painters and their true Christian spirit which, he felt, was distorted and finally submerged by the voluptuous naturalism and paganism of the later Renaissance. His influence was strong, therefore, on both her theme and her tone, though certainly not on the plan she devised for her work nor the details of its execution.[2]

Her best account of her purpose, as well as an apologia for her work, is found in a letter to Lady Byron who may have suspected her of "Romish" leanings:

The study of art by enabling me to trace all the steps by which imagination became representations and allegories and symbols became facts, lays bare a good deal of the construction of that [the Roman Catholic religion] . . . while I am farther, than ever before in my life, from all capability of entering into this belief, I have more sympathy with its effects . . . a deeper and deeper conviction that this power must, like the ancient mythology, merge into poetry . . . it may, if I succeed, do something for the cause of true art—but certainly it will not aid the cause of superstition.[3]

During the forties, Anna had begun to write on art for the *Athenaeum*, the weekly periodical then edited by Charles Dilke, which was devoted to the dissemination of culture for a well-read public and unusually devoted to Art, in contrast to its notable companions, *Blackwood's*, the *Quarterly*, the *Edinburgh* and *Fraser's*. It often carried reports of Royal Academy lectures or reviews by its art critic, George Darley.[4] In 1845 and 1846, the *Athenaeum* printed most of the first volume of *Sacred and Legendary Art* and part of the second as a series of articles and a trial run for her book. Their reception had been decidedly favourable.

Although the work had been undertaken in 1842 with some kind of an agreement with John Murray, Anna transferred it to Longmans in 1846:

Mrs. Jameson presents her compliments to Messrs. Longman, and begs to know whether they would consider it expedient to undertake the publication of her work, entitled 'Legendary and Sacred Art,' containing an account of the lives, legends, habits, and attributes of the sacred personages whose stories have been illustrated in the pictures and sculptures of the Middle Ages. The work is in two volumes, of which one and a half are finished and the rest in progress. Mrs. Jameson thinks it right to add that Mr. Murray had undertaken the work, but, for reasons which shall be explained if necessary, Mrs. Jameson withdrew the book from his hands. [M 227]

Evidently Mr. Longman extracted an agreement from Anna to finish by a deadline date in return for a monetary advance: "I am sold into a double captivity; for, to enable me to do this [to take Gerardine abroad in 1846], I have done what I most hate—contracted to finish a book in a certain time." [M 228] And, as the date of publication approached, Anna was uneasy about the choice of binding for which she was evidently financially responsible: "I am afraid the book will be too expensive—that my vanity will be gratified at the expense of my pocket. I am afraid it will not do, and begin to wish I had followed my first thought, and published it cheaply. Who buys or reads expensive books in these days? *I* do not, certainly. . . . " [M 253]

The first edition was an extraordinarily handsome one and expensive (2 guineas) by the standards of the forties. Its type is clear and readable, its headings and sub-headings are effectively set off and it is lavishly illustrated by the author's own etchings and woodcuts. These were the labours of Anna and her niece while in Italy in 1846–7. Anna's drawings have a common tendency towards a soft prettiness of feature; in some cases they are more like each other than they are like their originals. But as illustrations in the days before photographic reproduction was practicable, in painstaking detail of attitude, costume or composition, they add much to the text.

The naming of the first edition, *The Poetry of Sacred and Legendary Art*, is difficult for us to reconcile, even with Anna's own definition of her terms:

I hope it will be clearly understood that I have taken throughout the aesthetic and not the religious view of those productions of Art which, in as far as they are informed with a true and earnest feeling, and steeped in that beauty which emanates from genius inspired by faith, may cease to be Religion, but cannot cease to be Poetry; and as poetry only I have considered them. [*SLA* Preface]

If confusion attends this equating of art and poetry, it was a confusion current in the nineteenth century. Rio had made the same identification; John Constable speaks of art as "poetry,"[5] and Ruskin gives an explanatory, if not a more clarifying statement of an obviously current conception:

It is only further to be noticed that infinite confusion has been introduced into this subject by the careless and illogical custom of opposing painting to poetry, instead of regarding poetry as consisting in a noble use, whether of colors or words. Painting is properly to be opposed to *speaking* or *writing*, but not to *poetry*. Both painting and speaking are methods of expression. Poetry is the employment of either for the noblest purposes.[6]

The third edition of Anna's work, revised and printed in 1857, dropped "The Poetry" from the title, and as *Sacred and Legendary Art* the entire series has been known in its many editions since. The volumes comprise, at the very least, a vast compendium of useful knowledge about art over a very wide range, from galleries to churches, from painting to sculpture, from the Ravenna mosaics to the works of the High Renaissance and of Blake, of whom, to her credit, Anna speaks with uncommon perspicacity for one of her time: "The most original, and, in truth, the only new and original version of the Scripture idea of angels which I have met with, is that of William Blake, a poet painter, somewhat mad as we are told, if indeed his madness were not rather 'the telescope of truth,' a sort of poetical *clairvoyance*, bringing the unearthly nearer to him than to others." [*SLA* I, 85]

Art as the handmaiden of Christianity is the basis of the volumes' plan. The Introduction sketches the difference between the "two great classes": the Devotional, "which portray[s] the objects of our veneration with reference only to their sacred character" and the Historical, into which a sacred subject falls "the moment it represents any story, incident, or action, real or imagined." Emblems commonly found in Christian art are listed and explained, sometimes with a knowledgeable nod to their pagan origin as in the case of "The Glory, Nimbus or Aureole . . . the colossal statue of Nero wore a circle of rays, imitating the glory of the sun," [*SLA* I, 23]; and "The Peacock, the bird of Juno . . . signifying the apotheosis of an empress [became] a general emblem of the mortal exchanged for the immortal existence." [*SLA* I, 29]

The first large division deals with the Angels, their history in literature and their representations in art, including a discursive paragraph
on winged beings in ancient art: "Thus, with the Egyptians, the
winged globe signified power and eternity, that is, the Godhead; a
bird, with a human head, signified the soul; and nondescript creatures,
with wings, abound not only in the Egyptian paintings and hiero-
glyphics, but also in the Chaldaic and Babylonian remains, in the
Lycian and Nineveh marbles, and on the gems and other relics of the
Gnostics." [SLA I, 53]

A record of the division of angels into hierarchies and choirs according to Dionysius the Areopagite is followed by a massive amount of
detail on the various angelic representations from the Ravenna mosaics
to Blake. The trend of the accompanying comments and statements
of preferences, eclectic and wide-ranging as they are, is to direct the
reader away from the realistic and "worldly." Michelangelo's angels,
for instance, do not conform to her notions of beauty or of good taste:

Michael Angelo rarely gave wings to his angels; I scarcely recollect an
instance, except the angel in the Annunciation: and his exaggerated human
forms, his colossal creatures, in which the idea of power is conveyed through
attitude and muscular action, are, to my taste, worse than unpleasing. . . .
The later followers of his school, in their angelic as in their human forms,
caricatured their great master, and became, to an offensive degree, forced,
extravagant, and sensual. [SLA I, 81]

John Ruskin made a judgment on Michelangelo that was similar but
couched in more sophisticated critical language:

It is very difficult to determine the exact degree of enthusiasm that the arts
of painting and poetry may admit. . . . An intimate knowledge of the passions
and good sense, but not common sense, must at last determine its limits. It
has been thought, and I believe with reason, that Michael Angelo sometimes
transgressed these limits; and, I think, I have seen figures of him of which it
was very difficult to determine whether they were in the highest degree
sublime or extremely ridiculous. Such faults may be said to be the ebullitions
of genius, but at least he had this merit, that he never was insipid, and
whatever passion his works may excite, they will always escape contempt.[7]

Anna finds examples of angels painted with spiritual grace befitting
their subject matter from Cimabue, Giotto and Angelico whose "conception of the angelic nature remains unapproached, unapproachable,"
through Titian, whose angels are "mind and music and love, *kneaded*,
as it were, into form and colour" and climaxing in Raphael who, "excel-
ling in all things, is here excellent above all. . . . No one has expressed
the action of flight like Raphael except perhaps Rembrandt."

Section One concludes with a detailed treatment of the archangels,
their legends and their various representations, catalogued in a tone

of high, informative seriousness. Anything approaching levity is so infrequent as to be treasured when it occurs, quite out of proportion to its real wit:

In the Cathedral at Orvieto, the Annunciation is represented . . . to the right is the angel Gabriel, poised on a marble cloud, in an attitude so fantastic that he looks as if he were going to dance; on the other side stands the Virgin, conceived in a spirit how different! . . . majesty at once, and fear, a look of insulted dignity, are in the air and attitude . . . but I thought of Mrs. Siddons while I looked, not of the Virgin Mary [SLA I, 125]

As the volumes continue, with section after well-organized section— the Four Evangelists, the Early Church Fathers, the Saints—one recognizes a monumental dictionary-task, painstakingly done, combined with an equally monumental exercise in taste-making. Anna's works go far beyond the guidebook compendium of information to the constant directing of response: though her perceptions are often acute and her pronouncements are always readable, the very plan on which her work is based guides her readers towards a moralistic, pietistic view of the world's great art, a view which, when inevitably diluted in the process of communication, could and did become distressingly shallow and sentimental. When one compares the first four volumes of the series with the final two, *The History of Our Lord*, completed after Anna's death by Lady Eastlake, the wife of Sir Charles Eastlake, Director of the National Gallery, one realizes that Anna's writing could be insidiously persuasive and that her opinions were probably widely popularized because of the ease and warmth with which she expressed them. Lady Eastlake, the former Elizabeth Rigby, who had written on art for the *Quarterly* and who, in the thirties, had probably been influenced by Anna Jameson towards a particular interest in German culture,[8] wrote a clear, but comparatively heavy expository prose. Her work is close to the informative objectivity of a dictionary; Anna's, embellished by the trills and grace-notes both of style and theme that had long since been satirized by "Christopher North" as he reviewed her *Loves of the Poets*, marks her as a constant and conscious rhetorician. To persuade, to convert and to lead are always her goals.

The reviews of her book seem to have been uniformly favourable, often enthusiastic. Anna reported to Ottilie a sale of six hundred copies of the first edition, satisfactory considering the two guinea price and her concern about the competition of Lord Lindsay's *Sketches of the History of Christian Art* (1847). Alexander Crawford, Baron Lindsay, had also been inspired and influenced by Alexis Rio and after a trip to Italy in 1840 he had undertaken to record his enthusiasm for its art. While in Italy with Gerardine, Anna had seen his book and, to her relief, had found it quite different from her own work: "I was frightened by the publication of Lord Lindsay's book, but I have seen a copy, and now I do not mind him; he takes a different ground from mine."[M 239]

A congratulatory note from the venerable and highly respected Maria Edgeworth earmarks the Puseyites, "a vast class of purchasers," as one powerful source of popularity for the Legends: "You ought to have 1000 from them net. I have seen, by turning over the leaves, a vast deal of curious information and such proofs of vast research and indefatigable perserverance and discrimination of work and judgment, as ought to bring you in another *thousand* and canonize you into the bargain." [E 255]

Somewhat late, but gratifyingly effusive, was a note from Henry W. Longfellow, begging her to accept a gift copy of his latest work in return for the pleasure that *Sacred and Legendary Art* had brought him: "How very precious it is to me! Indeed I shall hardly try to express to you the feelings of affection with which I have cherished it from the first moment it reached us, now a year ago. It most amply supplies the cravings of the religious sentiments, of the spiritual nature within." [M 264]

The *Athenaeum*, *Blackwood's* and the *Edinburgh Review* gave lengthy and flattering notices to her work, the latter stressing its antiquarian interest but also accepting it on its own terms as a history of art and calling for the addition of legends of the Madonna and of the Monastic Orders. *Blackwood's*, after several pages of commendatory comment, only adversely criticized Anna's use of "Catholic" where she meant "Romish", and heralded James's callow young gentleman as they concluded: "In taking leave of these two fascinating volumes, we do so with the less regret, knowing that they will be often in our hands, as most valuable for instant reference. No one who wishes to know the subjects and feel the sentiment of the finest works in the world, will think of going abroad without Mrs. Jameson's books."[9]

Anna's own reaction to her latest success and acclaim was temperately and wisely stated in a letter to Ottilie, marvelling that in the midst of the widespread revolutionary uprisings of 1848 anyone could be found to care about her books: "But in ten years hence, where shall we be? and all these revolutions? . . . When they are become merely things of the past, if remembered at all, we are at least certain that Raphael and Mozart and Shakespeare and Goethe will be just where they are now, always a presence." [N 167]

19

Highlights, 1848-1854

THE URGE TO TRAVEL was never far from Anna's thoughts. When tied to her family by cares or by writing deadlines she was restless and planned escapes; whenever occasion allowed, she did escape, obviously finding stimulation and interest in new places far outweighing the difficulties of arrangements and the sheer discomforts of nineteenth-century tripping. In the autumn of 1848, as soon as her *Sacred and Legendary Art* was ready for the printers, she "ran away for change."

She went to Ireland "of all the places in the world, because I felt ashamed I had not visited my native land." The "Irishness" of the Murphys had not been a social asset to Anna in her younger days. Only as she felt secure in position and reputation did she begin to joke and even to boast a little about her background, at first only to Ottilie and later to Lady Byron. Now, however, both her loyalty of race and her sympathy for the Irish people in the decade of the "great hunger" roused her to undertake a tour from Dublin, west through Galway, and then through Limerick, Tipperary, Clonmel, Waterford, and Wexford, back to Dublin. There was a ten-day visit at Langford with the Edgeworth family whom she found "as charming as the world had believed them. Maria Edgeworth lively and full of natural sympathies at the age of eighty-one." But her trip was not so much a holiday as a mission. In Dublin she stayed with the Lord Chancellor, Mr. Mazière Brady, whose good sense and concern for Ireland impressed her. When she returned to England, she wrote to Sir Robert Peel, reporting her observations and urging his perseverance in an enlightened Parliamentary policy toward Ireland. *En route*, she was often disheartened by the "horrible misery" she describes in a letter to Robert Noel:

You will now ask me what are my general impressions. I have seen enough to make me hopeless, but yet I hope. In the north the linen trade is prospering, every loom at work. In the west and south, all society appear to be falling into a state of dissolution. The failure of the potatoes has changed the face of the country. The people die, or emigrate, or crowd into the poor-houses. . . . If governments can profit, as we hope they can, in these enlightened times, by the past, Ireland will not have suffered in vain. But when I was there I could not speculate and philosophize; I could only feel sick at heart, viewing the horrible misery which met me at every step—large buildings, *once* mills and manufactories, all empty, idleness and desolation and starvation everywhere. [M 255]

Though the worst years of the potato famine were over before Anna took her trip, her letter and the following one to Peel (April 4, 1849) add to the monumental evidence of Ireland's misery and England's confusion of policies:

Ealing April 4 [1849]
I hope Sir Robert Peel will not think these few words an invasion of his few days of peace and leisure—I have waited till now to venture some expression of the gratitude and veneration and sympathy which has filled my mind—he will allow me I hope to thank him for his two speeches on Ireland. . . . I returned before Christmas from a tour of three months in Ireland . . . I have seen and heard what will never leave my memory. Not that I despaired. I knew there was a future behind the dark clouds—a light, a hope but all was so distant! the present so terrible! the contradictions and anomalies so perplexing, so startling, so incredible—the very air so poisoned with falsehood—the dissolution of the social elements into a sort of primeval barbarity so inconceivable to those who had not seen it with their own living eyes and the impending *worse* than the shadow of the valley of death—the individual suffering to be passed thro' before the latter could be achieved—so awful that to perceive either hope or charity required an amount of *faith* which I could not be surprised to find wanting often where it was most needed.[1]

As she continues her letter, Anna's timidity of approach is forgotten in a strong defence of the Irish people and an indictment of the English press and of religious bigotry:

Sir, you are right in saying that the Irish as a nation are not disloyal but the intelligent lower classes (and how intelligent and acute and well informed some of those ragged ruffians were!) distinguished England from the English "government"—the word "government" had to them no good meaning—they pronounced the word as if it were a personified enemy . . . and then the incalculable mischief done by a portion of the English press (the Times for instance) by the tone of hatred and scorn of the people as a race and of hopelessness and sneering contempt of all that was said or attempted in their favour which was copied, repeated and disseminated as the feeling of the English people towards Ireland—this was blistering—festering the minds of those who were really loyal . . . while your second speech—battering down difficulties and prejudices gave me a hope that even the dreadful bigotry of a religious party powerful in England, yet more powerful in Scotland—the bugbear hitherto of enlightened statesmen—may give way before you. . . . Only go on! what is mere office to the power you can wield?[2]

She also informs Peel of Lord Chancellor Brady's plan to frame a bill changing, in favour of the Irish, conditions under which land is held, "to enable the Irish Court of Chancery to grant long and improving leases of lands now held under the court from year to year . . . and also one to facilitate the transfer and secure the letter to property. I hope I am not guilty of any feminine want of discretion in repeating this—probably you may know it—if not—some passages of your speech made me think you would like to know it—as a fast remedy?"[3]

To her pleading, Anna received a politician's guarded reply:

DRAYTON MANOR, APRIL 8, 1849

MY DEAR MRS. JAMESON,

—Your letter reached me just as I had concluded reading an article in the 'Edinburgh Review' on 'Sacred and Legendary Art,' and was rejoicing in the tribute of full approbation paid to your 'eloquent and beautiful volumes.'

I did you injustice in feeling some momentary surprise that you could turn from the splendid visions of St. Christopher and St. Catherine to the personal examination of the terrible realities of the west of Ireland.

I wish you could not confirm my mournful impressions as to the present, and my gloomy anticipations of the future. I would willingly have resigned even the great satisfaction I have derived from concurrence in my general views and sentiments, expressed with much force and feeling, for an assurance from your pen that my apprehensions as to the extent and rapid increase of moral and social evil were without foundation.

That assurance, however, you cannot give me, and all that is left for us is to cherish the hope that this chastening of the Almighty may be sent for some beneficent purpose; and that, by awakening us to a true sense of our danger, it may stimulate exertions that would not otherwise be made for the social improvement of Ireland. . . . [M 258]

The only pleasant part of the Irish trip was the visit made to Maria Edgeworth and her family. Maria at eighty-one was still warm in her affections and wide in her interests, living "with great elegance" and doing "immense good." The ensuing correspondence, carried on by a sister-in-law after Maria's death in May of 1849, demonstrates sincere mutual esteem, evidence of Anna's talent for quickly adapting and ingratiating herself to others, particularly useful to her when travelling.

This trip included extremes of experience more various than she had encountered since her Canadian travels. In one letter she reports calling at a Dominican educational institution where she was lodged in the priory and "oh! how you would all have laughed to see me drinking whiskey punch with the Reverend Fathers." The final paragraph of the same letter describes "the most dreadful scene I think I ever witnessed, the parting of about 50 emigrants from their relations; the howling, sobbing, shrieking of about 150 wretches, some whom in their desperation almost threw themselves under the Engine, was too much." [E 253]

After her return, benefited by change and perspective, Anna could regard Gerardine's marriage with equanimity. In the autumn of 1849 she wrote to Catherine Sedgwick:

I hold to the right of every human being to work out their own salvation; and the old have a right to advise, but no right to prescribe an existence to, the young. So Geddie has married the man whom she preferred from the first moment she saw him, and as yet they are enchanted with each other. They are now in Scotland, residing among his friends and relations, and they return to Rome, which will be their residence for some years, in about three weeks. Then I lose my child. . . . [M 262]

In the last decade of her life she was more free to travel than she had ever been before. When she was in London, working or visiting, she lived for several years with her married sister Camilla Sherwin, but she still considered as her base the home at Ealing which she largely supported. She was often on the Continent in these last ten years, so often that she is frequently counted with the expatriate English who made Italy their home. She certainly belongs to the large group of both English and Americans for whom Italy with its sunshine, art treasures and low living costs was a constantly beckoning Mecca.

In the fall and winter of 1850–1 she paid a visit to Germany and to Ottilie, staying with her in Vienna, the scene of the crisis of twenty years before, assuring her friend as she leaves that none of the old attraction and affection is lost: "My thoughts have been so near you, you ought to have *felt them as a pressure*. Did you? No one can be to me what you are. I may be happy or not happy beside you, but to *be* beside you is different, is more to me than to be anywhere else in the world." [N 172] Anna and Ottilie spent the Christmas of 1850 together in Vienna, and Anna wrote home of a splendid Weihnacht festival with many gifts for herself, necessitating a rather expensive outlay in return. She was never in a position of freedom from financial worry. A surprising amount of space in the letters home from this trip is taken up with financial instructions to her sisters, both the unmarried Charlotte and Eliza, living with Mrs. Murphy at Ealing, and the married Camilla, who at this time was furnishing for rental two floors of her London house. Such admonitions as this one give no shining impression of the intelligence of Anna's sisters; they were by now women in their mid-forties, but were obviously less than capable and dependable as household accountants: "I hope that you have all that can make the house comfortable—and receive your money regularly from Glyns and keep accounts punctually and that you begin in the new year without debt and all accounts made up and paid to the 31st."[4] Until 1850, she was certainly accustomed to receiving her allowance from Mr. Jameson; she asks her sisters to let her know whether her "usual Bill has arrived from Canada" because if so, "I will send dear Mama a little more money—trusting always—that your house accounts are quite straight—and that Eliza keeps her promise—never to draw her monthly money from the Bankers till the accounts for the previous month are made up and settled."[5]

Anna's enjoyment of German society was a compensation for such incessant petty worries, however; she was still attracted to the intellectuals and the minor royalty to whom Ottilie had first introduced her and she found the amenities of Vienna, both cultural and physical, particularly delightful:

The theatres are however very cheap and are a great pleasure to me.—the Burg. Theatre which is the court Theatre at Vienna,—is small, but most elegant—the whole of the boxes belong to the chief Nobles, Bankers and c. and it is with great difficulty we get stalls—the prices are, however, never raised—the acting is the finest in Germany, the actors are engaged for life— and when superannuated—dismissed with a good pension . . . I have never seen such perfect acting anywhere—even at Paris—another advantage at Vienna is the excellence of the Hackney coaches, they are like Gentlemens carriages. . . .[6]

She was now past fifty-six and had evidently aged drastically in the twelve years since her return from Canada. The pleasing portrait of her done by H. P. Briggs, in 1835, would now be a poor likeness; always inclined to weight, she had become quite heavy. Her red hair she describes as "nearly white" and moreover, in a rueful letter from Vienna she asks her sisters for some remedy, for she finds it "falling off dreadfully" and has scarcely any left in the front. She now dreads the winter weather most terribly—from this time on her letters contain bitter complaints about the cold and about debilitating ailments which must have been of a rheumatic or arthritic nature and which finally made her very lame. By both choice and vocation she was still the indefatigable traveller, however, and every trip was in large measure a working as well as a social tour.

In 1852 Anna prepared for publication a new and abridged edition of *Winter Studies*, published by Longmans as *Sketches in Canada and Rambles among the Red Men*. Such a title seemed to Anna Jameson neither ludicrous nor tasteless; she chose it herself and she reports her project to Ottilie with some pride, explaining the "Traveller's Library" of which it was a part:

I have been busy . . . on a second edition of the Canada book (for our rail-road literature), which reminds me to ask you if you have heard of the great book shops at all our Railway Stations, and the determination to put down all immoral and unhealthy publications and to supply a cheap and whole-some literature for the popular appetite? (the determination being on the part of the people, not any other interference). For this purpose they reprint in a small form and a large type and for a shilling (½ a florin) travels, tales, poems, translations, and try to banish the vile trash which has been engendered by our free press, 'as the sun breeds maggots in a dead dog.' [N 184]

At this time *Sacred and Legendary Art* was in its second successful edition. *Legends of the Monastic Orders* had been issued in the fall of 1850 and was doing well: "700 copies sold before the first of October" and a new edition imminent. She had found the subject-matter rather more difficult to deal with: "there is a reality in these monkish personages which puts them beyond the reach of poetry, and that reality is sometimes horrible." [N 167] *Legends of the Madonna*, again a more compatible subject, was published in 1852; Anna admitted that she had gained some "reputation" from it, but she confided its pitifully small financial return to Catherine Sedgwick:

My books have gained me some reputation perhaps and, what is better, have given pleasure to such minds as yours. The profit is so small that it is not worth mentioning. The produce of the 'Madonna' (of which 1,030 copies sold this year) is 49 £, which I shall receive at Christmas—very encouraging, it it not? But I go on with my allowance, and my little pension, and scribble, scribble, for love, if not for money. [M 278]

Anna was a recognized and celebrated art authority, the recipient of homage and requests for advice. The following letter is from George Combe, a son-in-law of Sarah Siddons and a well-known phrenologist in the day when the so-called science of character analysis by head-contours commanded more respect and popularity than it does now:

I am writing for the Phren. journal an account of the real skull of Raphael which I minutely examined and measured in Rome. Without telling you at present what it is like, will you be so obliging as to inform me if you know of any work of Raphael's successfully embodying the expression of energetic powerful passion referable to the lower propensities? Michael Angelo's

Christ in the last Judgment and his Statue of Moses, I take as examples of great expression of the propensity of Destructiveness combined with Self-Esteem. Has Raphael produced anything like these? . . .[7]

An aristocratic art patron, Sir Francis Egerton, 1st Earl of Ellesmere, wrote to her describing certain pictures in his collection, a Velasquez which he had bought in Madrid for £17 and a Rubens, which "if Rubens did not paint it, the devil did."[8]

When the new Crystal Palace was built in 1854 "nearly *twice* as large and lofty as the Crystal Palace of 1851" [N 194], she was commissioned to do the catalogue of sculpture, an undertaking published along with several other critical catalogues as *Companion to the Court of Modern Sculpture*. An article on Tom Taylor's *Benjamin Robert Haydon*, written for the *Edinburgh Review* of October, 1853, gained respect then and long afterward as a writer for the same periodical in 1876 looked back at it in approval:[9]

About three-and-twenty years ago Mr. Tom Taylor gave to the world an excellent and judicious life of Benjamin Haydon, in which he said, with great feeling and a proper degree of reticence, all that could or need be said of that most unfortunate of artists and of men. The biography was reviewed at the time in these pages by one who combined with a feminine delicacy of appreciation for the artist a vigour of style and power of criticism which has not often been surpassed in writing on the fine arts. . . . the tragic tale of Haydon's sufferings and death, . . . may be found related with consummate delicacy and judgment in the article to which we now refer. [M 277]

But the rewards in prestige were never matched by financial gain and Anna's situation was constantly precarious since she was always in suspense about the arrival of her allowance from Canada and particularly so when travelling. As she prepared to leave Dresden for England in February, 1851, she reported to her sister Charlotte the arrival of an unsettling communication from Mr. Jameson. She had not heard from him for many years; only sporadic reports from others had reached her and they had referred ominously to his heavy drinking:

[It is] the first letter I have had from him for seven years—it is very disagreeable—confirms I am sorry to say all the reports I have heard of his habits of drinking—it is so confused I cannot well make it out clearly—but he says, that, from considerations of health he is obliged to resign the chancellorship—he says he has been promised a retiring pension but is in doubt whether he shall get it—he enquires what are my pecuniary resources? —I have written a very guarded answer—but a very true one—guarded I mean in expression—before I can do more than merely acknowledge the letter I must take legal advice, meantime he says he has sent the last half yearly remittance—and I hope it is safe at the Bankers . . . do not let anyone know the contents of Jamesons letters till I return—I am not frightened—in fact I hardly know what to believe. . . .[10]

The history of Robert Jameson's Canadian career is depressingly contradictory to the picture of the "Excellent Chancellor" that his wife had predicted he would be. It is impossible to assess to what degree his professional unpopularity came from his own incompetence and to what degree it stemmed from the growing determination of the Upper Canadian Bar to control its own courts without overseas appointees. Though Jameson was the first Speaker of the Legislative Council of the combined provinces, though he held Upper Canada's senior legal position and for two terms was Treasurer of the Law Society of Upper Canada, the highest office of the Upper Canadian Bar, a movement was on foot to replace him as Vice-Chancellor as early as 1841: "As the Legislature are not inclined to give the Speaker of the Council any salary, if he already has as much as £1000 a year from the public funds, they hope that Mr. Jameson will resign the more laborious duty of Chancellor and remain here as Speaker. . . . I fear he is however a failure in both capacities."[11]

In 1848 the Baldwin-Lafontaine Reform party came to power. Shortly thereafter, the Government undertook the reform of the Court of Chancery, increasing the number of judges to three. William Hume Blake became Chancellor of Upper Canada, the office formerly vested in the Lieutenant-Governor. For a short time Robert Jameson continued to sit on the bench as Vice-Chancellor, side by side with Mr. Blake. In December, 1849, he retired on a pension of £750 a year. Anna Jameson received the word of his change in status and income about fourteen months later, a delay which even considering slowness of communication and her travels seems over-lengthy. At least as early as 1845, Robert Jameson had begun to buy land in Toronto, and shortly after his retirement from the bench Anna's allowance was stopped altogether, the understanding being that she would inherit his property purchases. But for the time being, her secured income was gone, the basis of living for her mother, sisters and herself, and she was understandably anxious.

Early in 1851 her friends and writing associates nominated her for Her Majesty's Pension List, the movement seeming to centre around the *Athenaeum* offices. Mrs. Procter, one of her oldest friends, was a moving spirit and Thackeray seems to have been the executive officer as the correspondence was between himself and Lord John Russell. Anna later named John Murray and Thackeray as her trustees [M 267]:

My Dear Mrs. Jameson,

—I am very nearly as pleased as you are, and shall gladly be your god-father to promise and vow the necessary things in your name. I saw Lord John Russell yesterday, and thanked him, and told him how happy some people were made, and what you said about your mother, which touched the premier's heart. And I wished *I* had a couple of trustees and a pension.

For yours very truly,

W. M. Thackeray

The year 1851, that of the "Great Exhibition," was one of national pride and excitement in which Anna participated eagerly. Because of the pressure of work in the preparation of *Legends of the Madonna*, she cancelled plans, projected with Mr. Longman, for articles stemming from the Exhibition about the "tendencies of national character as displayed in national art" and "the condition of the producers and workers in each country . . . this last topic growing on men's minds." [M 268] But nothing could dim the enthusiasm which she shared with her contemporaries, as the Exhibition with its grand Crystal Palace caught and held the imagination of the mid-Victorian English. The Crystal Palace was "amazing" in its height and size and when the Queen arrived to take her place on the throne with its great tree behind, its palm trees around and its thirty-foot glass fountain playing in front, "so beautiful a spectacle I never saw" . . . "the splendid colours, the music, the acclamations and really affectionate welcome of the people became almost overpowering." [N 176]

The Exhibition became both focal point and touchstone for national pride and for national self-examination. Most of its visitors felt some strong response to it, but few were as articulate as Anna, who, after her twenty-second visit, recorded her feelings on the incongruous contrast that was so integral a part of nineteenth-century England and which the Exhibition both symbolized and transcended:

For truly the spectacle now presented in this country is without a parallel, and I am sometimes glad that just at this period strangers should see how much order is compatible with liberty, how much loyalty is compatible with much grumbling, and unfortunately how much poverty and misery is compatible with wealth and prosperity. It is a strange spectacle and one not easily understood. [N 179]

Finally, she describes with particular vividness the triple English benignity of the crowd, the police and the Queen:

It was the *last* day on which the people were admitted [to the Crystal Palace]. There was an enormous assemblage. At 5 o'clock the bell rang for all to go out as usual, but on this occasion the people would not go. . . . the bells rang louder and louder,—no one would go. The organs played God Save the Queen, the people joined their voices, then they burst into acclamations; the voices rose, died away; rose and swelled, till the shouts were deafening. . . . But soon the shadows fell, night came on. There was a sea of human faces around me, and below me 60,000 people dimly seen, and all talking, singing, shouting with a joyous, kindly, feeling,—but nobody would go. . . . At last, when two hours had thus passed and the moon had risen, the Police gently interfered to urge the people to be reasonable and move towards the doors, but they would not hurry, and at length a troop of Engineers, quite unarmed, under the direction of the head of police, formed a line holding each other's hands and thus gradually swept the vast multitude towards the doors. There was no force, no resistance, no accident, no injury to any person, or any object. It was altogether the most sublime and picturesque spectacle I ever beheld in my life. . . . [N 182]

In these years, Anna's energy, industry and enthusiasm for a great range of people and projects did not slacken. They are years of harvest, with reputation secure, status accepted and enjoyed and in her correspondence a noticeable absence of the dramatizing self-pity that used to mar it. In her fifties her presence was considered a social and a literary asset to widely diversified groups in England, Germany and Italy. Even Henry Crabb Robinson, who had, years before, recorded his extremely unfavourable impression of Anna, mellowed his judgment, terming her "more mild and generally agreeable than she used to be."[12] Idiosyncrasies of manner, appearance and personality were far easier to tolerate in a successful authoress than in a struggling young woman who might be suspected of pushing into literary society, and he was pleased to be her guest at tea, though his reappraisal stops short of unqualified approval: "Mrs. Jameson improves on me, she seems more honest than I thought her."[13]

Anna's reputation had been made and her position secured by hard and unremitting work, by constant study, perhaps by a judicious opportunism in the matter of some of her friendships in the early years, but above all by her journalist's talent of assessing the market and writing for it. In significant measure, she was the type of her own reader; as the Victorian merchant's daughter longed to rise, intellectually and socially, so Anna had aspired and, self-propelled, had succeeded. Technically, her teacher's talent for organization of material and for its dissemination in didactic-moralistic channels was her great strength; her natural bent and her governess' career combined to give her handling of the most massive amount of information a lucidity which, if over-simplified, was both readable and "learnable." Above all, she had the toughness, the discipline and, by the fifties, the confidence of the professional journalist without a trace of cynicism about her readers. They, in large numbers, accepted her instruction. From the publication of *Visits and Sketches* in 1834, her works reflected, at the same time as they help to create, the taste of mid-nineteenth century England and America.

Contentment and enjoyment, in both her life and her work, are far more evident in Anna's middle age than in her earlier years. "My horizon widens around me," she writes to Lady Byron, and "I think every day that death will have the more and yet the more to kill in me . . . pray for me that I may not be a fool to the end and die, like a miser clutching his gold as long as his hand can grasp it."[14]

20

A Year of Misfortune

IT SEEMS CERTAIN that if Anna Jameson could look back to mark the milestones in her own life, the year 1854 would have been one of them, and a sombre one indeed. Mrs. Murphy died early in the year. She was very old and had suffered a period of failing health during which her daughters had nursed "dearest Minnie" with the care and devotion they had shown to Denis Murphy through his much longer illness. Then too, since 1851 when the news of her husband's resignation with its dismal implications had come from Canada, Anna had been dreading, but rather expecting to have to make the Atlantic voyage again: "I have had bad news from Canada. That unhappy man has been ill from the effects of intemperance for many months, and they fear for his life. If he dies, they say I *must* go to Canada, to settle his affairs. I will avoid it if possible, but I am in dreadful suspense. I do not receive the money which was settled by law. . . ." [N 95]

Though her pension from the Queen removed the most acute problems of poverty, £100 per annum did not provide a recompense for a separation allowance of £300 a year which, after his retirement, her husband was unwilling or unable to pay. She wrote to John Lees Alma of Niagara to determine Robert Jameson's condition and his reply justified her fears: "Well, he confirms all the worst as regards Mr. J's health and the dreadful habits into which he has fallen." [N 177]

Mr. Jameson may have been totally debilitated from drink; certainly his wife thought so. His situation was a lonely one: in 1844 he had sold the house, which had been finished and first occupied during Anna's Canadian visit, to Frederick Widder, a Commissioner for the Canada Company. For some time Jameson retained a room or rooms in the house, but in 1846 the sale was completed and he moved to another address. There are no records to be found of either Jameson or his activities in the 1850s until the notice of his death in early August of 1854 and the will which was written and signed shortly before:

In the name of God Amen. I Robert Sympson Jameson feeling myself at the point of death I wish to bequeath all my property on Queen Street to my joint friends George and Emma Maynard dated this thirty first of July one thousand eight hundred and fifty four the same to be divided hereafter according to their will and pleasure that have been my kindest friends on this side of the world my personal property to go the same way.[1]

With her mother's health failing quickly and her sisters dependent upon her, the knowledge that she had no part in her husband's estate was a considerable shock as Anna had every right to expect that she would be recompensed in property, at least to the amount of yearly income that she had waived for her husband's land purchases. Furthermore, the Vice-Chancellor's pension had been £750 a year, the registry office records a payment by Mr. Widder of £2000 for the house and, at the time of Mr. Jameson's death, he was the owner of considerable land—Jameson Avenue, in the west end of Toronto, still commemorates his name and holdings. Evidently Robert Jameson's surviving family shared Anna's dismay: she wrote to Ottilie of her brother-in-law Joseph's concern and of a visit to him in Ripon where he was a canon of the Cathedral. Anna made no legal claims upon the estate although she thought of doing so and was, for a time, encouraged by her brother-in-law. The Registry Office reports a deed poll of June, 1855, certifying the existence and contents of the will for Joseph Jameson. However, Anna had legal advice from her friend, Bryan Procter; he counselled her against legal action and she took none.

She was probably misinformed about her husband's beneficiaries. The Reverend George Maynard was an Anglican clergyman of considerable means and a family of four daughters. It is unlikely that the following letter, written to Ottilie, bears the true facts: "Mrs. M—, to whom the property is left, is a married woman who has a husband living; for the sake of money he has permitted an intimacy. The Will, in which no mention is made of Mr. Jameson's brothers and sister, was written a few hours before his death, and his hand *held* and guided while he wrote." [E 284] The truth cannot be ascertained now, but it seems more likely that, as the will states, the Maynards were "the kindest" and almost the only friends left to Robert Jameson when he died.

The story of Anna and Robert pointed from the first toward a sad finish, though it is difficult to believe that Elizabeth Barrett's account of the original cause of the rift, as she wrote it to Mary Russell Mitford, is not over-dramatized. Robert Jameson, says Miss Barrett on the authority of John Kenyon, vowed revenge on Anna because she had at first declined his offer of marriage; he persisted in his courtship with only revenge in mind. As soon as the two were married, he unmasked his real feelings toward his wife and his intention of having nothing to do with her henceforth.[2] The story, as told, bears striking resemblances to the account of the Byron marriage *débacle* which Ethel Colburn Mayne recounts in her *Lady Byron*, and its melodrama is more likely to have its basis in Anna's wounded romanticism than in Robert Jameson's frozen correctness.

A man would have needed a very strong nature to impress itself on Anna's own; this Robert Jameson did not have. "Amiable" and "inoffensive," the adjectives most applicable to him, are scarcely the ones needed to describe the man who could separate Anna Murphy from her family and replace the image of her father, so much the dominant figure in her family picture, with his own.

It may be that Robert Jameson or Anna herself suffered from some disability which made marriage, in any real sense of the word, impossible; Mrs. Murphy was told that her daughter's marriage had not been consummated. [M Preface] It is certain that by the time she was married, at thirty-one, Anna was far less able to receive offered affection with gratitude and reciprocation than to be the initiator in lavishing it—but only on those she deemed worthy. The self-dramatization which was, in her youth, so noticeable a part of her nature and so considerable a factor in the effectiveness of her writings, was also, no doubt, a complicating factor in her marriage. Her early assuming of the Ennuyée mask, the adoption of a role which involved self-deception far more significantly than any deception of the public, played its part in turning the game into reality and the role of the Ennuyée into her destiny.

Anna's frankest accounts of her feelings and her situation at the time of Robert Jameson's death are contained in her letters to Ottilie. "I do not feel grief, but I suffer *pain*," she writes, "Long habits of drinking have almost disturbed his intellect, and all his feelings toward me were very bitter . . . you will see that it is all sad and disgraceful. I wrote to him *kindly* before his death, but had no answer, and he refused to send a message to me." She dreaded most the possibility of having to go to Canada to settle affairs, but had sent "power of attorney" to a friend there, probably John Lees Alma, and she hoped to have the arrears of her income paid from the estate as a debt. Her decision against going to court certainly stemmed partly from her extreme unwillingness to undertake a Canadian trip, coupled with her extreme distaste for the procedures of "law and lawyers and suspense and pain—and all that is detestable." [N 194–7]

Finally, in January 1855 Anna writes of the loss of all hope of redress:

But my affairs are as bad as possible. Not only have I lost all I had a right to of my husband's fortune, but the debts which he owed to me likewise; so that I have less than nothing, and I can no longer support my sisters as I have done entirely for the last 14 years. All gone but the little pension from the Queen, and I cannot work as once I used to do. If my sisters could live without me I should go to a cheap country (Italy) and live there; but as yet all is dark. . . . [N 198]

Once again Anna's friends came to her support as they had done in the matter of procuring her a pension. Again it was Mrs. Procter who led the way, instituting a subscription fund which bought Anna an annuity of £100, a gift of £70 in money and much pleasure in the distinction of the donors, "the Queen, Prince Albert, Lord Lansdowne and others whose names I do not even know and to whom I am *personally* unknown." [N 201] An anonymous friend wished also to place at her disposal £50 a year. Though she refused the latter, saying that she would accept such bounty only from the Queen, she accepted the annuity with gratitude: "I am now taken out of that slavery to booksellers and bookmakers which I so hated and feared, and my sisters are safe. I had arranged their existence for this next year, but what was to become of them afterwards I could not tell. Now there is enough for all. . . ." [M 286]

It was at this time of assorted personal strains that Anna's friendship with Lady Byron came to its final breaking-point. For some time there had been rumbles of trouble, though on the surface the two remained close friends. Members of a literary coterie of aspiring young women with the Procters' daughter Adelaide, their leader, attended weekly gatherings at Ealing at which conversations ranged through the "Woman Question" in all its aspects. Anna Jameson was the mistress of the salon, but her friend Lady Byron was often present, adding her weighty moral arguments to the deliberations and the sponsorship of both name and fame to the group. No account of the final rift between the friends is really satisfactory, but it is certain that, as the Byron-Jameson friendship has been over-emphasized in some quarters, so the crushing effects of the quarrel on Anna have been overdrawn.[3]

In 1852 the daughter of Lord and Lady Byron, Ada, Lady Lovelace, died of cancer after a long and agonizing illness. Scattered throughout Anna's letters to Lady Byron and to Ottilie are references to the fascinating and clever Ada, suggestions that Anna would like to become intimate with the daughter as she had with the mother. It seems that she did so, though no letters between them remain, and that she was in Ada's confidence when Lady Byron was not. Lady Lovelace was a brilliant eccentric as befitted a Byron, a mathematical genius, or considered so in her day, and an obsessive gambler. She had caught the interest of Mr. Babbage, the inventor of the first calculating machine, and he was among those blamed by Lady Byron, whether justly or not, for abetting her daughter's ruin by gambling. Lady Lovelace attempted to devise a perfect betting system and gossipers reported that she had lost as much as £20,000 at the races and that when she died her husband was on the point of ruin from gambling debts which had been kept from the knowledge of her mother, but of which Anna Jameson was well aware. [N 177]

Lady Byron's overwrought nerves after her daughter's final illness were further strained by the publication in 1853 of Thomas Moore's *Memoirs, Journals and Correspondences*, a book which revived the public's interest in the Byron story. Anna writes to Ottilie of a revival of "all the old Byron scandal" and of her fears of further "horrible" revelations:

I am afraid that all the copies [of the *Memoirs*] were not destroyed. I am afraid that now Lady Lovelace is dead much will be said and spoken out which has hitherto been concealed. I shall be very sorry; for tho' I wish that justice may be done to her, so long misunderstood and traduced by the ignorant and the malignant, still I do tremble for the *consequences*. It is such a horrible, fearful, polluted tragedy, and if once the seal of silence be broken, where is it to end? What revelations may be poured upon an astonished world, God knows! She—Lady B—is ill from the agitation caused by all this. [N 191]

Unfortunately, complicating the picture and very possibly producing more tension and more hard feelings between Anna Jameson and Lady Byron, were certain financial dealings between the two entered upon many years before in the full flower of their friendship. Anna had reluctantly borrowed money from her friend, but only after making her own relative helplessness in financial contingencies abundantly clear:

You are free—you are rich, you have the assured power to do as you will and you will what is just. I am not free and I am poor and with the *will* to be just the *power* might be, from various accidents, taken away from me and no help. Thus it must follow that all else being equal, your confidence in me cannot be unlimited and entire. . . . I enclose *my* scheme written down in my own words that you may be sure I understand yours perfectly—

my scheme

I borrow from you 300 £ —you thereupon insure my life for 600 £ (I think, on reflection, I should prefer this to two insurances as it would simplify the thing).

The 300 £ you lend me I place at my bankers—and I use it as a fund for the following purpose—viz. to pay you regularly the yearly insurance say 27 £ and the interest of the money lent—12 £ a year I think,—and by paying down a sum of money to free myself advantageously from all dependence on my booksellers—I saw them on Thursday and found that this would be advisable.—I expect to repay you the 300 £ in two years. When it is repaid you will give me an acknowledgment that I have a right to the benefit of the insurance. If I die in the interim you have the 600 £ and I trust to your paying 300 £ to my sisters.[4]

The payment of the £300 is recorded in the bank books of Lady Byron's account with Drummond's. In 1844 and each succeeding year until 1851 there is record of a premium payment of £13.12. No such payment is recorded in 1852, the year of Lady Lovelace's death; instead there appears the record of a payment by Mrs. Jameson to Lady Byron of £12.[5] Thereafter no record remains of the history of the loan and the insurance policy—but money dealings between the two, especially when Anna's income was so precarious and her responsibilities proportionately so great, cast an ominous shadow on the friendship. Anna's will, dated the 15th of June, 1855, mentions a loan of £300 from Mr. John Scott Russell, engineer, naval architect and designer of the *Leviathan*, the wonder-ship of its day. Mr. Russell was her friend and later her executor; her debt to Lady Byron may well have been discharged with his help. It was Anna's nature to give freely to family and friends; the same cannot be said of Lady Byron, whose various financial dealings with others often occasioned unhappiness and recriminations.

The actual occasion of the quarrel is not recorded; its aftermath was marked by at least one attempt at reconciliation on Anna's part:

If the past my once so dear and kind friend, cannot be restored—at least it cannot be obliterated.

Many things may pass away, but not the least particle of memory as far as you are concerned. It grieves me that pain has come between us—that you are alienated from me and that I can comfort you no more—but let me only know that you are happy—if ever you are happy or happier let me only hear it—no matter thro whom—whatever the healing influence I shall bless it and love it for your sake. . . .[6]

The tenor of Lady Byron's part in the quarrel is best illustrated by the following letters, the only two which Anna kept out of all those which Lady Byron had written to her over the years [E 280-1]:

BRIGHTON, JANUARY 23, 1854

When I received your letter, I was on the point of writing to ask how your mother was, not having heard since the Noels left me. Though I declined to make use of your kind offers in regard to my Daughter's Monument, and to the Robertson concerns, I do not see what *that* has to do with mutual good-offices in matters which are wholly unconnected with either, and the fact that I accepted other proofs of your goodwill since the time when we differed on certain points, gave me a right to expect that you would permit me to render any trifling services in return.

Your habit of fixing your attention exclusively on some particular passage in my letters, apart from the context, or from previous communication, is the cause of your doing grievous wrong both to yourself and me. By thus *selecting* certain words, you deceive yourself as much as anyone else would be deceived by such a representation.

You say "*Be* just," as if I had been unjust! My justice toward you has been *Gratitude*—How could it be otherwise when you, who could so often command the first place in the regard of others, were generously content, as you have told me, with the second in *mine*? But our differences are not, I believe, personal. They depend at least *more* upon my being unable to acquiesce in some of your views on general questions. Would you have me say I think these right when I do not?—Would you have me concur in them when put into practice by you?—Would such a course be more faithful to friendship than to truth?—Of this be assured, that I should live to see my error. It will be a far less effort to me to acknowledge it than to maintain an opinion contrary to yours, especially when I think of you as watching by a death-bed. —In that sorrow I offer my deep sympathy, dear Mrs. Jameson.

Yours faithfully,
A. I. NOEL BYRON

BRIGHTON, FEBRUARY 13, 1854

MY DEAR MRS. JAMESON,—

I must trouble you with the correction of a date, of some importance to Truth.

You say, "I never believed your feelings alienated from me, TILL you told me they were."

Now, on the contrary, in the close of the year 1852, when my whole being was so absorbed that I could not have borne any added excitement or agitation, whilst you were accusing me of being false to friendship, I maintained that I was "as ever your friend"—this passed in writing, for we did not then meet, owing, as I told you, to the peculiar circumstances of my position.

The year following, in Dover St. you drove me, by your persevering attacks, to say something about "alienation"—but if you would look to *facts*, my subsequent intercourse with you, my visits in your society, would shew how far that *word* was from being verified—

You tell me you have "shielded the memory of Lady Lovelace from the cruel world." If the world is cruel, let it alone. If the "Repentance" which is now by her own direction in her own words, inscribed on the Monument to her at Kirkby Mallory, cannot disarm the Pharisees, they must be left to convince themselves. Your reiterated expressions of *Forgiveness*—in fact so many accusations, might need Forgiving, if I were not in so many respects, still your Debtor, in spite of yourself, always so truly

Your friend,
A.I.N.B.

All those who have written of the quarrel have over-emphasized its effect on Anna Jameson. Undoubtedly she was hurt, deeply; certainly she also broke off communication with her constant friends, the Noels, rather than risk withdrawal of Lady Byron's impervious favours from them. Anna both grieved and dramatized her grief as she wrote to Robert Noel in October 1854:

DEAREST NOEL:

—It is a hard struggle but I cannot see you nor speak to you nor write to you about the relative things—you are in every way bound to Lady Byron; be to her all you can and ought to be—leave me alone—I will not see again any friend who reminds me of her. These long years—ten years now—in which I have suffered—first for her, then thro' her—the idea of having been sacrificed when I so entirely loved and trusted—the expression of that face as I last saw it—these have pressed into my life deeper and deeper with time. You do not understand how it is—but be assured that I will do my best and work on bravely. That I may do so—let me not see you—dear Noel—not yet —at least.[7]

However, when this break came, Anna Jameson was a woman of sixty, with several works in progress and dependents, as always, to provide for. To Ottilie, she seems not to have mentioned the quarrel. She wrote briefly of it to Elizabeth Browning: "I got a blow which I expected but could not bear at first quite well—I think my feeling must have been something like yours, dearest Ba—in regard to one very near to you—I stood appalled and petrified before that inexorable temper— but am now comparatively well and at work again."[8]

Mrs. Browning replied with warm sympathy and with an assessment of Lady Byron which recent research bears out:

On another subject I am tenderly afraid of speaking—only, you are better, I perceive clearly, and it is reasonable and natural of you to be better. For my part I have an instinct against certain natures—in women especially. You may stand up very straight and it may be less from strength, than from an unemotional stiffness. You may stand like a card, or like a stone—It's easy to stand if you've no joints—that pretension to the calmness of absolute justice is . . . horrible—now really there's no other word for it!—and it always ends in gross injustice, always, always,—and if it didn't, it would be horrible just the same in my mind. Dearest Mona Nina, throw it all off—like a bad bad dream—There must be a reaction in a wide soul like yours—you must recoil, after having suffered. I am only glad that I do not know her by your means. I assure you, I feel so on this subject that I could not bear the touch of her hand.[9]

Anna did suffer loss, certainly emotional, perhaps financial as well, but to picture her thereafter as a broken old woman is unjust to her always volatile, often self-pitying, but diversified and constantly energetic temperament. It is more fitting and probably more just to echo Fanny Kemble's wise if cynical comment on the break-up of the friendship:

I do not pity Mrs. Jameson very much in her relations with Lady Byron. I never thought theirs a real attachment, but a connection made up of all sorts of motives, which was sure not to hold water long, and never to hold it after it had once begun to leak. It was an instance of one of those relationships which are made to *wear out*, and as it always appeared so to me, I have no great sympathy with either party in this foreseen result.

I pity Mrs. Jameson more because she is mortified than because she is grieved, and I pity Lady Byron because she is more afraid of mortifying than of giving her pain. It is all very *uncomfortable*; but real sorrow has as little to do with it now as real love ever had. . . .[10]

Alternatively, a comment of some quarter century later provides an apt last word: "Never was there so silly a rupture of the kindly relations of half a lifetime."[11]

Anna's reputation was now such that she could assemble, have published and be sure of a reading public for a collection of her *memorabilia*, a pleasant, less arduous undertaking than most of her writing chores. *A Commonplace Book of Thoughts, Memories and Fancies* is an innocuous and, to our eyes, undistinguished collection, gently interesting for the opinions expressed, the anecdotes about the famous recorded and for the strange and remarkable fat cupids which, etched by the authoress, adorn the work. In its day, however, it was well received, not only as an entertaining book for the respectable reader, but one which was guaranteed, by its writer's reputation, to be improving as well.

The *Athenaeum* objected to Mrs. Jameson's possible breaches of confidence with her friends:

Is Mrs. Jameson sure how far O.G. whose initials it is not hard to unriddle meant her ingenious plea for suicide (p. 34) to figure in print?—and the Kemble sisters wished to encounter what the one may have said about Mozart and the other apropos of 'the tune of Imogen'? We hold that such things are not Mrs. Jameson's own, precisely to use as she will. . . .[12]

The *Spectator*, however, appreciated its merits without such carping reservations:

The characteristics which we last week noticed as appertaining to real conversation belong to this book. It is brief, various and sometimes pithy. If it has not the weight which attaches to the talk or thoughts of some eminent men, it has great refinement without conventional timidity in handling certain questions . . . a very pleasant Jamesoniana, not only agreeable but instructive.[13]

The collection is certainly informative and opinionated, replete with food for polite conversation. Anna's sarcastic attack on Thackeray's thundering public denunciations of Swift and Sterne is its most memorable page; Mrs. Jameson did not often venture to ridicule a contemporary. That she did so on this occasion testifies once again to real, if sometimes latent, critical perception:

> Fancy a hundred years hence some brave, honest, human-hearted Thackeray standing up to discourse before our great-great grandchildren in the same spirit, with the same stern truth, on the wits, and the poets, and the artists of the present time! Hard is your fate, O ye men and women of genius! Very hard and pitiful, if ye must be subjected to the scalpel of such a dissector! . . . How much wiser and better, not to have to shudder before the truth . . . not to have to tremble at the thought of that future Thackeray, who "shall pluck out the heart of your mystery," and shall anatomise you, and deliver lectures upon you, to illustrate the standard of morals and manners in Queen Victoria's reign. [CB 245]

In these years many of Anna Jameson's casual relationships remained on a happier basis than her closer involvements. A correspondence with Mrs. Gaskell evidently began at the latter's request for an autograph note, but developed into a warm interchange, both of letters and of visits. Mrs. Gaskell valued Anna's judgment as a literary critic; she asked for her opinion, particularly about the two-volume publication of *North and South*:

> The story is huddled and hurried up [in its serial publication] especially in the rapidity with which the sudden death of Mr. Bell succeeds to the sudden death of Mr. Hale, but what could I do? Every page was grudged me, just at last, when I did certainly infringe all the bounds and limits they set me as to quantity. . . . I feel as if I must throw myself back a certain distance in the story and rewrite it from there. . . . Would you give me your *very* valuable opinion as to this? [E 297]

Mrs. Gaskell also wrote of her delight at her gift-copy of *The Commonplace Book*—"it is like looking into deep clean water"—and of her troubles in writing the life of Charlotte Bronte, "a most difficult undertaking." [E 294–8] Anna, in common with many others, did not freely approve of the *Life* when it was published. She wrote of it to Ottilie as a kind of curiosity, with a deliberate suspension of judgment on it. She defended Mrs. Gaskell to her *Athenaeum* colleague, Henry Chorley, however, in terms which evidently piqued him, as he protested her "fierce attack" [E 300]:

Your humour of toleration does not include the idea that a critic can have feelings to be hurt—or a conscience as much worthy of respect, as are sentimental attempts to repair that which requires neither sentiment or false colouring, if it is reparable—and I rather wonder you ask such a callous fellow as myself to tea on Thursday. Let me say, that when I go out for release and relaxation from a sad and wearying life, it is no pleasure to be publicly singled out for a fierce attack by one who does not find it convenient to listen to defence: and that I think your desire to bless Mrs. Gaskell (whom I like and admire quite as much as you can do, though I don't fancy her infallible) need not quite have been accompanied with such a vigorous exhibition of a counter spirit (to put it elegantly) against

> Your old and sincere friend
> H. F. CHORLEY

Anna's nature was never an easy one; as her fame had grown, so had her confidence to speak when and as she desired. A core of firm friends and scores of acquaintances were hers, but she could be, and often was, trying to the patience of intimates and casual acquaintances alike. Fanny Kemble's letters demonstrate years of affection, impatience and intermittent strain in her friendship for Anna Jameson. For one period Anna dangerously alienated herself from the Kembles by a series of tiffs with Adelaide; differences of opinion existed and she unwisely sought Fanny's support against her sister. Again, as in the case of Sarah Siddons, Anna had attempted to become a biographer of one of the Siddons family, this time of Mrs. Harry Siddons, Fanny's aunt, who had died in 1845. Once again, she was disappointed; Mrs. Siddons' son and son-in-law would not grant her permission. She had been encouraged in this project by Lady Byron, a friend of Mrs. Harry Siddons', and she was suspected by certain of the Kemble-Siddons clan of self-interest. With both her acuteness and her ready wit in full play, Fanny's various references to Anna, many of them veiled as "Mrs. J." or "Mrs. —," give Anna a full dimensional reality that the more conventional tributes usually lack. "Mrs. — talks sentimental morality about everything, her notions are pretty near right which is the same as pretty near wrong,"[14] says Fanny, in a context which is unmistakably Anna's. On another occasion, she writes to her great friend, Harriet St. Leger that, though Anna is clever, she is also silly: "If I wished to be saucy, which I never do and never am, I should tell you, being an Irishwoman, that it was Irish and therefore capable of a sort of intellectual bull."[15] Always, however, she writes the annoyance out of her system and returns to a more charitable and affectionate estimation of Mrs. Jameson: "The finer elements of her character have become more apparent and valuable to me the longer I have known her . . . I compassionate and admire her very much."[16]

In spite of the increasing physical disabilities of age and the accumulation of misfortunes that she suffered in 1854, her sixty-first year, Anna lost neither capacity for industry nor zest for life. By some, she was called irascible—but no one called her dull.

21

The Final Years

IN 1855, Anna Jameson entered what was, for her, a new arena—the field of the public lecture. Her first speech, "Sisters of Charity, Catholic and Protestant, at Home and Abroad," was delivered on February 14, 1855, at the home of Mrs. Reid, a friend of long standing, and was printed later in the year. *The Communion of Labour: A Second Lecture on the Social Employments of Women* followed in 1856. Anna's always lively concern for the position of women, demonstrated particularly in her *Characteristics, Visits and Sketches, Winter Studies and Summer Rambles*, and *Social Life in Germany*, had been supplemented by practical experience in her years of intimacy with Lady Byron and participation in her many philanthropic concerns. Since 1843, however, when her anonymous *Athenaeum* article on the Royal Commission *Report* had caused her some embarrassment, she had not been a public crusader.

In many ways, she was admirably fitted for the lecturer's role: as an author of prestige, as a tireless traveller and examiner of the evidence in her own and other countries and as a speaker: "what distinguished Mrs. Jameson above everyone I ever knew was one especial charm which no picture could ever give or perpetuate. It was her voice. Gentle, low and sweet. . . ."[1] Finally, because her reputation in latter years was primarily that of an art and literary critic, she could not be accused of pleading her own special cause when she dealt with the position of women. Her words carried more weight for that reason:

When Mrs. Jameson spoke, a deep silence fell upon the crowded assembly. It was quite singular to see the intense interest she excited. Her age and the comparative refinement of her mental powers, had prevented her sphere of action from being 'popular' in the modern sense; and this, of course, created a stronger desire to see and hear her of whom they knew little personally.

Her singular low and gentle voice fell like a hush upon the crowded room, and every eye bent eagerly upon her, and every ear drank in her thoughtful and weighty words.[2]

From 1853 to 1856 England was embroiled in the Crimean War and Florence Nightingale was engaged in her epoch-making nursing experiment at Scutari. Anna's lectures were timely; though she seems to have had no direct contact with Miss Nightingale, there are several admiring references to her in letters: "I feel *ashamed* of all. The only bright spot to me is Florence Nightingale . . . some of our horrid religious bigots are inclined to turn against her." [N 209] Her friends were by no means unanimous in Miss Nightingale's favour. To one of Anna's encomiums, Elizabeth Browning wrote a sharp and ironic reply, indicating, however, that she shared Anna's admiration of the Continental nursing order, the Sisters of Charity and would look upon them as models of achievement:

Every man is on his knees before ladies carrying lint, calling them 'angelic she's', whereas, if they stir an inch as thinkers or artists from the beaten line (involving more good to general humanity than is involved in lint), the very same men would curse the impudence of the very same women and stop there. . . . For the future I hope you will know your place and keep clear of Rafaelle and criticism; and I shall expect to hear of you as an organiser of the gruel department in the hospital at Greenwich. . . .[3]

At least as early as 1852 Anna had shown an interest in the administration of hospitals on the Continent by various nursing orders, in particular by the Sisters of Charity. Her first lecture's plea is for the founding of a Protestant nursing sisterhood in which young women would be trained to nurse in and administer hospitals, female prisons, reform schools and the entire spectrum of social service work. Her second lecture is a continuation and a broadening of the first. She considers the matters of training and pay and documents her words with examples from her own observations of the working of European institutions.

Between the two lectures Anna had visited France, Germany and northern Italy; in Paris, Vienna, Milan and Turin she had inspected every hospital which would admit her. All of her findings she documented with her customary precision, the result constituting an impressive report on the Continental practice of nursing together with an eminently reasonable argument for similar services in England. Most cleverly, she appealed steadily and provocatively to her self-consciously Protestant audience to do as well in training and using all the faculties of its women as did the Roman Catholic Church. Sir George Cornewall Lewis, Chancellor of the Exchequer, wrote to her in thanks for a printed copy of her second lecture, though he disagreed with her project for a Protestant nursing sisterhood and declined to advance it in any practical way.[4]

Anna's lectures were both an indication and a result of the increasing interest in the amelioration of social conditions for all ages and sexes, and particularly, at this juncture, for women. Her last public appearance before her death was at meetings of the Society for the Promotion of Social Science at Bradford, for which she had purposely returned from Italy. These went on for several days, commanding widespread interest and the presence of many notables: the President, Lord Shaftesbury, the aging Lord Brougham and "about 3000 persons of all ranks, a large number of ladies." [N 228] Anna was among those who spoke and she wrote to Ottilie with enthusiasm, approving all the conference questions and reporting major speeches until finally: "Here was an end to me. I could no longer attend the meetings and was confined to my room all day, with illness and fatigue." [N 229]

Anna's beliefs relating to men and women had not changed markedly from her early writing days when the Alda-Medon dialogues introduced *Characteristics of Women*. But as her reputation grew, so grew her confidence in her authority to speak, an authority she retained through prudence: "I will not mix myself up with any of the different sects of opinion, moral or religious, that is certain."[5] She added to these her sound journalistic talents for seeking out the evidence she wanted and presenting it persuasively. Her broad statements of principle, found in the Alda-Medon Introduction to *Social Life in Germany*, are also incorporated into the lecture, the "Communion of Labour." They are listed here as she wrote them down for Ottilie:

I believe that God created the human race, *one* in species, male and female; the two sexes being equally tho' differently endowed.

I believe that the Gospel of Christ recognises mankind, male and female, as one body, one church, both sexes being *equally* rational beings with improvable faculties, *equally* responsible for the use or abuse of the faculties entrusted to them, *equally free*, to choose the good and refuse the evil, equally destined to an equal immortality; and I insist that any human and social laws which are *not* founded in the recognition of this primary law, are and must be false in the general principle, and in the particular application and in result, equally injurious to both sexes.

I believe that neither the law of nature, nor the Gospel law, makes any difference in the amount of virtue, self-control and purity of heart and person required from man and woman equally, and I insist that all conventional laws and all relations and contracts between the two sexes which admit or create inequality in this respect, and let loose the passions of the one sex to prey on the other, introduces a horrid treacherous warfare between the sexes, depraving and degrading both, and by the eternal law of Justice, even more fatal to the oppressor than to the oppressed.

There are in nature masculine and feminine attributes, but there are not masculine and feminine virtues and vices—whatever is morally wrong, is equally wrong in man and in woman and no virtue is to be cultivated in one sex, that is not equally required by the other.

I believe marriage to be the holiest as it must have been the first of all human institutions. But, a solemn contract equally incurred by two human beings equally responsible, is, before God and man, equally binding on both. And therefore any conventional law binding the one party and absolving the other as regards the most sacred of all the obligations incurred by such a contract—mutual truth, in word and act—must of necessity place both parties in a false position and render the whole contract of marriage a standing lie.

Lastly—

The natural and Christian principles of the moral equality and freedom of the two sexes being fully recognised, I insist that the ordering of domestic life is our sacred province indissolubly linked with the privileges, pleasures, and duties of maternity, and that the exclusive management of the executive affairs of the community at large belongs to men as the natural result of their exemption from the infirmities and duties which maternity entails on the female part of the human race.

And by maternity I do not mean the actual state of motherhood—which is not necessary nor universal—but the maternal organisation, common to all women. [N 234]

Anna's most direct influence on the "Rights of Women" movement came through her encouragement of a group of young women, friends and associates of Adelaide Procter, the daughter of her old friend. All of these girls were eager, aspiring reformers; among them at least two, Emily Faithfull and Barbara Bodichon, became memorable women, the former as a printer and publisher, a pioneer in advocating the employment of women in various fields hitherto closed to them, and the latter as one of the founders of Girton College, Cambridge. This group of girls was encouraged by Anna to make her stopping place their headquarters, whether it be her rooms at Bruton Street in London or the home at Ealing. She was their patroness and she called them her "adopted nieces."

She suggested the idea of the *Englishwoman's Journal*, a periodical which was designed to open new avenues for women, particularly for the large and growing group who needed to work to maintain themselves or members of their family. One of the group recalled Anna's reiterated concern for employment opportunities: "There are 800,000 women over and above the number of men in the country; and how are they all to find husbands, or find work and honest maintenance? The market for governesses is glutted."[6] The two editors of the

Englishwoman's Journal were Miss Bessie Parkes, afterwards Mme Belloc, and Miss Barbara Leigh Smith, later Mme Bodichon. The periodical was printed by Emily Faithfull with a group of female helpers. Miss Faithfull was given recognition for her pioneer efforts by the Queen, became "printer to her Majesty," and in 1863 founded the *Victoria Magazine.*

The correspondence of Anna's last years was much concerned with the affairs of her "nieces." In 1859, through her influence, Adelaide Procter joined the Committee for the Promotion of Social Science. "[Our] various talents, in whatever way they gave token, she nurtured with counsel and assistance,"[7] one of them reminisced, and recalled various pleasant excursions taken by the group at Anna's expense, while she, their hostess, remained at home, working.

A letter from Mme Bodichon, in Algiers with her husband in 1859, demonstrates her affection and respect for Anna Jameson, by the detail of its account of her life and work and by the cordiality of its tone. To her "nieces," Anna was not ill and failing in health as she seemed to many of her contemporaries. It seemed quite possible to Mme Bodichon that Anna should come out to Algiers "some winter" and "have some months here to study the inhabitants. The journey is not very difficult and every day becomes easier." [E 330] She expected encouragement from Anna for all her projects, enjoyment of all her impressions of the strangeness of North Africa and, on her side, confidently wished her older friend success in "the many ideas you spoke to me about at Brighton." [E 330]

Anna had developed from the ambitious, literary young governess to the eminent, responsible author; her influence on these young girls and on the "woman question" in general is both a credit to her growth and evidence of it. In spite of an unhappy marriage and the life-long necessity to provide for herself and others, she had not become an aggressively militant feminist. From the beginning, she had proselytized for reforms in education and opportunity for women, at first cannily indirect in her statements, then gradually bolder in the expression of her opinions. She had never become defensive and bitter against the male sex in general, whose company, admiration and friendship she very much enjoyed. Such adaptability of temperament could, and sometimes did, make her seem a turncoat in the eyes of a rampant feminist. But she was incapable of the harshness of judgment of Harriet Martineau, or of Lady Byron who had said of Gerardine's marriage: "It would have made a better Romance if Macpherson had been blown up."[8] Sometimes to the detriment of her reputation with one or other of her circle, Anna, the woman, never became completely submerged in Mrs. Jameson, the author-critic-crusader. She was involved primarily with people not with "questions" or "movements" and she was concerned to be held in affection and esteem. Of this she was well aware; "a woman's idea of Fame," she had once written to Ottilie, "is always love *generalised*." [N 165]

In the last years of her life, the closest and warmest of Anna Jameson's friends were Ottilie von Goethe and the Brownings. To the latter she looked as to superior beings, though she remained sceptically aloof from Elizabeth Browning's interest in spiritualism as she had done from Harriet Martineau's enthusiasm for mesmerism. Her own conviction of an external intelligence needed, she wrote, "no chairs or tables or mediums while between me and the spiritual world higher spirits and intellect—such as yourself and your husband and other gifted beings stand as interpreters—I believe as humanity progresses it will become more spirit and less matter—but it is slow work."[9]

Though she admired Browning, both man and poet, her rhapsodies on his works could be tempered by impatience and a schoolmistress' admonitions to clarify his obscurities: "*Do* dear Browning, think of this—all judges—good judges, are agreed as to the wondrous wisdom and subtlety of thought—and all agree as to the obscurity in the expression of the thought."[10] Less urgently, but with a similar critical admiration, she wrote of *The Statue and the Bust* and *Men and Women* to Elizabeth Browning:

I have been reading his two volumes with the deepest attention and interest —I am struck with absolute wonder by the depth and reach of intellect they display. . . . I could complain of that singularity of form and expression which renders them difficult reading but then if it were quite otherwise it would not be R.B. The diction has individuality as well as peculiarity . . . only I wish one could have pleasure unmixed with perplexity the first time of reading—on the whole, my idea of the Poet's *power* is raised.[11]

Early in 1856, Anna's sisters, led by Camilla, Mrs. Sherwin, proposed a scheme for augmenting the family income by opening a house at Brighton where they would take paying guests. Anna's acquiescence in the venture included, of course, her financial backing, as she explained to the Brownings:

. . . my sisters feel—with reason—that as I am the only resource, if anything happens to me—what is to become of them?—So I have yielded to their wishes—and all the money I can spare for the present, I have given to Camilla for her speculation—it promises well—I have limited the sum because I will not trifle with those means, which must supply the daily requirements of *all*—I must not risk our *home*.[12]

Camilla's scheme was not a success; Anna's sisters seem to have been unfitted for any sort of business undertaking. Anna reported to Ottilie a total loss of the money she had invested. Henceforth the sisters made Brighton and not Ealing their home and though Anna disliked Brighton and called it a vulgar showplace, she had to consider it her head-quarters when in England.

However, it was less difficult for Anna Jameson to adapt herself to a change and a place which she heartily disliked than it would have been to many another; she had always been a wanderer and in spite of poor health and increasing discomfort and lameness, she kept astonish-ingly active. In 1855, Ottilie von Goethe wrote to Sybilla Mertens of Anna and of a visit they had enjoyed:

Seit 10 Tagen ist die Jameson hier, und obgleich sie etwas von dem irlän-dischen Kobold Leptmann hat, ein Geist, von dem man nicht einen Augen-blick die Augen wegwenden darf, weil er sonst verschwindet, so sind wir doch auch wieder manche gute Stunde zusammen und Du kannst Dir denken, wie nach Jahrelanger Trennung es mir wohlthut. Wir haben auch glücklicher Weise, wenn wir auch in den äusseren Richtungen verschieden sind, dass sie nähmlich ihr ganzes Leben fleissig und ich mein ganzes Leben faul, doch wieder gemeinschaftliche Interessen. So ist sie jetzt wieder sehr activ, obgleich sie eigentlich angegriffen und körperlich auch nicht mehr ihre alten früheren Kräfte hat.[13]

In the last five years of her life she was three times in Italy: for some months in 1855, for an entire year during 1857–8 and again for a shorter time in 1859. There she was a senior member of the expatriate group for which the Brownings provided one of the more constant cores and around whose edges swirled an ever fluctuating stream of British and Americans. They were all pilgrims to the monuments of Roman and Renaissance artistic achievement, they were all searching for inspiration for their own artistic endeavours and they basked in the reflected warmth of past culture as they did in the actual warmth of the Mediterranean sun.

Here in Rome, living on the first floor of an old palazzo, nearly opposite the ferryway across the Tiber, "affording a pleasant view of the yellow river and the green banks and fields on the other side,"[14] Anna enjoyed an always agreeable fame, meeting many travellers who sought introductions to her and becoming intimate with a few who, like herself, were dedicated to the service of art in one or other of its forms. One of the latter was William Wetmore Story, a Bostonian of impeccable background and legal training with a life-long passion for sculpture. He and his family lived in Rome for many years where his studio was, as Henry James expressed it, a centre of "sculpture, poetry, music, friendship."[15] John Gibson, a sculptor whose bust of Mrs. Jameson, a forbidding piece of work, is in the National Portrait Gallery, was another welcome member of her circle as was his American protégé, Harriet Hosmer, whom Anna advised about circumspect behaviour among Rome's artist colony. Jackson Jarves, the American collector whose writings constituted a missionary effort for art in America and whose assemblage of early Italian paintings form the basis of Yale's collection, was introduced to Mrs. Jameson by the Brownings, and was very probably influenced personally by her as he professed himself influenced and educated by her writings.[16]

Nathaniel Hawthorne, introduced by Mr. Story in 1858, gives a detailed description of the elderly Anna, the most vivid surviving impression of her appearance in the last years of her life: "I had expected to see an elderly lady, but not quite so venerable a one as Mrs. Jameson proved to be; a rather short, round and massive personage, of benign and agreeable aspect, with a sort of black skullcap on her head, beneath which appeared her hair, which seemed once to have been fair, and was now almost white. I should take her to be about seventy years old."[17] In fact, Anna was then sixty-four. She had, however, lost the ruggedness of health which had enabled her to be the intrepid traveller of her earlier days. Hawthorne found her quite lame—"it looks fearfully like the gout, the affliction being apparently in one foot. The hands, by the way, are white, and must once have been, perhaps now are, beautiful. She must have been a perfectly pretty woman in her day,—a blue or gray eyed, fair-haired beauty."

Hawthorne's record of his first meeting with her closes with expressions of esteem mixed with a certain relief at the affability of his reception: "She began to talk to us with affectionate familiarity, and was particularly kind in her manifestations towards myself, who, on my part, was equally gracious toward her. In truth, I have found great pleasure and profit in her works, and was glad to hear her say that she liked mine. . . . She is said to be rather irascible in her temper; but nothing could be sweeter than her voice, her look, and all her manifestations today." Anna subsequently gave Hawthorne an exhausting educational-artistic tour of Rome, wringing from him a rueful comment: "It was impossible not to perceive that she gave her companion no credit for knowing one single simplest thing about art. Nor, on the whole, do I think she underrated me; the only mystery is how she came to be so well aware of my ignorance." Finally he records with both appreciation and relief the end of his "apprenticeship" to Anna's art instruction:

She is a very sensible old lady, and sees a great deal of truth; a good woman, too, taking elevated views of matters; but I doubt whether she has the highest and finest perceptions in the world. . . . I bade her farewell with much good feeling on my own side, and, I hope, on hers, excusing myself, however, from keeping the previous engagement to spend the evening with her, for, in point of fact, we had mutually had enough of one another for the time being.

Although Hawthorne's reminiscences do not attribute to Anna Jameson an absolute excellence in critical perceptiveness, their pleasant tone compensates for an earlier, analogous, but waspishly unkind judgment by John Ruskin:

Mrs. Jameson was staying also at Danieli's, to complete her notes on Venetian legends: and in the evening walk we were usually together, the four of us;—Boxall, Harding and I extremely embarrassing Mrs. Jameson by looking at everything from our pertinaciously separate corners of an equilateral triangle. Mrs. Jameson was absolutely without knowledge or instinct of painting (and had no sharpness of insight even for anything else); but she was candid and industrious, with a pleasant disposition to make the best of all she saw, and to say, compliantly, that a picture was good, if anybody had ever said so before. Her peace of mind was restored in a little while, by observing that the three of us, however separate in our reasons for liking a picture, always fastened on the same pictures to like; and that she was safe, therefore, in saying that for whatever other reason might be assigned, other people should like them also.[18]

Ruskin's words and tone are not surprising; the importance of his reminiscence is in establishing Anna Jameson as a companion on those walks, however much he denigrates her critical powers.

Her lengthy visit to Rome in 1857–8 brought her great satisfaction, reuniting her with her niece Gerardine in fact, as in theory she had long ago become reconciled to the marriage. At this time Gerardine resumed working for and with her aunt as she had done on their first trip abroad. Anna's sight had been failing for some years. One of her girl protégés recalled how, at Ealing, she used to sit up writing until three or four in the morning, saying that she could best concentrate on her work when the rest of the household was asleep: "Although she had a lamp made especially to serve her nightwork—a lamp consisting of two low sockets, with supports for green shades over short opera candles—still there were times when she could hardly see."[19]

For this reason, her niece undertook a set of about thirty etchings for a new edition of *Sacred and Legendary Art*. Though Anna never really forgave Robert Macpherson who had robbed her of a "daughter," she took comfort in her niece's maturity, her responsibility and her satisfaction with her marriage. Macpherson had ensured the family's future by the happy accident of finding Michelangelo's painting, *The Entombment.* For many years he kept it, calling it "Gerardine's Fortune," before selling it to the National Gallery. [M xiv] Anna could not fail to see proof of the reports that Elizabeth Browning had often sent her by letter: that her niece had become a happy matron, that Mr. Macpherson had a thriving business in photography and that, as Anna once acquiesced in a reply to Mrs. Browning, "all is well as God has ordered it."[20]

In the winter of 1859 she again visited the Macphersons in Rome, beginning work on *The History of Our Lord*, the final two volumes of her *Sacred and Legendary Art*, and going from there to Florence where she continued her work, though intermittently ill and at times very lame. The Brownings were in Florence, their welcome and affection an unfailing antidote to "the 'tinkling cymbal' of company talk."[21] Still indomitably a traveller, she went on in the spring to join Ottilie in Germany for a visit of several months. She left her friend in the fall to return to England and the social science meeting in Bradford. While there, she records what must surely have been one of the bleakest and is certainly the most tantalizingly unfinished of her many encounters. She drove to Haworth with a clergyman who was to deliver a sermon: "Haworth, you know, was the home of Charlotte Brontë, where she died. We were received by the feeble, desolate old man, her father, and—I shall tell you the rest when I see you." [E 335]

After a visit to Fryston, the home of Monckton Milnes, and another to Mrs. Gaskell in Manchester, Anna came back to her sisters' home at Brighton, though in fact she spent most of her time in London. From her rooms in Conduit Street she went daily back and forth to the Print Room of the British Museum where she was assembling her final two volumes and, very possibly, was planning one more, a life of Christ and St. John the Baptist. [M 310]

Early in March, she returned to her rooms in a snow storm. The cold which followed developed into bronchial pneumonia and on March 17, 1860, she died. She was buried at Kensal Green with her father and mother.

Although Robert Jameson had felt no obligation to his wife in the disposal of his property, Anna clung to the empty shell of her marriage to the very end of her life. In February 1860, a month before her death, she had corrected a biographical account of herself for a contemporary collection. The compiler had spoken erroneously of Robert Jameson's official position in Upper Canada and of a "severance" between the couple. The proof is corrected in Anna's handwriting, thus: "Mr.

Jameson was Chancellor of the Canadas—and there was no 'severance.' "[22]

There were many who mourned Anna Jameson. Elizabeth Browning wrote agitatedly of the loss of "a very dear friend, dear, dear Mrs. Jameson."[23] To Gerardine she wrote in comfort for "losing (as far as the loving can lose those whom they love, as far as death brings loss) that great heart, that noble human creature." [M 314] Catherine Sedgwick's memorial tribute, written to her niece, is lengthy and gracious, bestowing on Anna an accolade that she would have certainly enjoyed: "She impressed me as the best talker I ever heard and I have heard many gifted "unknown" and many known and celebrated. Mrs. Kemble, who has had far more extended opportunities than mine, as she has been familiar with men trained to talk in the London social arena, I have heard assign the first place to Mrs. Jameson."[24]

Strangely contrary and certainly erroneous in the matter of conversational facility was the obituary in the *Athenaeum*, signed "H. M." and almost certainly written by Harriet Martineau. Though she gives Anna Jameson credit for unremitting industry and achievement, she is gratuitously denigrating on the personal side. Deaf herself, she was remarkably incompetent to judge in another the qualities of voice and conversation. Shortly after Anna's death, Harriet Martineau made her the subject of one of her *Biographical Sketches*, somewhat redeeming her earlier error by a reasoned criticism of Mrs. Jameson's works and a just, even generous, estimate of her personality, "that of a warmhearted and courageous woman, of indomitable sociability of nature, large liberalities, and deep prejudices." She finds that too much of Mrs. Jameson and too many of her experiences are allowed to obtrude upon her works, "but long after they have ceased to be sought and regularly read, some touch of nature in them . . . will remind a future generation that in ours there was a restless, expatiating, fervent, unreasoning, generous, accomplished Mrs. Jameson . . . a great benefit to her time from her zeal for her sex and for Art."[25]

Almost immediately Anna's friends rallied to raise a fund for her sisters who were now deprived of the support of her pension. Robert Browning's sincere grief was expressed in bad-tempered indignation at the sisters, to whom, however, a pension was granted:

I suppose I may not indulge in a 'sfogo' about the projected subscription, as I am resolved I shall not contribute a farthing thereto. . . . My flagging in this case is limited to refusing to give a farthing to the interesting relatives who worried our friend to death, as I very well know. All her life long, they sucked her dry of the necessary oil of gladness and (occasionally) milk of human kindness; and now there is an end to the supply from her, I don't intend to offer the least squeeze from my nipples. If there is any surplus—now that a pension is secured to them—I advise the administrators of the fund to expend it on a votive tablet to Lady Byron, whose share in the worrying quite deserves one.[26]

The responsibility of finishing Anna's work was accepted by Lady Eastlake. On March 21 she had written of Anna's death to a friend:

I am sure that our thoughts are meeting on one painful subject. You had not known the dear lady so long as I, but still I know that you are now deeply lamenting her. I fear you, like most of her friends, were totally unprepared for this sad event.
I shall miss her sorely. She was ever kind to me—excellent in judgment and advice, a very *strong* woman, though never approaching the man—profound and conscientious in all she did, and devoted to such good works as the world knew nothing of. We shall not see her like again. Sir Charles laments her deeply.[27]

Lady Eastlake, who had referred to Anna Jameson in an earlier letter as "a woman of very determined mind who has worked beyond her strength. . . . She is full of art,"[28] found with the unfinished manuscript a plan of the whole and a mass of memoranda:

Mrs. Jameson's order is beyond all praise, and much facilitates the work. The sisters and Mr. Longman are rather frightened at the difficulty of selecting illustrations, but that's the pleasantest and easiest part in my view, especially as Mrs. Jameson has left notes and specimens from which she was to have made a selection.[29]

The two-volume *History of Our Lord* was published in 1864, a considerable tribute to the esteem in which Anna Jameson's works were held and the concern of friends, family and publisher to see the series finished.

William Cullen Bryant, writing her obituary in the *New York Evening Post*, April 6, 1860, voiced that esteem:

It is with great regret that we place on record the death of Mrs. Anna Jameson, an author who has done more than any other of the present day, and certainly more than any other who ever wrote in our language, to open the general mind to the principles of art, and train it to a ready perception and feeling of the highest beauty in works of painting and sculpture.[30]

Eighteen years later, an anonymous journalist in the *Saturday Review* paid his tribute to her name, while sketching the decline in respect for her aesthetic judgments:

. . . Mrs. Jameson died eighteen years ago, and the present generation has outgrown her aesthetic views. If her books on *Sacred and Legendary Art* still survive, theirs is a kind of life corresponding somewhat to the *succès d'estime* awarded to inconsiderable works by honored names. . . . Though the opinions may be now somewhat faded, the interest of the intellectual character remains.[31]

As time passes and the explorers of the nineteenth century investigate its bypaths, a renewed awareness of Anna Jameson's works as creators and reflectors of the taste of her time becomes evident. Henry James placed her compilations among "the very few books in our language, belonging in form to literature, in which the principles of painting, or certain specific pictures, are intelligently discussed."[32] In *The Consort of Taste*, a contemporary assessment of influential figures in nineteenth-century art criticism, John Steegman adds a solid testimonial to Anna Jameson's importance. He calls her "rather a compiler than a thinker, perhaps"; but "a woman of wide experience and immense industry in her field, whose labours still bear fruit." Mr. Steegman speaks of her influence on Elizabeth Eastlake, beginning with *Visits and Sketches* in which "she [Mrs. Jameson] stepped as a pioneer into a new world of contemporary German thought. Although that was a world that very soon did become familiar in this country, Mrs. Jameson was among its first interpreters." In summary he concludes: "When Anna Jameson died in 1860, worn out by overwork and underpayment, a new era of art history and criticism had already begun with Morelli, Crowe and Cavalcaselle. She is therefore a most important link between old and modern criticism."[33]

Anna's influence on popular taste in America has been acknowledged by Howard Mumford Jones in *O Strange New World*. He speaks of her "enormous appeal" and the innumerable American reprints of her various works, particularly of her art compilations: "Mrs. Jameson was informative. Her works are still in demand in public libraries . . . to the influences she released, coupled with the appeal of John Ruskin, the Americans owe the many sepia prints of Guido Reni's *Dawn* that used to hang over library shelves and on the walls of American schoolhouses."[34]

Van Wyck Brooks in his *Dream of Arcadia*, a history of American writers and artists in Italy, refers to Anna Jameson as a "short, round, competent, energetic and comely Anglo-Irishwoman" who was "very influential," not only spreading a knowledge of art among the public by her writing, but exercising influence on artists themselves. John Gibson said he owed his start to Mrs. Jameson's praise in her *Diary of an Ennuyée* and "it is quite possible that her interest in the primitives was not without effect on Browning's taste."[35]

Though Anna Jameson's influence does not shine with the romantic glamour of a Madame de Staël's, it was none the less real, an informing and directing force in the nineteenth century. By ambition, hard work, acuteness in assessing public taste, and Irish luck in anticipating it, she both catered to and, to some extent, directed popular culture on two continents, during and considerably beyond her lifetime. Her life, with its complexity of pattern, and her works, with their diversity of theme, weave the complete tapestry; either one without the other leaves the pattern incomplete, less than truth and less than justice to her achievement.

> *Indeed, if it were not for the other side of the*
> *tapestry, it would seem not at all worthwhile for*
> *us to stand putting in more weary Gobelin stitches*
> *(till we turn into goblins) day after day, year*
> *after year, in this sad world.*

[Elizabeth Barrett Browning to Anna Jameson, August 1855]

BIBLIOGRAPHY, NOTES AND INDEX

Bibliography

THE MATERIAL in this bibliography has been arranged under the following headings:

A. CHIEF MANUSCRIPT COLLECTIONS
B. UNCOLLECTED MANUSCRIPT MATERIAL
C. ANNA JAMESON. WORKS. FIRST EDITIONS
D. ANNA JAMESON. WORKS. EDITIONS QUOTED IN THE TEXT
E. BIOGRAPHICAL AND CRITICAL MATERIAL. BOOKS
F. BIOGRAPHICAL AND CRITICAL MATERIAL. ARTICLES
G. ROBERT JAMESON. BIOGRAPHICAL MATERIAL
H. GENERAL BACKGROUND. HISTORICAL, SOCIAL, CRITICAL

A. CHIEF MANUSCRIPT COLLECTIONS

Goethe and Schiller Archives, Weimar: About 410 letters in all, 309 from Anna Jameson to Ottilie von Goethe; 84 from Ottilie to Anna Jameson, and the rest to and from various friends.

The Lovelace Papers: Private Collection. About 200 letters to and from Anna Jameson and Lady Byron.

Wellesley College Library: 78 letters in all, 64 from Elizabeth Browning to Anna Jameson; 8 from Anna Jameson to Elizabeth Browning; the rest, correspondence with Robert Browning and John Kenyon.

Yale University Library: 30 letters to and from Anna Jameson.

The Houghton Library, Harvard University: 26 letters from Anna Jameson to various people.

The University of Illinois Library: About 27 letters from Anna Jameson to various people.

New York Public Library: 16 letters to and from Anna Jameson.

Armstrong-Browning Library, Baylor University: 6 letters.

Cornell University Library: 4 letters.

University of Toronto Library: 3 letters; John Payne Collier. *Notes and Emendations to the Text of Shakespeare's Plays* (London, 1853). Autographed with marginalia by Anna Jameson.

Detroit Public Library: Letter from Miss Emily to Miss Kate Mason.

British Museum: Add. Mss. 1843—(1849), 40532, 40541, 40601, 28510. Letters to Sir Robert Peel and biographical notice.

Toronto Public Library: State Papers Upper Canada; Baldwin Correspondence; Letters from William Hume Blake to Robert Baldwin; *Diary* of Henry Scadding; 3 letters.

The last Will and Testament of Anna Jameson. London, Somerset House, 1860

Voyage to America. Private Collection, Toronto. 66 drawings by Mrs. Jameson, illustrating her tour in Canada and the United States: 25 drawings of scenery in Italy and on the Rhine.

The Last Will and Testament of Robert Sympson Jameson. No. 445 G R Registry Office, Toronto.

The following libraries have one or two items of interest: Huntingdon, the Universities of Kentucky, Rochester, Duke, Brown, Columbia, Edinburgh, Liverpool, the Birmingham and Nottingham Public Libraries, the Bodleian and the Victoria and Albert Museum.

B. UNCOLLECTED MANUSCRIPT MATERIAL

THE FOLLOWING ITEMS are from a catalogue of Christie, Manson and Woods, Monday, December 20. 1886. They represent a further large mass of manuscript material dispersed and not yet located.

Lot No.

149   Jameson (Mrs.): Common-Place Book, Poetry and Prose, partly original, partly selected from English, French, and Italian authors, in 3 Vols., small 4to., manuscript, with sketches in pen and pencil. (1811–20)

150   Jameson, Poems and Extracts from her Diary during her first Italian Tour, 4to., manuscript, with pen-and-ink sketches. (?1833–4)

151   Jameson, Residence in Germany, manuscript, containing extracts in German (partly in the handwriting of Gerardine, 1844–47) part of which is a transcript by Mrs. Jameson of Ottilie von Goethe's critical remarks upon several literary lights of Germany, 4to., Russia

153   Jameson, Six Portfolios of MS Notes; her original Sketch and Draught of her Works upon Sacred and legendary Art and two Note-books—Agreements with Longman and Co., etc.— Catalogue of Mr. H. A. J. Munroe's Pictures.

154   Jameson, Projects for giving Employment to Ladies in the reformation of fallen Women, etc.—Papers and Autograph Letters on these subjects from and by distinguished Women and Men.

155   Portfolio of about 270 Drawings, Etchings, and Proof Prints —but chiefly Drawings (prepared for the engraver)—after pictures described in Mrs. Jameson's Works, some unpublished; an interesting collection, with references, corrections, and memoranda in Mrs. Jameson's handwriting.

156   Etchings, from designs by Mrs. Jameson, 100 plates, proofs before letters, mounted in a vol.—Drawings by Gerardine, Mrs. Jameson's Niece—2 vols.

166   Jameson (Mrs.) Correspondence, comprising 122 Autograph Letters of Literary and Artistic Celebrities. [These include letters from: Carlyle (T), Thackeray (W. M.) 2 letters, Dickens (C.), Wordsworth (W), Emerson (R. W.), Morgan (Lady), Tieck, Webster (Daniel), Siddons (Mrs.), Landseer (Sir E.), Millais (Sir J. E.), Princess Metternich, and the Duke of Wellington.

C. ANNA JAMESON. WORKS. FIRST EDITIONS

A First or Mother's Dictionary for Children. London, 1825.

The Diary of an Ennuyée. London, 1826. First issued anonymously as *A Lady's Diary.*

Memoirs of the Loves of the Poets. 2 vols. London, 1829.

Memoirs of Celebrated Female Sovereigns. 2 vols. London, 1831.

Characteristics of Women. 2 vols. London, 1832.

Memoirs of the Beauties of the Court of Charles II. London, 1831.

Fantasien. Fancies: A series of subjects in outline, designed and etched by M. Retzch. With prefatory remarks by Mrs. Jameson. London, 1834.

Visits and Sketches at Home and Abroad. 2 vols. London, 1834.

Winter Studies and Summer Rambles in Canada. 3 vols. London, 1838. A selection from this work was published by Longmans in 1852 under the title *Sketches in Canada and Rambles among the Red Men.*

Pictures of the Social Life of Germany, as Represented in the Dramas of Princess Amalie of Saxony. 2 vols. in one. London, 1840.

Handbook to the Public Galleries of Art in or Near London. London, 1840.

Companion to the Private Galleries of Art in London. London, 1844.

The Decoration of the Garden Pavilion in the Grounds of Buckingham Palace. Engraved under the supervision of L. Gruner, with an Introduction by Mrs. Jameson. London, 1846.

Memoirs of Early Italian Painters. 2 vols. London, 1845.

The Relative Position of Mothers and Governesses. London, 1846.

Memoirs and Essays on Art, Literature and Social Morals. London, 1846.

Sacred and Legendary Art. 2 vols. London, 1848.

Legends of the Monastic Orders. London, 1850.

Legends of the Madonna. London, 1852.

A Commonplace Book of Thoughts, Memories and Fancies, Original and Selected. London, 1854.

Handbook to the Court of Modern Sculpture. In *Official Handbooks of the Crystal Palace.* 2 vols. London, 1854.

Sisters of Charity, Catholic and Protestant, at Home and Abroad. London, 1855.

The Communion of Labour. London, 1856.

The History of our Lord, as Exemplified in Works of Art. 2 vols. London, 1864. Begun by Anna Jameson and completed by Lady Eastlake.

Early Canadian Sketches. Introduction by G. H. Needler. Toronto: Burns and MacEachern, 1958.

D. ANNA JAMESON. WORKS. EDITIONS QUOTED IN THE TEXT

Characteristics of Women. 2 vols. London, 1832. 1st edition.

Characteristics of Women. 2 vols. London, 1858.

A Commonplace Book of Thoughts, Memories and Fancies. New York, 1855.

The Diary of an Ennuyée. London, 1826.

Memoirs and Essays on Art, Literature and Social Morals. London, 1846. 1st edition.

Memoirs of Celebrated Female Sovereigns. London, 1869.

Memoirs of the Loves of the Poets. Boston, 1857.

Visits and Sketches at Home and Abroad. 2 vols. in one. New York, 1834.

Winter Studies and Summer Rambles in Canada. 2 vols. in one. New York, [1839?].

Sacred and Legendary Art. 5th ed; London: Longmans, 1866.

E. BIOGRAPHICAL AND CRITICAL MATERIAL. BOOKS

Artom-Treves, Guiliana. *The Golden Ring: The Anglo-Florentines, 1847–1862.* Translated by Sylvia Sprigge. London: Longmans, 1956.

Brooks, Van Wyck. *The Dream of Arcadia.* New York: Dutton, 1958.

Browning, Elizabeth Barrett. *The Letters of Elizabeth Barrett Browning.* Edited by F. G. Kenyon. 2 vols. London: Smith, Elder, 1897.

———. *Letters of Elizabeth Barrett Browning to Mary Mitford.* Edited by Betty Miller. London: John Murray, 1954.

Browning, Robert. *Dearest Isa: Robert Browning's Letters to Isabella Blagden.* Edited by C. McAleer. University of Texas Press, 1951.

————. *Leters of Robert Browning*. Edited by T. L. Hood. London: John Murray, 1933.

————. *The Letters of Robert Browning and Elizabeth Barrett, 1845–1846*. 2 vols. London: Smith, Elder and Co., 1899.

Campbell, Thomas. *The Life of Mrs. Siddons, 1755–1831*. London, 1839.

Carlyle, Thomas. *Letters of Thomas Carlyle*. Edited by C. E. Norton. 2 vols. London: Macmillan, 1888.

————. *Thomas Carlyle, Letters to his Wife*. Edited by Trudy Bliss. London: Victor Gollancz, 1953.

Channing, William Ellery. *The Correspondence of William Ellery Channing and Lucy Aikin, 1826–1842*. Edited by Anna Letitia Le Breton. Boston: Roberts, 1874.

Eastlake, Elizabeth (Rigby), Lady. *Letters and Journals of Lady Eastlake*. Edited by Charles Eastlake Smith. 2 vols. London: John Murray, 1895.

Ebisch, Walther and Levin L. Schücking. *A Shakespeare Bibliography*. Oxford: Clarendon Press, 1931.

Fields, James T. *Yesterdays with Authors*. Boston: Houghton Mifflin, 1900.

Hawthorne, Nathaniel. *Notes of Travel*. 4 vols. Riverside Press, 1900.

Hayter, Alethea. *One Sultry August*. London: Faber, 1965.

Emerson, R. W. *English Traits*. Boston: Phillips, Sampson and Co., 1856.

Heine, Heinrich. *Shakespeares Mädchen und Frauen*. Vol. V of *Heine's Sämtliche Werke*. Leipzig: Der Tempel, 1930.

Hopkins, Gerard Manley. *A Hopkins Reader*. Edited by John Pick. Oxford: Oxford University Press, 1953.

Houben, H. H. *Ottilie von Goethe, Erlebnisse und Geständnisse, 1832–1857*. Leipzig: Klinkhardt und Biermann, 1923.

Jaggard, William. *Shakespeare Bibliography*. Stratford: Shakespeare Press, 1911.

Jameson, Anna. *Anna Jameson: Letters and Friendships, 1812–1860*. Edited by Mrs. Steuart Erskine. London: T. Fisher Unwin, 1915.

———. *Letters of Anna Jameson to Ottilie von Goethe*. Edited by G. H. Needler. London: Oxford University Press, 1939.

Jones, Howard Mumford. *O Strange New World*. New York: Viking, 1964.

Kahn-Wallerstein, Carmen. *Die Frau vom Andern Stern: Goethes Schwiegertochter*. Bern: A. Francke, 1948.

Kemble, Frances Anne. *Notes on some of Shakespeare's Plays*. London: Bentley, 1882.

———. *Records of a Girlhood*. New York: Henry Holt, 1883.

———. *Records of Later Life*. 3 vols. London: Bentley, 1882.

Killham, John. *Tennyson and the Princess*. University of London, 1958.

Macpherson, Gerardine. *Memoirs of Anna Jameson*. Boston: Roberts Brothers, 1878.

Marchand, Leslie. *The Athenaeum*. Chapel Hill: University of North Carolina Press, 1941.

Martineau, Harriet. *Harriet Martineau's Autobiography*, Memorials by Maria Weston Chapman. 3 vols. London: Smith, Elder, 1877.

———. *Biographical Sketches*.

Mayne, Ethel Colburn. *The Life and Letters of Anna Isabella, Lady Noel Byron*. London: Constable, 1920.

Robinson, Henry Crabb. *On Books and Their Writers*. Edited by Edith Morley. 3 vols. London: J. M. Dent, 1938.

Ross, Janet. *Three Generations of Englishwomen: Memoirs and Correspondence of Mrs. John Taylor, Mrs. Sarah Austin and Lady Duff Gordon*. London: John Murray, 1888.

Schoolcraft, Henry Rowe. *Personal Memoirs of a Residence of Thirty Years with the Indian Tribes on the American Frontier*. Philadelphia, 1851.

Sedgwick, Catherine. *The Life and Letters of Miss Sedgwick*. Edited by Mary Dewey. New York: Harper, 1871.

Smiles, Samuel. *A Publisher and His Friends: Memoirs and Correspondence of John Murray*. London: John Murray, 1911.

Steegman, John. *Consort of Taste, 1830–1870*. London: Sidgwick and Jackson, 1950.

Steegmuller, Francis, *The Two Lives of James Jackson Jarves*. New Haven: Yale University Press, 1951.

Taplin, Gardner. *The Life of Elizabeth Barrett Browning*. Yale: Yale University Press, 1958.

Taylor, Tom. *Life of Benjamin Robert Haydon*. 3 vols. London, 1853.

Thackeray, William Makepeace. *The Letters and Private Papers of W. M. Thackeray*. Edited by G. N. Ray. 4 vols. Cambridge: Harvard University Press, 1945.

Wilson, John. *Christopher North, A Memoir of John Wilson*. Compiled by Mrs. Gordon. 2 vols. Edinburgh: Edmonston, 1863.

F. BIOGRAPHICAL AND CRITICAL MATERIAL. ARTICLES

Bluhm, Heinz. "The Newberry 'Goetheana': A Preliminary Report on the Chicago Find," *Newberry Library Bulletin*, V, no. 5, Aug., 1960.

Boyce, George K. "From Paris to Pisa with the Brownings," *New Colophon*, III, 1950.

"Life of Mrs. Siddons by T. Campbell", *Blackwood's Edinburgh Magazine*, XXXVI, July-Dec., 1834.

"Characteristics of Women", *Blackwood's Edinburgh Magazine*, XXXIII, Jan.-June, 1833.

"Characteristics of Women, Moral, Poetical and Historical; Visits and Sketches at Home and Abroad", *Edinburgh Review*, LX, July 1834– Jan. 1835.

Cunningham, Allen. "Biographical and Critical History of the Literature of the Last Fifty Years," *Athenaeum*, Dec. 28, 1833.

"The Diary of an Ennuyée," *Monthly Review*, new series, I, Jan.–June, 1826.

"A Few Hours at Hampton Court," *Blackwood's Edinburgh Magazine*, XLVIII, July–Dec., 1840.

"Germany and the Germans," *Quarterly Review*, LVIII, Feb.–April, 1837.

"Harriet Martineau and Mrs. Jameson," *A New Spirit of the Age*. Edited by Richard Hengist Horne. 2 vols. London, 1844.

Hayens, Kenneth. "Heine, Hazlitt and Mrs. Jameson," *Modern Language Review*, XVII, 1922.

"Loves of the Poets by Mrs. Jameson," *Blackwood's Edinburgh Magazine*, XXVI, July–Dec., 1829.

"Lady Travellers," *The Quarterly Review*, LXXVI, 1845.

"The Life of Mrs. Siddons, by Thomas Campbell," *Blackwood's Edinburgh Magazine*, XXXVI, 1834.

"Memoirs of Anna Jameson, by Gerardine Macpherson," *Littell's Living Age*, vol. 139, 1878.

"Monologue or Soliloquy on the Annuals," *Blackwood's Edinburgh Magazine*, XXVI, July–Dec., 1829.

"Mrs. Jameson's Memoirs of the Beauties of the Court of Charles II," *The Times*, Oct. 16, 1838.

Nethercot, Arthur H. "The Reputation of John Donne as a Metrist," *Sewanee Review*, XXX, 1922.

"Noctes Ambrosianae," no. XLVII, Dec., 1829, *Blackwood's Edinburgh Magazine*, XXVI, July–Dec., 1829.

"Noctes Ambrosianae," no. LIX, Nov., 1831, *Blackwood's Edinburgh Magazine*, XXX, July–Dec., 1831.

"Noctes Ambrosianae," no. LXIV, Dec., 1832, *Blackwood's Edinburgh Magazine*, XXXII, July–Dec., 1832.

"The Position of Women," *Westminster Review*, Jan., 1841.

"The Poetry of Sacred & Legendary Art," *Blackwood's*, LXV 181–9.

"The Rights of Women," *Quarterly Review*, LXXV, Dec. 1844–March 1845.

Scadding, Henry. "Mrs. Jameson on Shakespeare and the Collier Emendations," "The Week," Toronto, 1892.

"Shakespeare in Germany," *Blackwood's Edinburgh Magazine*, XL (1836).

"Sketches on the Road," *Fraser's London Magazine*, V, 1822; VI, 1822.

"Thoughts on Orpheus," *Blackwood's Edinburgh Magazine*, XLIV, 1838.

"Two Ladies," *Blackwood's Edinburgh Magazine*, CXXV, Jan.–June, 1879.

"Winter Studies and Summer Rambles in Canada," *British and Foreign Review*, VIII, Jan.–April, 1839.

"A Wreath on the Grave of the Late Anna Jameson," *The Argosy*, XXXI, Jan.–June, 1881.

G. ROBERT JAMESON. BIOGRAPHICAL MATERIAL

Arthur, Sir George. *The Arthur Papers: Being the Canadian Papers, Mainly Confidential, Private, and Demi-official of Sir George Arthur, K.C.H., Last Lieutenant-Governor of Upper Canada*. Edited by C. R. Sanderson. 3 vols. Toronto: Public Library and University of Toronto Press, 1957.

Coleridge, Hartley. *Letters of Hartley Coleridge*. Edited by G. E. and E. L. Griggs, London: Oxford University Press, 1936.

Coleridge, Hartley. *Poems by Hartley Coleridge with a Memoir of his Life*. Edited by Derwent Coleridge, 2 vols. London, 1851.

Coleridge, Hartley, "Sonnets to R[obert] J[ameson]," *Fraser's London Magazine*, VII, 1823.

Connolly, B. W., S. J. "After 100 Years—A Jesuit Seminary," *Philosopher's Quarterly*, 1944-5.

Dent, John Charles. *Canadian Portrait Gallery*. 4 vols. Toronto: Magurn, 1880–1.

Griggs, Earl Leslie. "Four Letters of Hartley Coleridge," *Huntingdon Library Quarterly*, IX 1945–6.

"Jameson, the Rev. Joseph," *Alumni Cantabrigienses*. Compiled by J. A. Venn. Part II, 1752–1900.

Lamb, Charles. *Letters*. Edited by E. Lucas. *Everymans Library*. 2 vols. London: J. M. Dent, 1909.

Read, David B. *The Lives of the Judges of Upper Canada and Ontario from 1791 to the Present time*. Toronto: Rosewell and Hutchison, 1888.

Riddell, Hon. William Renwick. *The Legal Profession in Upper Canada in its Early Periods.* Toronto: The Law Society of Upper Canada, 1916.

Riddell, Hon. William Renwick. "The Ordinary Court of Chancery in Upper Canada," *Essays and Addresses,* vol. 15. Osgoode Hall.

Robertson, John Ross. *Landmarks of Toronto,* 6 vols. 3rd series. Toronto: J. R. Robertson, 1898.

Robinson, Henry Crabb, *Diary, Reminiscences and Correspondence.* Edited by Thomas Gadler. 3 vols. London: Macmillan, 1869.

Ryerson, Egerton. *The Story of My Life.* Edited by J. G. Hodgins. Toronto: Wm. Briggs, 1883.

Scadding, Henry. *Toronto of Old.* Toronto: Adam, 1873.

State Papers, Upper Canada. No. 121. Goderich to Colbourne, March 26, 1833; No. 215, Glenelg to Head, Aug. 3, 1837; Nov. 24, 1837. Toronto Public Library.

Wordsworth, William. *The Letters of William and Dorothy Wordsworth.* Edited by Ernest de Selincourt. Oxford: Clarendon Press: 1935–9.

H. GENERAL BACKGROUND. HISTORICAL, SOCIAL, CRITICAL

Allston, W. *Lectures on Art and Poems.* Edited by Dana. New York: Scribners, 1850.

Austen, Jane. *The History of England in Love and Friendship and Other Early Works.* Preface by G. E. Chesterton. London: Chatto and Windus, 1922.

Brand, Charles Peter. *Italy and the English Romantics.* Cambridge: Cambridge University Press, 1957.

Cruse, Amy. *The Englishman and His Books in the Early 19th Century.* London: Harrop, 1930.

Craig, Gerald M. *Early Travellers in the Canadas 1791–1867.* Toronto: Macmillan, 1855.

Dunham, Aileen. *Political Unrest in Upper Canada. 1815–1836.* London: Longmans, 1927.

Enfield, D. E. *L.E.L.: A Mystery of the Thirties.* London: Hogarth Press, Leonard and Virginia Woolf, 1928.

Ermatinger, Charles Oakes. *The Talbot Regime.* St. Thomas: Municipal World, 1904.

Landon, Fred. *Lake Huron* in *The American Lakes Series.* Indianapolis: Bobbs-Merrill, 1944.

Hall, S. C. *Retrospect of a Long Life, 1815–1883.* New York: D. Appleton, 1883.

Herold, J. Christopher. *Mistress to an Age.* New York: Bobbs-Merrill, 1958.

Hewlett, Dorothy. *Elizabeth Barrett Browning.* London: Cassell, 1953.

Howitt, Mary. *An Autobiography.* Edited by Margaret Howitt. 2 vols. London: Isbister, 1889.

Hudson, G. R. ed. *Letters of Browning, Story and Lowell.* London: Bowes & Bowes, 1965.

James, Henry. *William Wetmore Story and his Friends.* London: Thames and Hudson, 1903.

Loskiel, George Henry. *History of the Mission of the United Brethren among the Indians of North America.* Translated from the German by Christian Ignatius Latrobe. London, 1794.

Macready, W. C. *Diaries.* Edited by W. Toynbee. New York: Putnam, 1912.

Mineka, Francis E. *The Dissidence of Dissent: The Monthly Repository 1806–1838.* Chapel Hill: University of North Carolina Press, 1944.

Middleton, Jesse A. and Fred Landon. *The Province of Ontario: A History, 1615–1927.* 4 vols. Toronto: Dominion Publishing House, 1927.

Neff, Wanda Fraiken. *Victorian Working Women.* London: Allen, 1929.

Oliphant, Mrs. and E. R. Oliphant. *The Victorian Age of English Literature.* 2 vols. London: Percival and Co., 1892.

Ossoli, Margaret Fuller, Marchesa. *The Writings of Margaret Fuller.* Selected and Edited by Mason Wade. New York: Viking, 1941.

Peacock, Carlos. *John Constable*. London: John Baker, 1965.

Planché, J. R. *Recollections and Reflections*. 2 vols. London: Tinsley Bros., 1872.

Price, Lawrence Marsden. *The Reception of English Literature in Germany*. Berkeley: University of California Press, 1932.

Rubenius, Aina. *The Woman Question in Mrs. Gaskell's Life and Work*. Upsala: University of Upsala Press, 1950.

Schlegel, August Wilhelm von. *Lectures on Dramatic Art and Literature*. Translated by John Black. Revised by Rev. A. J. W. Morrison. London: Bell, 1876.

Schoolcraft, Henry Rowe. *Algic Researches*. 2 vols. New York, 1839.

——— *The Indian Fairy-Book*. New York, 1856.

Staël-Holstein, Anne Louise Germaine, Baronne de. *Corinne; or Italy.* . . . Translated by Isobel Hill; with metrical versions of the odes by L. E. Landon. New York: Pooley and Co., [187?].

Notes

INTRODUCTION

1. Henry Crabb Robinson, *On Books and Their Writers*, ed. Morley (London, 1938), I, 441.

2. John Steegman, *Consort of Taste, 1830–1870* (London, 1950), 187.

3. Harriet Martineau, *Harriet Martineau's Autobiography* (London, 1877), I, 265.

CHAPTER 2

1. *Little Louisa* was republished as *A First or Mother's Dictionary for Children* (London, n.d.).

2. Toronto Public Library, Scadding Collection, vol. 6.

3. F. A. Kemble, *Records of Later Life* (London, 1882), I, 78.

CHAPTER 3

1. H. A. C. Sturgess, M.V.O., librarian of the Middle Temple, has supplied the following information: "Robert Sympson Jameson, admitted to the Middle Temple on February 6th, 1818. Third son of Thomas Jameson, late of Somerly nr. Christchurch, Hants., esq. dec'd. Called to the bar 28th November, 1823."

2. William Wordsworth, *The Letters of William and Dorothy Wordsworth*, ed. de Selincourt (Oxford, 1935–9), no. 499.

3. Hartley Coleridge, *Poems by Hartley Coleridge*, ed. Coleridge (London, 1851), I, lvii.

4. Hartley Coleridge, *Letters of Hartley Coleridge*, ed. Griggs (London, 1936), no. 22, 1822.

5. Robinson, *On Books and Their Writers*, I, 171.

6. Charles Lamb, *Letters*, ed. Lucas (London, 1909), 216. Lamb also reports the printing of four sonnets by Hartley Coleridge addressed to R. S. Jameson, which first appeared in the February 1823 edition of *Fraser's London Magazine*.

7. *Ibid.*, II, 217, 221.

8. *Ibid.*, II, 235.

9. Robinson, *On Books and Their Writers*, I, 262.

10. Henry Crabb Robinson, *Diary, Reminiscences and Correspondence*, ed. Sadler (London, 1869), II, 46.

11. *Ibid.*, II, 111.

12. David B. Read, *Lives of the Judges of Upper Canada and Ontario from 1791 to the Present* (Toronto, 1888), 188. "Cases in Bankruptcy by Thos. C. Glyn, Esq., of Lincoln's Inn, Barrister at Law and Commissioner of Bankruptcy, and Robert S. Jameson, Esq., of the Middle Temple, Barrister at Law, containing reports of Cases decided by Lord Chancellor Eldon and by Vice Chancellor Sir John Leach. From Michaelmas Term, 1821, to the sitting before Michaelmas Term, 1824, and a Digest of all the contemporary cases relating to the Bankruptcy Laws in the Courts." See also British Museum Catalogue.

13. Barry Cornwall was the pen name of Bryan Waller Procter, lawyer and poet, associated at this time with *Fraser's London Magazine*. He was the son-in-law of Basil Montagu.

14. *A Dictionary of the English Language* by Samuel Johnson and John Walker with the pronunciation greatly simplified and on an entirely new plan and with the addition of several thousand words (2nd ed.; London, 1828).

CHAPTER 4
1. C. P. Brand, *Italy and the English Romantics* (Cambridge, 1957), 16.
2. "The Diary of an Ennuyée," *Monthly Review* (new series), I, 1826, 414–26.
3. "Memoirs of Anna Jameson, by Gerardine Macpherson," *Littell's Living Age*, 138, 637.
4. Robinson, *On Books and Their Writers*, I, 441.
5. *Ibid.*, I, 407.

CHAPTER 5
1. For detailed reminiscences of the Montagus and the Procters see F. Kemble, *Records of a Girlhood* (New York, 1883), 127ff.
2. Cf. "Mrs. Arkwright," G. Macpherson, *Memoirs of Anna Jameson* (Boston, 1878), 15.
3. A parallel incident occurred in 1840 when Anna accompanied Lady Byron to a sitting with Benjamin Haydon: "Mrs. Jameson seemed annoyed, and found fault with the head. . . . I said 'Come, don't look criticism,' which annoyed her more. . . . Lady Byron was fidgety, and the head turned out bad." *Life of Benjamin Haydon*, ed. Taylor (London, 1853), III, 158.
4. The sketch was reprinted in *Visits and Sketches*, I, 288.
5. The *Cambridge Bibliography* lists as Anna's first published work "*Cadijah, or the Black Palace*. A Tragedy in Five Acts, 1825." There is no record of this work elsewhere. Mr. Bateson, General Editor of the *Cambridge Bibliography*, has informed me that he considers it an erroneous entry.
6. Thomas Carlyle, *Thomas Carlyle, Letters to His Wife*, ed. Bliss (London, 1953), 93.
7. Robinson, *On Books and Their Writers*, I, 442.
8. Read, *Lives of the Judges*, 189.
9. "A Wreath on the Grave of the Late Anna Jameson," *Argosy*, XXXI, Jan.–June, 1881, 449.
10. J. C. Dent, *Canadian Portrait Gallery* (Toronto, 1880), II, 57–66; III, 52. Dent uses the expression "personal deficiences." Needler is more explicit: "Vice-Chancellor Jameson's 'infirmity' as Premier Robert Baldwin euphemistically called it, was evidently that he drank himself to a premature death." [N xxi].
11. Cf. Brand, *Italy and the English Romantics* and G. Artom-Treves, *The Golden Ring: The Anglo-Florentines, 1847–1862* (London, 1956) for further amusing and informative detail on the English abroad.

CHAPTER 6
1. T. Carlyle, *Letters of Thomas Carlyle*, ed. C. E. Norton (London, 1888), II, 243.
2. "Monologue, or Soliloquy on the Annuals" *Blackwood's Edinburgh Magazine*, 1829, 949–50.
3. *Ibid.*, 951.
4. Brand is of the opinion that the enthusiasm for Italy and all things Italian began to change to enthusiasm for Germany about 1830. Brand, *Italy and the English Romantics*, 23.
5. A. H. Nethercot, "The Reputation of John Donne as a Metrist," *Sewanee Review*, XXX, 1922, 468.

6. A similar strong partisanship for Mary Queen of Scots is found in Jane Austen's early work, *The History of England in Love and Friendship and Other Early Works* (London, 1922).

7. Enfield. *L.E.L.: A Mystery of the Thirties* (London, 1928), 61.

8. "*Loves of the Poets* by Mrs. Jameson," *Blackwood's Edinburgh Magazine*, XXVI, 1829, 529.

9. *Ibid.*, 539.

10. J. Wilson, *Christopher North: A Memoir of John Wilson* (Edinburgh, 1863), II, 205.

11. "*Loves of the Poets* by Mrs. Jameson," *Blackwood's Edinburgh Magazine* XXVI, 1829, 529.

12. *Ibid.*, 539.

13. L. Marchand, *The Athenaeum* (Chapel Hill, 1941). Enfield also discusses the influence exerted by publishers on the periodical press in *L.E.L.*, 91.

14. "*Loves of the Poets* by Mrs. Jameson," *Blackwood's Edinburgh Magazine*, XXVI, 1829, 539.

15. "Noctes Ambrosianae," LIX, *Blackwood's Edinburgh Magazine*, XXX, 1831, 841.

16. *The Times*, London, Oct. 16, 1838.

CHAPTER 7

1. See A. Cruse, *The Englishman and His Books in the Early 19th Century* (London, 1930) for an account of women's education which demonstrates the truth of Anna's criticism. John Killham has a valuable chapter on the topic in *Tennyson and the Princess* (London, 1958).

2. T. Campbell, *The Life of Mrs. Siddons, 1735–1831* (London, 1839), 170.

3. *Ibid.*, 192.

4. *Characteristics of Women* (London, 1858), Preface; II, 310.

5. F. Kemble, *Notes Upon Some of Shakespeare's Plays* (London, 1882), 57.

6. "*Characteristics of Women, Moral, Political and Historical*"; "Visits and Sketches at Home and Abroad," *Edinburgh Review*, LX, 1834–5, 180–6.

7. "*Characteristics of Women*," *Blackwood's Edinburgh Magazine*, XXXIII, 1833, I, 139–41.

8. *Ibid.*, III, 404.

9. "*The Life of Mrs. Siddons* by Thomas Campbell," *Blackwood's Edinburgh Magazine*, XXXVI, 1834, 358.

10. *Ibid.*, 354–5. The *Edinburgh Review* article was coincident with this one but Anna waited for some years more for official recognition from the *Quarterly*.

11. H. Heine, *Shakespeares Mädchen und Frauen* (Leipzig, 1930), 111.

12. K. Hayens, "Heine, Hazlitt and Mrs. Jameson," *Modern Language Review*, XVII, 1922, 42ff.

13. A. Cunningham, "Biographical and Critical History of the Literature of the Last Fifty Years," *Athenaeum*, Dec. 1833, 894.

14. J. P. Collier, *Notes and Emendations to the Text of Shakespeare's Plays* (London, 1853). The marginalia were described by Henry Scadding in his pamphlet "Mrs. Jameson on Shakespeare and the Collier Emendations."

15. G. M. Hopkins, *A Hopkins Reader*, ed. Pick (Oxford, 1953), "Letter to Alexander Baillie;" Sept. 6, 1863.

CHAPTER 8

1. A. Dunham, *Political Unrest in Upper Canada* (London, 1927), 157 and note.

2. *State Papers Upper Canada*, CO 43/44, 121. Goderich to Colborne, March 26, 1833.

3. Robinson, *On Books and their Writers*, I, 442; 262.

4. For this particularly well-documented phase of Anna Jameson's life, see Needler; H. Bluhm, "The Newberry 'Goetheana': A Preliminary Report on the Chicago Find," *Newberry Library Bulletin*, V, 1960, 183 ff; H. Houben, *Ottilie von Goethe*; Kahn-Wallerstein, *Die Frau vom Andern Stern*.

5. Houben, *Ottilie von Goethe*; "die Jameson," though it sounds odd to our ears, was not a term of contempt, but simply a form of reference to Mrs. Jameson until the friendship consolidated to a first name basis.

6. C. Kahn-Wallerstein, *Die Frau vom Andern Stern: Goethes Schwiegertochter* (Bern, 1948), 89.

7. Houben, *Ottilie von Goethe*, 13–14.

8. *Ibid.*, 15.

CHAPTER 9

1. Cf. Steegman, *Consort of Taste*, ch. 1.

2. The popular biography by Louis Kronenberger, *Marlborough's Duchess*, bears out Mrs. Jameson's suspicion.

3. Robinson, *On Books and their Writers*, I, 350.

4. "Characteristics of Women," *Edinburgh Review*, LX (1834–35), 180.

5. *Ibid.*, 198.

6. Houben, *Ottilie von Goethe*, 41.

7. "Germany and the Germans," *Quarterly Review*, LVIII (1837), 326.

CHAPTER 10

1. C. Sedgwick, *The Life and Letters of Miss Sedgwick*, ed. Dewey (New York, 1871), 277.

2. J. Ross, *Three Generations of Englishwomen* (London, 1888). A broad and informative selection of the letters of Mrs. Austin, her mother, Mrs. John Taylor, and her daughter, Lady Duff Gordon.

3. Houben, *Ottilie von Goethe*, xiii–xv.

4. *Ibid.*, 48.

5. *Ibid.*, 34.

6. The Newberry Library Goethe collection may well thrown light on this small but teasing mystery.

7. Houben, *Ottilie von Goethe*, 48–9.

8. *Ibid.*, 54.

9. *Ibid.*, 41.

CHAPTER 11

1. This makes no mention of Robert Jameson's letter which Macpherson says is dated October 30th and which is quoted above.

2. W. F. Neff, *Victorian Working Women* (London, 1929), 209; cf. also A. Rubenius, *The Woman Question in Mrs. Gaskell's Life and Work* (Upsala, 1956).

3. Mrs. Jameson was often one of the breakfast party at Rogers', whose gatherings were noted for their assembling of London's wit and talent. Mrs. Jameson's letters to Ottilie at this time provide a kind of check-list of literary London.

4. Catharine Parr Traill gives an account of static electricity in *The Backwoods of Canada* (1836), very possibly the book which Anna sent to Ottilie at this time. Mrs. Traill's tone is similar to Anna's—mystification and awe at the strange phenomenon.

5. Washington Irving is described by Fanny Kemble as an intimate friend of her family [K 564]. We may suppose that Anna Jameson's introduction was through the Kembles. Her correspondence had continued with Fanny since the latter's removal to America and the young sister Adelaide had continued to be a friend and protégé of Anna's [N 37, 61].

6. The American copyright law operative in 1833 protected only authors publishing in America. The authors of works published in Britain could be, and were, pirated mercilessly.

7. "Memoirs of Anna Jameson," *Littell's Living Age*, vol. 139, 637.

CHAPTER 12

1. Percival Ridout, described as a "distant relation of the Ridout who married Mathilda Bramley," Thomas Ridout, Surveyor General of Upper Canada, 1810–21. For Ridout family history see Mathilda Edgar, *Ten Years of Upper Canada in Peace and War* (Toronto, 1890).

2. "Captain James Fitzgibbon (1780–1863) served as a non-commissioned officer in the Napoleonic wars, came to Canada in 1802, and got his commission in 1806. He distinguished himself in the war of 1812, and was acting adjutant-general in the rebellion of 1837." [N 74, n. 4].

3. W. E. Riddell, "The Ordinary Court of Chancery in Upper Canada," *Essays and Addresses*, XV (Toronto, n.d.), 13; *idem*, "The Courts of Upper Canada," in J. E. Middleton and F. Landon, *The Province of Ontario*, II (Toronto, 1927).

4. Read, *Lives of the Judges of Upper Canada* (Toronto, 1888), 196.

5. *The Arthur Papers*, III (Toronto, 1925), 453.

6. J. R. Robertson, *Landmarks of Old Toronto*, I (Toronto, 1896), 493. For a complete history of the Jameson house, 1837–1961, see "After 100 Years: A Jesuit Seminary," *The Philosopher's Quarterly*, 1944–5; also Eric Arthur, *Toronto, No Mean City* (Toronto, 1964).

7. Toronto Public Library. Unpublished letter addressed to Inman Esq., c/o Mr. Forbes. *Characteristics of Women* was published in New York in 1839 by Saunders and Otley. The Dedication and Preface are dated Toronto, January 1, 1837.

8. There are various mentions of John Lees Alma in Anna Jameson's letters to her family and to Ottilie von Goethe. He was Irish, the son of a friend of Denis Murphy. After a time in South America he settled in Niagara Falls where he became a prosperous merchant. He is buried in St. Mark's Churchyard, Niagara, and in the church is a memorial window to him, dedicated in 1890. The University of Toronto Library copy of Mrs. Jameson's *Sisters of Charity, Catholic and Protestant, at Home and Abroad* (London, 1855) is a presentation copy from the author to John Lees Alma.

9. Detroit Public Library. Mss. Emily Mason to her sister Miss Kate Mason. July 23, 1837.

10. Toronto Public Library. Scadding Collection. *Diary*.

11. Henry Scadding, "Mrs. Jameson on Shakespeare and the Collier Emendations," *The Week*, 1892, 11–12. For further information regarding Mrs. Jameson's sketches of the Canadian tour see *supra*, chap. XV.

12. *Ibid.*, 11.

13. *Ibid.*, 11.

14. *Ibid.*, 14.

15. J. Ross, *Three Generations of English Women*, I (London, 1888), 116. Lord Colborne was Commander-in-Chief of the forces, Sir Francis Bond Head was Governor of Upper Canada and Lord Gosford, whom the *Cambridge History of the British Empire*, VI, calls "a genial but undistinguished nobleman," was Governor of Lower Canada.

16. F. Kemble, *Records of Later Life,* I (London, 1882), 123.
17. *Ibid.,* I, 124.
18. *Ibid.,* 125.
19. Ironically, Fanny Kemble's marriage was no more successful than Anna's had been. She was divorced from Pierce Butler, mainly because of a general independence of mind which made her unfit for the nineteenth-century role of wife and mother in which she was cast. Specifically, she could not reconcile herself to her husband's family being slave owners, nor could she refrain from what they considered unwomanly meddling in their concerns—clearly spoken sympathy for the Abolitionists. She returned to the stage and then to a more congenial career of Shakespeare readings, in the manner of her famous aunt, Mrs. Siddons.
20. Sedgwick, *Life and Letters,* 272.
21. *Ibid.,* 241.
22. *Ibid.,* 378.
23. *Ibid.,* 379.
24. W. E. Channing, *The Correspondence of William Ellery Channing and Lucy Aiken,* (Boston, 1874), 182.
25. W. Allston, *Lectures and Poems,* ed. Dana (New York, 1850), 377; V. W. Brooks, *The Dream of Arcadia* (New York, 1958), 13–25.
26. Saunders and Otley published the 3 vol. London edition in 1838; Putnam published a 2 vol. American edition in 1839 as well as a 2 vol. in one edition, probably 1839.
27. Ross, *Three Generations of Englishwomen,* I, 117.

CHAPTER 13
1. The value of the "Summer Rambles" as a keenly observant early Canadian travel account is attested by its modern reprints. As well as the McClelland and Stewart edition of 1923, the Nelson edition of 1943 and the McClelland and Stewart New Canadian Library edition of 1965, Gerald Craig has included selections from Anna Jameson's Canadian tour in his *Early Travellers in the Canadas, 1791–1867.* These editions consider the work for its backward glance at early Canada. The original text has been cut in each case to omit the German part of the "Winter Studies" material. Anna's words have been used as authoritative illustration by many authors specializing in historical or biographical study. Ermatinger's use of her material in *The Talbot Régime,* Fred Landon's in *Lake Huron,* and Chase and Stellanova Osborn's in *Schoolcraft-Longfellow-Hiawatha* all give evidence of the regard in which her observations are held.
2. Colonel Fitzgibbon was a colourful and an important figure in Upper Canada. He commanded the Militia at the time of the Rebellion of '37; Mrs. Jameson's description of him, in "Winter Studies," 94 ff., is a lively and a valuable record. Her account of the visit of White Deer, 24 ff., is impressive for the objectivity of its reporting.
3. H. R. Schoolcraft, *Personal Memoirs of a Residence of Thirty Years with the Indian Tribes on the American Frontier* (Philadelphia, 1851), 563.
4. *Ibid.,* 568.
5. *Ibid.,* 567.
6. *Ibid.,* 561–2.
7. *Ibid.,* 634. Three stories attributed to Mrs. Schoolcraft's translation are printed in the Mackinaw section of "Summer Rambles": "The Forsaken Brother," "Mishosha" or "The Magician and his Brother" and "The Origin of the Robin." One further tale, "An Allegory of Winter and Summer" is printed in the Sault section of the book, attributed to Mrs. Johnston, through the translation of her

daughter. All four of these stories appear in Mr. Schoolcraft's *Algic Researches* of 1839, and three of them in his *Indian Fairy Book* of 1856. Mr. Schoolcraft commonly uses proper names for his characters: the forsaken brother is Sheem; Winter and Summer are Peboan and Seegwun; the robin-boy is Iadilla. In Anna Jameson's versions these characters are unnamed. The language of the versions is, however, very similar, in some cases identical. It is an interesting insight into Anna's perspicacity as a bookmaker that she published these tales before Schoolcraft's own collection was printed.

8. Toronto Public Library. Scadding Collection, Vol. 6. "Letter to Rev. McMurray."

9. G. H. Loskiel, *History of the Mission of the United Brethren* (London, 1794), part III, 23–5.

10. A selection of sketches, with an introduction by Professor Needler, was published in 1958 by Burns and MacEachern under the title of *Early Canadian Sketches*. The original album is the property of Mrs. Watson Bain, Toronto.

11. "*Winter Studies and Summer Rambles in Canada,*" *British and Foreign Review*, VIII, 1839, 134–5.

12. *Ibid.*, 137.

13. *Ibid.*, 144.

14. *Ibid.*, 148.

15. *Ibid.*, 153.

16. W. H. Thackeray, *The Letters and Private Papers of William Makepeace Thackeray*, ed. Ray (Cambridge, 1945), I, 377.

17. "The Position of Women," *Westminster Review*, Jan. 1841, 16.

18. *Ibid.*

19. "The Rights of Women," *Quarterly Review*, LXXV, 1845, 113. The comment refers to Anna's remarks in *Winter Studies.*

20. *Ibid.*, 116–7.

21. John Killham, in *Tennyson and the Princess* has several pages of analysis of Anna Jameson's contributions to the 19th century feminist controversy in England up to 1839.

CHAPTER 14

1. *Dictionary of National Biography.*

2. Sedgwick, *Life and Letters*, 277.

3. Lovelace papers, A. J. to Lady B. [March 11, 1841].

CHAPTER 15

1. Mr. Malcolm Elwin in *Lord Byron's Wife* gives us the authentic Lady Byron, far truer to the real Annabella than Ethel Colburn Mayne's romanticized heroine. The Jameson-Byron letters in the Lovelace papers give considerable further evidence of the validity of Mr. Elwin's judgements.

2. Lovelace papers, A. J. to Lady B., [July 9, 1840].

3. When she grew up, Marie was known as Ada Leigh. She lived in Paris where homes for women were named after her. She married the Bishop of Ontario, John T. Lewis, D.D., L.L.D., and died and was buried in Toronto, Canada. E. C. Mayne, *The Life and Letters of Anna Isabella, Lady Noel Byron* (London, 1920), 367 and note.

4. Mayne, *The Life of Lady Byron*, chap. 23.

5. Lovelace papers, A. J. to Lady B., Tuesday [April 26, 1842].

6. *Ibid.*, A. J. to Lady B. [July 5, 1842].

7. *Ibid.*, A. J. to Lady B. [March 31, 1843].

8. *Ibid.*, A. J. to Lady B. [July 18, 1842].
9. *Ibid.*, A. J. to Lady B. [July 20, 1842].
10. *Ibid.*, A. J. to Lady B. [July 20, 1842].
11. *Ibid.*, A. J. to Lady B. [Dec. 13, 1840].
12. *Ibid.*, A. J. to Lady B. [Nov. 11, 1842].
13. *Ibid.*, A. J. to Lady B. [March 2, 1843].
14. *Ibid.*, A. J. to Lady B. [Sept. 22, 1843].
15. *Ibid.*, A. J. to Lady B. [Sept. 24, 1843].
16. Killham, *Tennyson and the Princess*, 110–19. The *Athenaeum* article was rewritten as "Women's Mission and Women's Position" and published in *Memoirs and Essays*, 1846.
17. Lovelace Papers, A. J. to Lady B. [July 29, 1844].
18. *Ibid.*, A. J. to Lady B. [September 18, 1844].
19. *Ibid.*, A. J. to Lady B., [August 16 (?), 1844].
20. Cf. *Harriet Martineau's Autobiography*, ed. M. W. Chapman, for an incomparable record of Miss Martineau's strange and diverse personality; also Vera Wheatley, *The Life of Harriet Martineau*.
21. *Ibid.*, A. J. to Lady B., November 5, 1842.
22. J. T. Fields, *Yesterdays with Authors*, (Boston, 1900), 378.
23. Lovelace papers, A. J. to Lady B. [February 25, 1843].
24. *Ibid.*, A. J. to Lady B. [March 23, 1843].
25. *Ibid.*, A. J. to Lady B. [January 26, 1844].
26. *Ibid.*, A. J. to Lady B. [November, 6, 1842].
27. *Ibid.*, A. J. to Lady B. [February 27, 1843].

CHAPTER 16
1. Robinson, *On Books and Their Writers*, I, 441–2.
2. Macready, *Diaries*, ed. W. Toynbee (New York, 1912), I, 496.
3. S. Smiles, *A Publisher and His Friends: Memoirs and Correspondence of John Murray* (London, 1911), 334.
4. *Athenaeum*, February 1842.
5. British Museum. Add Mss. 1843–[1849], 40532, 40541, 40601.
6. Steegman, *Consort of Taste*, 187.
7. Lovelace papers, A. J. to Lady B. [March 2, 1845].
8. H. M. Jones, *O Strange New World* (New York, 1964), 109 and note 58.
9. Sir Kenneth Clark, *The Gothic Revival* (Harmondsworth, 1960). See the chapter on Pugin, in which this point is made, very forcibly.
10. See Chapter II. "Of Mothers and Governesses" draws on Anna's lengthy experience as a governess as well as on various statistics available to her.

CHAPTER 17
1. E. B. Browning, *Letters of Elizabeth Barrett Browning*, ed. Kenyon (London, 1897) I.
2. G. B. Taplin, *The Life of Elizabeth Barrett Browning* (New Haven, 1958).
3. Lovelace papers, A. J. to Lady B. [October 27, 1846].
4. *Ibid.*, A. J. to Lady B. [Nov. 12, 1846].
5. Wellesley Mss., 8, E. B. B. to A. J. [Feb. 8, 1847].
6. Yale Mss. R. B. to A. J. [April 1, 1847].
7. Lovelace papers, A. J. to Lady B. [Nov. 12, 1846].
8. Wellesley Mss. 14, E. B. B. to A. J. [Aug. 11, 1849].
9. *Ibid.*, 10, E. B. B. to A. J. [Aug. 5, 1847].
10. *Ibid.*, 19, E. B. B. to A. J. [Dec. 10. (1850?)].
11. Jones, *O Strange New World*, 109.

CHAPTER 18

1. Henry James, *The American*, 63. Rinehart, from the 1877 edition.
2. F. Steegmuller, *The Two Lives of James Jackson Jarves* (New Haven, 1951), 129.
3. Lovelace papers, A. J. to Lady B. [Feb. 4, 1847].
4. Marchand, *The Athenaeum*, 344. George Darley was art critic for the *Athenaeum* from 1834 to his death in 1846.
5. Peacock, *John Constable: The Man and his Work*, Ch. I.
6. John Ruskin, *Modern Painters*, III, "The Grand Style."
7. *Ibid.*, III, 29.
8. Steegman, *Consort of Taste*, 185–7.
9. *"The Poetry of Sacred and Legendary Art," Blackwood's Edinburgh Magazine*, LXV, 181–9.

CHAPTER 19

1. British Museum. Add. Mss. No. 40601.
2. *Ibid.*
3. *Ibid.*
4. Yale Mss. A. J. to her mother [Jan. 1, 1851].
5. Yale Mss. A. J. to her sister Charlotte [Jan. 25, 1851].
6. Yale Mss. A. J. to Mother and sisters [Oct. 31, 1850].
7. Yale Mss. George Combe to A. J. [1845].
8. Yale Mss. Sir Francis Egerton to A. J.
9. Cf. A. Hayter, *One Sultry August* (London, 1965). Miss Hayter describes the circumstances of Haydon's death and a group of Victorians, among them the Brownings, the Carlyles and Mrs. Jameson, who were associated with him in the days preceding his suicide.
10. Yale Mss. A. J. to Charlotte Murphy [Feb. 4, 1851].
11. *Arthur Papers*, III [1945], 475.
12. Robinson, *On Books and Their Writers*, II, 730.
13. *Ibid.*, 734.
14. Lovelace papers, A. J. to Lady B. [Oct. 27, 1846].

CHAPTER 20

1. Registry Office, Toronto, No. 445 GR. Aug. 15, 1854.
2. *Letters of E. B. B. to M. M.*, ed. Miller (London, 1954), 97–8.
3. Ethel Colburn Mayne radically over-estimates the effect of the rift on Anna Jameson.
4. Lovelace papers, A. J. to Lady B. [July 15, 1843].
5. Mr. Malcolm Elwin verified this information from the bank books of Lady Byron: Lady Byron paid Anna Jameson £300 on 26th August 1843. Thereafter, for eight years from 1844 to 1851 inclusive, appears the entry on 18th September, "Law Life Assurance Co. 1 yr on £300 upon life of Anna Jameson £13. 12. 0." There is also a payment on 1st February 1847 to "A. Jameson £160." On 20th September 1847 she received from Mrs. A. Jameson payment into her account of £25. 12. 0., and on 16th September 1852 she received from Mrs. Jameson £12. On 9th March 1852 Lady Byron paid Scott Russell £600.
6. Lovelace papers, A. J. to Lady B., [May 16, 1853].
7. *Ibid.*, A. J. to R. Noel [October, 1854].
8. Wellesley Mss., 46, A. J. to E. B. [Feb. 10, 1856].
9. *Ibid.*, 17, E. B. B. to A. J. [May 4, 1850].
10. Kemble, *Records of Later Life*, 578.

11. *Littell's Living Age*, Vol. 139, 1878, 636ff.
12. *Ibid.*, Vol. 44, 1855, 95ff.
13. *Ibid.*, Vol. 44, 98.
14. Kemble, *Records of Later Life*, III, 104.
15. *Ibid.*, III, 337.
16. *Ibid.*, III, 112.

CHAPTER 21
1. "A Wreath on the Grave of the Late Anna Jameson," *Argosy*, XXXI, 1881, 456.
2. Parkes, *Vignettes*.
3. Wellesley Mss. 41, E. B. B. to A. J. [1855].
4. Harvard Mss. A. L. S. Lewis, Sir G. C. [London] 28 Dec. 1859.
5. Wellesley Mss. 51, A. J. to E. B. B. [N.D.]
6. "A Wreath on the Grave of the Late Anna Jameson," *Argosy*, XXXI, 1881, 455.
7. *Ibid.*, 455.
8. Lovelace papers, Lady B. to A. J. [July 18, 1849].
9. Wellesley Mss. 38, A. J. to E. B. B., Jan. 12, 1854.
10. *Ibid.*, 45, A. J. to R. B. [n.d.].
11. *Ibid.*, 58, A. J. to E. B. B. [n.d.].
12. *Ibid.*, 44, A. J. to E. B. B., Feb. 1, 1856.
13. Houben, *Ottilie von Goethe*, 210 .
14. Hawthorne, *Notes on Travel*, III, 354.
15. H. James, *William Wetmore Story* (London, 1803), 317; See also Hudson, ed. *Letters of Robert Browning, W. W. Story and J. R. Lowell.*
16. Steegmuller, *James Jackson Jarves*, 129.
17. Hawthorne, *Notes on Travel*, III, 354–67.
18. Ruskin, *Works*, XXXV, 373–4.
19. "A Wreath on the Grave of the Late Anna Jameson," *Argosy*, XXXI, 1881, 454.
20. Wellesley Mss. 49, A. J. to E. B. B. [July 12, 1854].
21. *Ibid.*, no. 49, A. J. to E. B. B. [Jan. 12, 1854].
22. British Museum. Add. Mss. 28510.
23. Browning, *The Letters of Elizabeth Barrett Browning*, II, 365.
24. Sedgwick, *Life and Letters*, 381.
25. Martineau, *Biographical Sketches*, 435.
26. R. B. Browning, *Dearest Isa: Robert Browning's Letters to Isabella Blagden*, ed. McAleer (Austin, 1951) 73.
27. E. Eastlake, *Letters and Journals of Lady Eastlake*, ed. Smith (London, 1895), II, 137.
28. *Ibid.*, 91.
29. *Ibid.*, 137.
30. *Littell's Living Age*, 69, 1860, 445.
31. *Ibid.*, 139, 1878, 636.
32. James, *The Painter's Eye*, ed. Sweeney, 34.
33. Steegman, *Consort of Taste*, 187.
34. Jones, *O Strange New World*, 109.
35. Brooks, *Dream of Arcadia*, 38, 78.

Index